# ROBBING THE ONE-ARMED BANDITS

## An Encyclopedic Guide to Finding and Exploiting Advantageous Slot Machines

D0381468

## CHARLES W. LUND

**Robbing the One-Armed Bandits,**
**Second Edition**

Published by:    **RGE Publishing**
414 Santa Clara Avenue
Oakland CA 94610
(510) 465-6452
FAX: (510) 652-4330
Web site: www.rge21.com
e-mail: books@rge21.com

Second Edition, First Printing
1 2 3 4 5 6 7 8 9 10

ISBN 0-910575-13-4

# Disclaimer:

*1) Neither the author nor the publisher intends this book as an encouragement to anyone to gamble. Gambling is always risky. A player may suffer financial losses even when he has the advantage. If you use the information in this book to attempt to win at gambling, you may lose your money.*

*2) Neither the author nor the publisher is an attorney. Any advice in this book which may be construed as legal advice is absolutely not intended as such. The author's references in this book to the legality or illegality of any act are based upon the author's best information at hand. Be aware, however, that all laws, and especially gambling laws, differ widely from county to county, state to state, and country to country. New laws are often enacted, and old laws often change. Always check the laws in your locale if you are unsure of the legality of any action you may take in a gambling casino. Neither the author nor the publisher wishes to encourage anyone to violate any laws.*

# Table of Contents

## Odds & Ends

## Appendix

# Introduction

*by Arnold Snyder*

When I started playing blackjack back in the mid-seventies, slot players were considered the dregs of the casino. Card counters have traditionally viewed themselves as the only smart players in the casino, the only players who were using strategies based on intelligence and logic, and whose efforts gave them an advantage over the house. In fact, the only slot machines that got any respect in the counters' eyes were those rare video blackjack machines that were exploitable via basic strategy and/or card counting. Most blackjack slots, however, were not so exploitable.

In 1988, blackjack expert Stanford Wong radically altered this perspective with the publication of *Professional Video Poker* (Pi Yee Press). Suddenly, a new breed of player appeared on the scene — the video poker (VP) pro. More gambling experts and authors expanded on Wong's seminal work. Lenny Frome, Dan Paymar and Bob Dancer became the new video poker gurus. Paymar even started publishing a newsletter, *Video Poker Times,* which became the voice of the Las Vegas VP community, where new variations of machines were analyzed as soon as they appeared in the slot jungle.

Then, a couple of years ago, a new type of slot machine was introduced — "Piggy Bankin'." Similar to the progressive machines that had ever-growing dollar jackpots, these machines banked "credits" from previous play. One attractive feature was that you could see the banked "coins" on the display so that you could estimate the average profit derived from playing the slot machine until the bonus was obtained. Unlike the VP progressives, the Piggy Bankin' payout would not go to some other player on a connected bank of machines, either; the machines were independent.

Stanford Wong provided some of the initial Piggy Bankin' analysis in his *Current Blackjack News* newsletter, and soon the pros were buzzing. New banking machines appeared; Shopping Spree, Safe Cracker, Temperature's Rising; the banking slots began taking over the casinos' slot departments.

My eyes were opened to the realities of advantageous slot play last year when a pro player invited me to stay in one of his comped suites in a major Nevada casino. Solely as a result of his play on the casino's $1 and $5 slot machines, he not only had full RFB, but multiple suites of comped rooms that he was filling with his friends. He was comped just as fully as any high stakes blackjack player. This player was also to become one of the first slot pros I knew to be barred from the slot departments of some major casinos in Nevada.

What's that? Thrown out of a casino for beating slot machines? Can this really happen? Unfortunately, this is one more area where we may extend our analogy of advantageous blackjack to slot play. Some casinos are now barring the really good slot players.

When I first saw Charles Lund's photocopied, self-published, 75-page report, "Advantageous Slot Machines," about eight months ago, I realized immediately that Lund was breaking new ground for serious advantage players. I called him and talked to him at some length about how he'd collected his data for analysis and whether he thought he could expand his text into a book-length manuscript.

Lund explained that he had a Ph.D. in statistics from Virginia Polytechnic Institute and State University, and that he had simply applied standard statistical sampling and analysis techniques to the slot machine data that he and his wife had personally collected. He said he would be more than happy to provide me with his raw data in order to expand his report into a book. I sent him a contract and asked him to start working on the project immediately.

Along the way, we decided against publishing all of his raw data; instead, he would provide a technical Appendix which would provide an explanation of how he collected and analyzed data for his studies. There were various practical reasons for this change of course. First, the raw data itself would be meaningless without a fairly detailed explanation of how the various machines worked. With some two dozen machines analyzed in his report, this technical data and the explanation of how it was analyzed for each type of machine would make this book very complex, tedious, and difficult for the average player to understand. I was already collecting photos of the various slot machines so that explanations of the workings could be graphically displayed.

To further complicate matters, some of these slot machines that Lund had analyzed in his initial report were already fast becoming obsolete. Many new machines had entered the market, some of which had already become more popular than the machines in Lund's initial analyses. As a player, he was already collecting data on these new machines! How many of them did I want to include in this book?

We decided that it would be far more valuable to the masses of players to provide playing advice on twice as many machines, without a lot of technical data, than to fill the book with vast quantities of statistical analyses on fewer machines. Hopefully, Lund's technical Appendix will satisfy the more mathematically inclined who would like an explanation of how he went about his analyses on the four dozen banking slots described in this book.

Meanwhile, while working on this book, Lund and his wife were permanently barred from the slot department of the then-new Bellagio Casino in Las Vegas. Lund acknowledges that they had been profiting about $500 per day each (on 25¢ slots!) when Bellagio security expelled them. To Lund's surprise, they were bluntly informed that Bellagio simply will not tolerate skillful slot players, and that he and his wife should also consider themselves barred from the slots at all of Steve Wynn's casinos, including Golden Nugget, Mirage and Treasure Island.

Is this fair? Is this legal?

The marketing concept behind the banking slots is not difficult to understand. As a player sees the credits building on the machine he is playing, getting ever closer to that "bonus round," he is tempted to continue playing longer than he would if no bonus round were impending. From the savvy player's perspective, and I don't necessarily mean the professional player but any player who has become familiar with how these devices work, it is now worthwhile to *shop* for the best machine in the slot department. Any player who sees two Piggy Bankin' machines available, one with 25 coins in the bank, the other with 10 coins in the bank, would be foolish to choose the 10-coin machine because breaking the bank will net the player a minimum of 10 coins as opposed to a minimum of 25 coins.

To continue with the shopping metaphor, the banking machines that are engaged in (or fast approaching) their bonus rounds, can be considered a casino's "loss leaders" — items available to the public that draw in customers, in hopes that the customers also purchase other items the store profits from.

A professional slot player, in essence, is like a supermarket shopper who only purchases the loss leaders. If you were to go into a grocery store and purchase nothing but the sale items, the loss leaders, the coupon specials, so that the store literally lost money on your visit, you would not expect to be barred from future shopping at that store. Lots of people do this. In fact, if any store attempted to throw you out because you were only purchasing sale items, you could sue them for false advertising, harassment, discrimination and other violations of local, state and federal consumer protection laws. There is, to be sure, an active subculture of grocery store couponomists (to borrow a term coined by Anthony Curtis) who trade coupons with each other, subscribe to their own newsletters and have their own websites. They never worry about the cashiers refusing to ring them up, or the store manager reading them their rights. It's not illegal to take advantage of a deal, even if you did not fulfill the purpose of the deal (from the store's perspective), which was to generate other profitable transactions from your business.

In May 1995, attorney Anthony Cabot wrote an article in *Casino Journal* (an industry trade journal) describing why Nevada casinos are so reluctant to throw out video poker professionals, who descend like vultures on banks of machines as soon as their progressive jackpots give the players any significant advantage over the house. Cabot explained that there is a state gaming regulation that defines any progressive jackpot — which is to say any

jackpot that accrues as a direct result of prior players' losses —
as money which the casino no longer owns, but which is merely
being held in "trust" for whatever member of the gaming public
ultimately wins it.

Cabot did not go into great detail as to why this regulation exists, but I can think of several good reasons for it. Gaming regulations require that slot devices pay back a certain percentage to the
players. Unless these amounts accrued in progressive jackpots
are figured into the moneys paid out, a casino could "reset" their
progressive jackpots any time they wanted. But since those accrued funds are figured into the machine's payout, if a casino
took them back, many machines would fail to meet these standards. And many casinos advertise payback percentages, such as
95%, 98%, etc. Unless these jackpot totals are figured into the
paybacks, the casinos would also be guilty of false advertising.
Cabot explained in his *Casino Journal* article that casinos may
not pick and choose which members of the public will be allowed
to stake their claim for that jackpot that is awaiting public distribution.

So, the video poker pros who are ejected from casinos today
are the more aggressive teams of players who attempt to take
over whole banks of machines by muscling out the casinos' regular customers. Such players are not ejected for being professional
players, but — at least ostensibly — for being rude, and causing
disturbances. To my knowledge, these types of team ejections
have not been challenged in the courts. Provided the slot surveillance videos do show that the team employed aggressive and
rude behavior to run off the casino's regular customers, the casino would probably prevail in the courts. Any business has the
right to eject unruly patrons whose behavior is disturbing other
customers. Neither the courts nor the general public condone
such behavior.

Unlike the progressive jackpot slots, however, the banking
slots do not display a dollar-and-cents total of accrued moneys
for distribution to the public. The payouts from the banked credits, to be sure, do get tallied into the machine's payback percentage, but these credits are not tied to any specific dollars-

and-cents jackpot that is displayed on the machine, or that is counted as money held in trust for the public. This factor alone probably means that casinos in Nevada, and most other states, may eject professional players from their banking slots at their whim, just as they may from their blackjack tables.

None of this is meant to imply that most skillful slot players should expect such treatment from the casinos. Lund himself has had very few difficulties of this sort. Also, most advantageous slot play is not at such high stakes as blackjack. But the reader should be warned that the casinos never take kindly to professional players. If you begin to utilize the methods that Charles Lund reveals in this book, it is best to keep your knowledge to yourself, and to go about your business of milking the slot machines looking as much like the average tourist as you can.

If you find this method of winning at the casinos enjoyable, then you may want to keep track of Lund's continuing work in this area. RGE plans to publish regular supplements to this book with information on new banking slots as they appear. As we go to press, Charles Lund has already produced the first such supplement, a 65-page report which describes and analyzes 16 additional new banking machines to appear in Las Vegas. We intend to update this book annually with the new machines as they appear. Until then, the truly dedicated can obtain Lund's supplements directly from RGE Publishing before they are available to the masses in book form. You'll find information about this on the back pages of this book.

Happy slot hunting!

— *Arnold Snyder*

# Preface

recent years, with the end of the mechanical slots and the beginnings of electronic mechanisms, there has been a considerable change in slot machines. Then with the development of video displays and computer mechanisms involving far more advanced programing, slot machines entered another seemingly endless arena.

In the drive to be competitive, companies have created a wide assortment of games specifically designed to appeal to the public and yet similar in many ways to the old style slot machines.

The degree of complexity involved in playing some of the newer slot machines has reached surprising levels. No longer are the machines just a matter of dropping in a coin or two or three or 45, 50, 100, ... or 225 (yes, there are some that will play 225 coins per spin) and then pulling the handle or pushing the spin button. Certainly, the casino and slot manufacturer do not care if an individual behaves in this manner; but such thoughtless play can be quite detrimental to the player.

It is true that modern slots carry instructions outlining how the machine is to be played. These instructions are generally rudimentary and often require an individual to play the machine to grasp the details of meaning in the instructions. More often than not, the manufacturer's instructions go unread by the player. This is to an extent encouraged by the manufacturer, as indicated by the placement of the pertinent information in locations other than at eye level.

Additionally, one must realize that the player has arrived at the casino to have fun, court Lady Luck, and play games, not to become embroiled in reading directions. Consider this: playing Monopoly may be enjoyable, but reading its instructions is not many people's idea of entertainment.

Coupled with this disinterest in reading the information on the slot machine itself is the lack of thought by even good slot players in coming to grips with the implications of the information when it has been read.

Because of these conditions, sizable numbers of players often instill value into a modern slot machine through their play and neglect to extract as much as possible of that value back out of the machine. These naive players often unknowingly leave slot machines in a valuable condition which can be exploited by any knowledgeable person possessing the proper playing strategy and a rather minimal bankroll.

The information in this text can be used in two distinct ways. First, depending on the type of slot machine, one can use this information to determine if the particular machine that one is playing has reached a stage where it will, on average, be of value to remain at the machine and continue to play until some potential value has been extracted from the machine.

However, the far more common use of this information will probably be to assist an individual to determine if a particular slot machine that some previous player has vacated is, on average, of value to play. If so, then armed with the additional enclosed strategy information, the individual can begin playing and attempt to remove that potential value.

The following material can definitely be used to select slot machines which are of value; the text will also explain how best to proceed to remove that potential value from the machine in the least expensive and most timely manner.

# Preface to Second Edition

During the intervening months since my first book, there have been substantial changes with regard to banking slot machines. To avoid problems that became apparent with the introduction of the first set of banking slots, certain modifications became necessary.

First, banking slot machines became of lower denomination and, as a consequence, of less potential value when left by novice players. Dollar denomination machines were converted to or replaced by quarter and nickel denomination machines.

Second, in conjunction with the above trend, banking machines were developed which were of necessity quarter or nickel denomination slot machines. The games generally involved the play of multiple credits. In some, one could play 45 credits per spin. Clearly, these machines had to be nickel denomination devices. Imagine a customer's outcry if the denomination was one dollar and he inadvertently hit the max bet button. A spin valued at 45 dollars compared to his anticipated one dollar expenditure would result.

Third, entirely new machines were introduced wherein the bonus round, while still of value, was given a random component. This was usually done by giving the participant in the bonus round a choice of several unknown alternatives, each of which had a different bonus amount.

I am at times literally amazed how rapidly the gaming industry is generating new versions of banking games. Competition, with the need to be first on the scene, has led companies to generate new games at a rather rapid pace. Some games, such as Jungle King and Merlin, are remakes with minor repackaging of previous similar games such as Empire, Isle of Pearls, and Spacequest, while Jewel in the Crown and Vacation U.S.A. are entirely new.

The degree of complexity involved in playing some of these newer games on slot machines has reached surprising levels. The complexity will almost undoubtedly continue to increase as different machines are introduced into the gaming environment. The potential slot player will find games mentioned which not only require one to take note of certain banked items but additionally to examine certain facets of the previous play.

The result of all of the above and other minor changes by manufacturers has been to generally make banking slot machines of less value when not played to completion of the bonus round.

Therefore, you will still be able to produce winning results using the information about banking slots contained herein; however, your sessions will be of less value than previously for the same amount of time and number of machines played.

# Banking

No casino could set all its slot machines to have 101% payback and stay in business for long. Occasionally, a casino will advertise that some of its slots have settings to pay over 100%. Then on entering, a player will find a multitude of slot machines with absolutely nothing to indicate just which machines have the "over 100% average payback."

The amount of play necessary to determine just which machine (or machines) possessed that extra edge would be extreme. The cost to a player to determine just which machine(s) could be beaten in the long run would be prohibitive. If one were to somehow learn that information from another source, the information would be worthless within days because the casino personnel would notice a person playing that particular machine too much and simply reset the machine to its standard percentage level while perhaps resetting some other slot machine to pay over 100%.

The point here is that when we speak of an advantageous slot machine, we are speaking of a type of slot machine that gives the player a temporary advantage. We are not speaking about some unknown machine or machines that the casino has hyped for publicity's sake while adjusting its internal settings to be slightly beneficial to the customer.

For a slot machine to be temporarily beneficial to the player, there must be some alteration (sometimes quite subtle) to the machine during its regular play. This alteration need not be distinct and noticeable to the player. In fact, one reason that novice slot players leave machines which would be valuable to continue playing is because the alteration which has made the machine valuable has occurred without a lot of fanfare. The change in the machine's status has been made quietly during the simple routine play of the slot machine. No jackpot bells went off; no "CALL ATTENDANT" sign lit up the monitor. But some subtle yet distinguishable thing has occurred.

The machine must enter a state or condition different from the previous state or condition in that the expected profits from slot play are on average more valuable than the credits being expended during the slot play.

This condition is generally accomplished through a system called banking. In banking as it relates to slot machines, credits, symbols, or some privilege is held in abeyance as a reward or bonus for continued slot play and this may be based on the previous play. The bonus is then awarded when a certain semi- difficult feat is accomplished on the slot machine.

As described above, banking is a technique that has been developed by slot manufactures to encourage slot players to remain at a particular machine and continue to play. It was well known that many slot players often left a machine when they had lost a certain amount, e.g. the twenty dollar bill initially inserted. Studies showed that banking often encouraged some of these losing players to insert additional funds and remain at the slot machine. In the course of a year, inducing additional play among only a fraction of the vast numbers of players could generate substantial additional gaming revenues.

Because of this extra play and the consequent additional profitability of slot machines that have a banking feature over conventional "unbanked" slot machines, banking seems to be here to stay and may well be added to more slot machines in the future.

Often a player on a banking machine will leave while the machine is in a state of increased value and advantageous to continue playing. This departure may be based on ignorance, or some pressing engagement, or possibly a lack of funds to continue playing, or any of a number of obscure reasons. But when this does occur, any person who recognizes the potential value of the machine can begin advantageously playing that very machine with the proper strategy.

A player will generally be better off financially if, instead of playing various slot machines in the hope of being lucky, he spends his time walking through the casino looking for a machine that has been vacated while in an advantageous condition.

# The Slot Card

Many think of a slot card as just one of those things that the casino has as a gimmick. Well, they're right; but it can be one of the nicest gimmicks to experience. A player who begins using a slot card will be absolutely shocked how rapidly slot points can be earned. This is because few people realize just how much monetary action they are giving the casino when they play at a slot machine. On any slot machine, even when an individual plays only one coin at a time, it is often amazing just how many pulls on the handle or pushes on the spin button can occur in a small period of time.

Not all of these spins of the reels are losers; after a hundred spins, the player may well be ahead financially or relatively close to the amount of funds with which he began. Yet those repeated wagers can add up to a sizable number of slot points.

Depending on the particular slot club, these slot points can then be converted into room rentals, meals, assorted logo items, and often everybody's favorite, cash. I must also suggest that any player carefully examine his options as to just what to obtain with his slot points. It may be surprising, but the alternatives to receiving cash for one's slot points are often better.

However, slot card points are a bonus and one should avoid letting these additional benefits distort one's perspective. Slot points are generally minuscule compared to the main objective—winning cash at the slot machines themselves.

A very good book about slot clubs for those playing in the Las Vegas area is Las Vegas Slot Clubs 2000/2001 by Charles W. Lund, who seems to be busy writing all the time. This book or its latest updated version can be obtained through RGE Publishing, 414 Santa Clara Avenue, Oakland CA 94610. Or go to their Web site catalog at *www.rge21.com.*

Slot points can be used directly to obtain various benefits from the casino. However, one's slot play can occasionally be more fully utilized to gain some otherwise lost bonuses. Basically, when playing larger denomination machines for substantial periods of time, ask the floor person or slot host for an appropriate complimentary. Don't hesitate to request some sort of legitimate offering from the slot host. But always ask politely and in such a manner that the host can politely refuse if the request can't be fulfilled. For example, ask, "Could you check our slot card and see if you can arrange for a buffet for my wife and me?" A player will often get the benefit of receiving two free buffets without losing any slot points.

The only time I tend to be more aggressive with phrases such as "I would like a complimentary meal for two to the coffee shop," is when I have been playing on a dollar or higher machine which doesn't for some reason have a working card reader. Then the situation is much more clumsy for the slot host because there is no record of just how long I have been playing; also the slot host does not want to lose what may be a "good" customer for the casino. One almost always gets the request in such cases.

In my wanderings through a blur of casinos, I have met individuals who seriously believe that if a player uses a slot card, the slot machine's computer is programed to make fewer slot payouts to the player, at least to the extent of the value of the slot points. This is such a falsehood that it is astounding to me that these people can believe their own words. Yet there is nothing that one can say to alter these people's distorted idea. Let me assure the reader that the slot manufacturer's creation functions independently of the slot card reader that is added onto the machine. Slot points simply function as a bonus.

Another complaint that I have heard about using slot cards is based on the idea that the IRS will get hold of those records and know just how much the individual profited playing slot machines.

Well, that's right! The government could actually get hold of the casino's records and check to see just how much one has won on the slot machines. But that would be a real variation of the government's activities in such a situation. Since the casinos are required to report all large winnings to the Internal Revenue Service, the government has much of the information that it wishes. The tax people are generally interested in sizable winnings and not in routine play at the machines. Consequently, whenever a player has a win of or exceeding $1200, the player is required to present proper identification and complete and sign a W-2G form. So the important information about sizable winnings flows to the government regardless of slot card use.

A second problem with the slot card for tax purposes is its misuse. For example, there are individuals who go into a casino and surreptitiously insert their slot card into various slot machines. If an individual without a slot card begins to play, this play is credited to the player whose card is in the reader because the new player usually doesn't even glance at the card reader. With several machines "working" for him, the individual may eventually accumulate enough points from the play of others to obtain a few free meals or items from the logo shop. Depending on the slot club, cash benefits may be obtained. But more significantly with regard to our tax discussion, the play of these other individuals, which would probably be financially negative, could be used as the basis of a deduction from slot winnings by obtaining a printout from the casino.

As I understand things, such activity is illegal, although I know of no case where someone was actually prosecuted. Usually the individual is simply told to stay out of the casino. Casinos generally counter this type of activity by instructing the change people and floor persons to remove slot cards from machines that are not being played whenever such a card is spotted. Additionally, some slot card mechanisms are designed to automatically terminate collecting information on slot play if the slot machine in which a card is inserted is not played within a specified time allotment (usually several minutes). As a further defense against such random card insertions, some casinos keep a running count on the number of slot cards issued to each account. Obtaining fifty extra slot cards in a month would certainly send off a few bells in the slot department.

If a player seriously wants to accumulate a few extra slot points that he deserves because he forgot and left his slot card out of the last machine played, let me suggest a mild remedy. When playing a slot machine, a player can simply put an extra slot card in the machine on each side of the machine being played. This is not an uncommon practice because many people often drop coins into adjacent machines as they play the machine that is in front of them. Then if someone does perchance begin to play one of these side machines without removing the player's slot card, . . . well, the player shouldn't disturb him. It's rude to interrupt a dedicated slot player.

Now a player can begin to get an idea of the informational problems associated with the use of slot cards from the government's and the casino's perspective. Incidental to all this, I should comment that generally the casino's record of one's losses at slot play can properly be used to offset taxes on winnings. This is commonly done by requesting a computer printout of one's slot play from the casino's slot club.

If a player is serious in his concern about the government's tax men following his casino action on the slot machines, let me make one suggestion. On many advantageous slot machines, it is possible to pull one's slot card from the machine prior to the winning of substantial funds in a final bonus round. Using this technique (appropriately pulling the slot card), one can generally make the machine appear to be a loser. I believe doing this to convince the IRS that a player has lost funds is an extreme move. However, I certainly approve of doing it to deceive the casino about how the player is faring.

A final word of caution about the use of slot cards is in store for the reader. Slot points are generally considered a promotional item or gratuity from the casino and do not have the same status as direct winnings. Thus, these points can be nullified at the whim of the casino. Clearly, this affects the use of slot points that accumulate on one's slot card.

My advice is to always extract the value from the slot card as soon as reasonably possible. This is based on the experiences that my wife and I personally had at the Tropicana Hotel and Casino in Las Vegas.

We eventually caught security people there involved in very questionable activities. However, the activities in this situation were not, strictly speaking, illegal in the sense of prosecutable, but were rather simply labeled poor business practices from the point of view of the Tropicana. This is further mentioned in the chapters Piggy Bankin', The Slot Point Fiasco, The Search, and Till Tapping, and was also partially covered in the local newspaper, the Valley Explorer.

The upshot of all this was that we were told to stay out of the Tropicana by the security department. It seems that Tropicana security doesn't mind watching everybody else but just doesn't want to be watched itself. When we were expelled from the Trop, there was $500 on our slot card. $296 was actual cash while $204 was in food comps. Through the intervention of the casino manager, we were eventually able to obtain the $296 in cash that we had on the slot card. However, we were not permitted to use the $204 of food comps since we were not permitted to enter the casino.

Although this is the only casino where we have ever had any problem with our slot card points, there are some good lessons to be learned from the experience. First, a player should generally remove the value from the card as it accumulates. Although he believes hisr conduct is above reproach and certainly doesn't expect to have any difficulty with the casino personnel, he simply shouldn't take a chance on any situation arising. Secondly, he should never show his slot card to the security personnel. It will not impress them that he is a valued customer. (This was my mistake in dealing with the Tropicana security.) Thirdly, it is best to remove the value from the card as soon as reasonably possible because there is an outside chance that the individual named on the card will die. Slot points do not become a part of an individual's estate and are simply forfeited back to the casino. Sure, that's another long shot, but still, why take a chance with any sizable amount of slot points? As an added precaution in that respect, it is a good idea to have a joint slot account with one's spouse.

As I stated before, my wife and I only had a problem with the confiscation of our slot points at the Las Vegas Tropicana and at absolutely no other of the sixty-plus casinos in Las Vegas. This should also not be taken as an indication that a similar action would occur at the Tropicana in Atlantic City. But then again,

I've heard that people who steal with their right hand know how to steal with their left.

# Additional Information

In the pages which follow this chapter, the most profitable method to play many machines will be described in varying detail. Some machines will be listed that have a banking feature but yet are still not profitable to locate in order to play. The information about the various advantageous slot machines has been obtained by me, my wife, and a few associates, and is based on those personal experiences. Also, all the data has been gathered in the Las Vegas area, which may distort the results somewhat because the competitive gaming environment results in smaller casino holds. In no case has a slot manufacturer supplied information that could be used to make exact determinations related to the advice presented. Although such data is a part of the slot manufacturer's knowledge, it is often held closely as a trade secret.

However, with hundreds of trials (slot plays) and some sophisticated analyses, considerable information about the workings of these advantageous slot machines has been obtained. The data collected has been given somewhat special treatment. The data does not include information involving very large wins on these slot machines. This is, in part, because such rare events have a radically distorting effect on comparatively small collections of data, and also because such wins are not a typical occurrence for the average individual playing for the relatively short period of time that such a vacation generally entails.

Omitting such pieces of data does, of course, affect the analysis. As a consequence, the results presented in the following chapters are somewhat on the conservative side, although mildly so. Since in no case were unusually large losses (which were never as big as the very large wins) removed from the collection of data, the final results presented herein are biased, in that the actual average wins should be very sightly larger. This bias is again increased somewhat when recommendations are made regarding when and how to play the various slot machines. I felt that since the reader will almost undoubtedly be using the findings presented herein, conservative and easily remembered rules and strategies should take precedence over a precision that could overwhelm some of the many readers.

I should also comment that the information collected has been abbreviated to assist the general reader, who is usually only interested in obtaining a profit from his slot play. Hopefully, the chapters which follow will prove useful to anyone visiting casinos and playing slot machines for even a short period of time.

I should mention that not every machine will be a winner and that the player will only have what is generally referred to as the long-run advantage. In other words, the information provided herein should make the player a winner with repeated play, and his various slot plays will make him a winner on average. However, playing advantageous slot machines correctly and under the proper conditions will not guarantee a win with each slot machine play. Because of the innate variability, some machines will wind up among one's losing experiences. Nonetheless, with repeated play under the proper conditions, one will in time be a winner.

When playing slot machines, there are some general rules to observe. First, it is far easier to use a bill acceptor than to hand-feed coins. Consequently, a player should generally use a reasonably sized bill for the particular denomination machine that is being played. Putting a hundred dollar bill into a nickel slot machine is ludicrous. The two thousand credits posted on the machine are far more than one can reasonably use in playing; and at the end of the slot play, the player will almost undoubtedly need a time-consuming hopper fill.

Another reason to use the bill acceptor is in case a special pay period arises. Some machines, e.g. Buccaneer Gold, have a special feature which involves a short play period, usually about thirty seconds, during which all the payouts are doubled. During such a period, the slot customer is well-advised to play the maximum number of credits per spin. But in order to play most rapidly during this time frame, the player should be playing credits rather than using the more time-consuming process of hand-feeding coins.

With regard to rapid play, one should note that some machines, such as Super 7's, have speed buttons. Although one will initially be fascinated with the play of the various slot machines, one will eventually become slightly bored and even find it a little amazing that others can find the machines intriguing. If one begins to find the slot play boring, one should set the speed button to its maximum. Over the course of many spins, the time to complete a particular game will be significantly reduced.

Another piece of good advice is to be sure to be fully paid by the slot machine when cashing out. First, a player should be sure that the credit meter reads zero. If it doesn't, the machine probably needs a hopper fill; a slot attendant will notice the machine's top light blinking and come to make the proper adjustment. Sometimes, the problem is simply that the machine has had a coin jam during the payout.

With slot machines, it is a good policy to record just how many credits one has prior to cashing out. Then when reaching the change booth and converting the dispensed coins back into paper currency, one can note if one receives the same amount as the slot machine indicated. If there is a shortage, simply tell the cashier or a floor person and the matter will be corrected with the player receiving the amount of the shortage, usually a coin or two. However, if perchance there are more coins than originally thought, then the player may have located an over-payer. These are discussed in a later chapter.

A player should generally avoid playing slot machines if he is underfinanced and doesn't have enough funds to play the machines properly to completion. If he does play into some monstrously awful slot machine that quickly depletes the money on his person, instead of leaving the machine when the funds are gone, he should call a floor person and ask to have the slot machine reserved while he goes to eat. The floor people at most casinos are empowered to reserve a machine for a period of roughly two hours. This should hopefully be enough time to obtain some additional funds to continue to play the machine to its completion. The player should never expect the machine to remain unnoticed while he goes to obtain additional funds.

In the course of playing advantageous slot machines, one will eventually notice that there are more than a few other individuals examining the same types of slot machines. These people are relatively easy to identify in the casino setting because they are routinely observing a select set of slots, and also their play follows certain standard practices. As soon as a particular objective is accomplished on a slot machine, they will terminate their play. It's hard to avoid noticing these same people day after day during casino visits.

These individuals are basically the competitors for the advantageous machines that inexperienced players leave. Competing with them to obtain machines of value is a skill all its own and learning how to compete better is something that simply takes time.

About the simplest trick these patrons sometimes use to get a desirable machine that they have just missed is to say to the person at the machine, "I was going to play that machine. I just went to get change." Simply remain at the machine and tell the individual that next time he should use the change light to get a change person to come to him.

If one sits down at a valuable machine and another person simply states, "I was waiting for that machine," one should pleasantly tell him, "And you still are." One should never be overly concerned about personal safety, because casinos have more than enough security personnel, backup, and plain clothes operatives to handle any violent situation. Since all the games are monitored, the entire incident will be on tape; and if one has only acted defensively, this will be noted.

As a final precaution concerning these competitors, a player should generally not wear a name tag (with complete name) or similar item while playing a valuable slot machine. If he does, he may find that he is suddenly paged for an important phone call. If he cashes out from the machine and leaves it unattended, he may well learn that the other party has the wrong person, who coincidentally has his same name.

It has been my opinion that waiting for machines is not a profitable use of one's time. Oh, certainly, if I were to see a valuable machine and the current player appeared to be inexperienced because of his style of play (usually playing max coins) and the player also had only a very few credits left, I would pause to see if he departed after using his few remaining credits.

But, based on my observations, advantageous slot machines are generally not worth waiting for. This is because many inexperienced players often simply get out more money when their credits are gone and continue to play their machine. So a wait of many minutes can often be all for naught. And then there's the real possibility that another person will come by and decide to also wait for the same machine. How can one resolve that situation?

The easiest solution to all this is to generally not bother to hang around waiting for machines. A player will find plenty of other machines in the time he would have wasted waiting. Also as a general rule, one shouldn't fret about failing to get a particular machine. Try to learn something from the experience and remember that one simply can't get and play all the machines available. Additionally, if one hasn't spent any appreciable amount of time waiting, then one doesn't feel much loss in not obtaining a particular machine.

It is also suggested that a player examine the casino funbook prior to playing. Occasionally, a casino will have a coupon in its funbook aimed at slot play. Although this is definitely the exception, it is wise to check the casino funbook before playing.

When playing advantageous slot machines at various casinos, one will notice that there are different pay schedules on some games that have the same name. Superficially, one might think that it is better to play the machine that has the best pay schedule. That would not necessarily be correct. Every casino can set the hold on its machines; consequently, a machine with a "generous" pay schedule may have a setting that holds more for the casino than a machine with a "less generous" pay schedule at another casino. A casual player cannot sort out this type of variation and should simply select and play all of any type of machine in the same manner.

In this regard, it should be noted that generally lower denomination slot machines have a larger hold than higher denomination slot machines. When I have noted this to affect the data of a particular type of machine, the relevant information has been included in the text.

In the data given in the following chapters, no attempt has been made to discriminate the nuances of variability among the numerous casinos in regard to their hold. However, if one plays for months, these small variations start to become apparent. The information given in this book is a compilation of the results of machines at all the casinos visited. The information concerning when and how to play various machines should be correct for any casino.

It is my opinion that variations in the hold for different casinos and also for different areas across the country will only affect the average profitability of a particular machine mildly and only change the average profitability by a very few credits at most.

# The Machines

## An American in Paris

*Synopsis: Play three credits per spin when any figure is one step from the end of a route which has fifty or more as the indicated bonus or two steps from the end of a route which has one hundred or more as the bonus or three steps from the end of a route which has a bonus of 150 credits. Terminate play when the requirements for play are not met.*

An American in Paris is, except for cosmetic variations, identical to Tour de Slot. Both these games are exclusive to Paris; even their sister properties, Bally's, etc. do not have these or similar versions of this game. With such limited distribution, it was debatable whether to include this game in the book. However, it was felt the game was of such a different variety that it would serve as an example concerning other games that might be developed and presented to the public. So the information is included.

The play on An American in Paris is composed of two parts. There is the spinning of the three reels with results which are paid as ordinarily through reference to the pay tables. Then additionally, there can be some reel alinements which effect a banking feature on the visual.

The visual, located above the reels, pictures a white circular area with a flag pole and French flag from which six routes each wind to one of six attractions of the city of Paris. To an extent, this compares to a six-legged octopus.

The routes, which are of varying lengths, are composed of distinct steps similar to the divisions on a sidewalk. Small figures each move from the central circular area to the end of their particular route. The movement of the figures follows the discrete pattern of the route and toward a number located near its end.

When a figure reaches the end of a route, you are awarded a bonus on the credit meter. The bonus is a number of credits equal to the number located near the end of the particular route. The figure is then returned to the white circular area to begin a new trip on the same route. The number near the end of that route and used to determine the last bonus is then altered.

The accompanying chart shows the relationship of the various destinations, route lengths, figures, and reel positions. On examination, you may be interested to note that each of the various figures is limited to appearing on one reel. Thus, you can move any figure only one step per spin.

A profitable method to play An American in Paris is to locate a machine on which any figure is one step from the end of a route which has fifty or more as the indicated bonus or two steps from the end of a route which has one hundred or more as the bonus or three steps from the end of a route which has a bonus of 150 credits.

After locating such a machine, you must play the maximum of three credits per spin until the appropriate figure is moved to the end of the route and the desired bonus is obtained.

Play is terminated if the machine no longer meets any requirement for play.

The advice given above is conservative. You can actually play machines with the figures at greater distances from the end of the routes. However, the play quickly begins to become marginal and, coupled with the fact that results on these games are quite variable, you will probably find more satisfaction in just playing machines with strong settings.

As a final suggestion, never be tempted by a bonus of less than fifty which has the figure only a single step from the route's end. On average, you will be financially disappointed. A figure only a single step from a small bonus is helpful during play for a larger bonus, but should not be played on its own merit.

| DESTINATION | ROUTE LENGTH (in Steps) | FIGURE | REEL POSITION (Left to Right) |
|---|---|---|---|
| Le Louvre | 10 | Male Pedestrian | 1 |
| La Seine | 4 | Scooter | 1 |
| Le Moulin Rouge | 5 | Auto | 2 |
| L'Arc de Triomphe | 6 | Balloon | 2 |
| La Tour Eiffel | 9 | Female Pedestrian | 3 |
| Le Port Alexandre III | 7 | Bicycle | 3 |

# Balloon Bars Balloon Race

*Synopsis: Never play.*

Balloon Bars Balloon Race is a banking game in which the item being banked is the height of the three balloons which are numbered 15, 40, and 100. The balloons are represented on the screen above the reels and the player is rewarded the number of credits of the balloon reaching the top of the screen. The balloon reaching the top will almost invariably be balloon number 15.

This game is difficult to analyze because there are no clear digital markings of altitude on the balloon background display. Although the balloons move a distinct number of steps during their rising, it is difficult to see with precision that, for example, balloon number 40 has three steps to go. But more significantly, the new player or total novice cannot hope to be able to evaluate the three balloons' positions properly.

Since you can't accurately appraise the item that has been banked, you should avoid this particular banking game.

# Big Bang Piggy Bankin'

*Synopsis: Play one credit per spin when there are forty or more credits in the bank. Terminate play when three "Break the Bank" symbols or equivalent are alined. [Note: Slot machine instructions commonly use the terms "aline" and "alinement" instead of the more common "align" and "alignment." As Webster allows both spellings, we shall adhere to the industry standard.]*

Big Bang Piggy Bankin' slot machines are similar in appearance to their predecessors, Piggy Bankin' slot machines. These newer machines bank an additional credit into the pretend piggy bank whenever you wager three credits and aline three blank symbols. The piggy bank, which can start at a number as low as five, thus grows until three "Break the Bank" symbols or an equivalent grouping containing some wild symbol(s) are alined on the payline.

In order to play these machines advantageously, you should find a piggy bank that contains at least forty credits and you should wager one credit per spin. Play should be terminated when three "Break the Bank" symbols or any of the equivalent groupings are alined.

The machines are rather time-consuming to play in order to break the bank. This large amount of play makes the results of individual machines rather volatile, and the winnings, which are averages experienced with long-run play, can be frustrating to obtain.

# Bingo

*Synopsis: Play to completion any fixed position bingo that is at least half done. Alternatively, determine the number of spot-credits of the previous player and decide if that number of spots additionally marked on the card will result in a bingo. Play in all cases should be at one credit per spin on one payline. Terminate play when a bingo is obtained.*

Bingo is exactly that, bingo. I am not going to clutter these pages with instructions about the basic game of bingo. If you don't know how to play bingo, you must have missed childhood.

So assuming you already have a reasonable grasp of bingo, I will proceed to explain the slot machine version called Bingo.

The slot machine version has five reels on a video screen. These five reels correspond to the five columns on a standard bingo card, which is displayed on the screen. The five reels often play as on an ordinary five reel slot machine. However, the reels, when coming to a stop, occasionally have one or more bingo balls (a maximum of five) displayed. When a bingo ball is displayed, the machine will simulate the drawing of a bingo number, not from the general collection of 75 bingo numbers, but only from the collection of the fifteen numbers associated with the column in which a particular ball appears. In this respect, the drawings in the game of Bingo differ from standard bingo.

Whenever a bingo ball leads to a number which is present on the displayed bingo card, the card is marked. The cards are marked in two distinct ways; but this phenomenon, should it occur on your bingo card, will be easily understood during the play of Bingo. It suffices that each number on the card is clearly marked when it occurs.

Note that if all fifteen numbers of a particular column have been drawn, then the appearance on the reels of a bingo ball associated with that column will not cause a number to be drawn.

Bingo numbers are drawn during the play of the game until a bingo is obtained. There are several types of bingos which we will discuss in greater detail later in this chapter. When the bingo occurs, the machine enters a bonus round during which you must select among five random alternatives to obtain an until-then-unknown amount of credits. With a minimum of assistance, the machine then resets for a new bingo game.

Surprisingly, there are actually two items banked in Bingo. One is the numbers that have been drawn and the second is the numbers marked on the cards. Fortunately, these two items are closely correlated. (Generally, for every number marked on a card, two other numbers have been drawn that were not present

on the bingo card.) As a consequence, we will only concern ourselves with the numbers that are marked on the card.

Additionally, we will forego any study of the pattern of the
marked spots (drawn numbers) on the cards. We will only deal
with the number of bingo spots (numbers) that are already
marked on a card.

But before we get into that discussion, I should explain how
to have the machine generate bingo numbers or, as we commonly
say, draw bingo numbers. Bingo numbers can be obtained by
playing a single credit on only one payline. The bingo balls
(numbers) do not have to be on a payline and function somewhat
similarly to a scatter pay. The consequence of this is that in all
cases, you should only play one credit per spin until the bonus is
obtained. Then, naturally enough, play should be terminated.

As was mentioned previously, there are several types of
bingos on a Bingo machine. After a bonus round, the player must
make a selection for a new bingo game prior to the amount of the
bonus being transferred to the credit meter. So the previous
player will, as far as our readers are concerned, decide which
bingo game is played. It is possible on a Bingo machine to terminate a bingo game and begin anew with a totally fresh card and
game. This can, in a very few cases, be a wise maneuver. But
that is to get ahead of ourselves. Generally, you will be completing the bingo game that the previous player has started.

On Bingo, there are sixteen different bingo games that may
be played. They are described in the accompanying table. This
collection of sixteen varieties of bingo can be divided into two
groups: fixed position bingos and variable position bingos.
There are eleven fixed position bingos: Four Corners, Small Diamond, Small Picture Frame, Letter T, Plus Sign, Letter X, Large
Diamond, Letter L, Letter N, Large Picture Frame, and Cover
All. The other group of five can each be won with a bingo in several assorted positions.

The reason for mentioning these two groups is because deciding if a machine is of value to play can be based, in part, on the
type of bingo that the previous player has begun.

The easiest way to decide if some Bingo machine is, on average, worth playing is to see if the previous player was playing a fixed position bingo. Assuming that to be the case, then if half the bingo is completed, play the machine until the bingo is obtained. As mentioned above, play at one credit on one payline until the bingo is obtained and then terminate play. This strategy will, on average, lead to positive financial results.

That is the simplest profit-making strategy that I know for playing a Bingo machine. It is, unfortunately, quite incomplete in that it omits the consideration of play on the five variable position bingos. Besides that, the strategy is rather weak in that it does not consider the coin input of the previous player. However, that strategy will, on average, make you a winner. Using that strategy, you will, however, pass by many valuable Bingo machines.

A much better strategy to use is also more complicated.

This strategy is based on two assumptions. The first assumption is that the cost of getting a bingo number on the card is a constant across the the entire drawing of the 75 numbers. In other words, the average cost to obtain the third number on the card is the same as the cost to obtain the fifteenth number on the card. This is not perfectly true and will be off somewhat more in a cover all game, but is a workable assumption for our analysis.

It is known that the bonus for obtaining a bingo is a function of the total amount wagered since the last bingo. This leads to the second assumption, which is that, in order for you (the second player) to be a winner, on average, the previous player must have put at least half the money into the Bingo machine prior to your obtaining the bonus from the bingo. This is actually, I believe, a little too high in that the previous player needs only to have inserted a slightly lower percentage. Continuing, the previous player's input being 50% or more should place you, the second player, in a definitely favorable position to exploit the previous player's slot play.

Unless we have patiently waited and watched the previous player's slot play, clearly we have no sure method of measuring that slot play. However, we can attempt to make a reasonable estimate of his coin input by using certain information on the machine.

The first bit of information is the previous player's last total bet. This is easily seen on the machine as total bet, which is the product of lines played and bet per line. So this last total bet is the first bit of information. We then assume that the player wagered exactly the same on each of his previous spins. This is not an unreasonable assumption and is common among many slot players. Then count the number of marked spots on the bingo card. Count the marked spots no matter how they are marked. Then multiply the number of marked spots times the total bet to get a product which is a certain number of what we will call spotcredits, for lack of a better name. This final product is a measure of the previous player's input. In one sense, this product is just a meaningless number; but it is an indicator or measure of the previous player's input into that particular Bingo machine. Let us call the measure of the previous player's input M.

Now you will find this Bingo machine, on average, to your financial advantage to play if you can be reasonably assured that, on obtaining the bingo for the bonus payment, your input will be less than or equal to the input of the previous player. The measure of his input was M and so the measure of your input should be less than or equal to M.

Since you will always be wagering on only one line at one credit per spin, your total bet will always be one. If you wager in this manner and obtain M bingo numbers, you will have inserted coinage which by our measure appears to equal that of the previous player's input. But if you bingo at or before getting M bingo numbers, you will, on average, have a profitable experience. This will be because an early bingo would indicate that you had inserted less than half the funds used to generate this bonus.

So with this strategy, you must first measure the previous player's input and then decide if obtaining additional bingo numbers numerically equal to his input will generate a bingo. If so, then the machine is, on average, worth playing.

Now if you're getting lost in all this verbiage, which is quite natural, let me assist you by giving a few examples.

Let's assume that you locate a Bingo machine at which the previous player has obtained six bingo numbers and his last total bet was five credits. The measure of his input in this case is 6 x 5 or thirty spotcredits. Now if you play with a total bet of one and obtain thirty more bingo numbers, your input will also be thirty spotcredits. Since there are six spots marked already, you can't possibly add thirty more markings to the bingo card without first getting a bingo. Therefore, you will bingo before you have put in 50% of all of the funds since the last bingo. Thus, on average, this Bingo machine is definitely a good play.

As a second example, let us assume that you locate a Bingo machine at which the previous player has obtained two bingo numbers and his last total bet was five credits. The measure of his input in this case is 2 x 5 or ten spotcredits. If you play with a total bet of one and obtain ten more bingo numbers, your input into the Bingo machine since the last bingo will also be ten spotcredits. Since there are two spots on the bingo card already marked, you will, at that time, have twelve spots marked on the bingo card. If, for some reason, you believe that twelve spots marked will form a bingo, then you should play the machine. Personally, I would generally avoid play on such a machine.

Now let's assume that in the above example, instead of two marked spots, there had been three. Then the measure of the the previous player's input is 3 x 5 or fifteen spotcredits. If you play with a total bet of one (and I know of no good financial reason to play more) and obtain fifteen more bingo numbers, your input into the Bingo machine since the last bingo will also be fifteen spotcredits. Since there are three spots on the bingo card already marked, you will then have eighteen spots marked on the bingo card. If you believe that twelve more spots marked for a total of eighteen will form a bingo, then you should play the machine. Almost certainly, eighteen spots on a bingo card will form a straight line or as the machine terms it, an Any Way bingo. Of course, if the game is Cover All, then you still won't have a bingo. So depending on what type of bingo is being attempted, you variously may or may not continue play on this Bingo machine.

As a final example, assume that the previous player has obtained two spots on a Cover All bingo and his last play was five credits per line on all five paylines. His last wager was a total bet of 25 credits. The measure of his input that we are using yields 2 x 25 (i.e. 2 spots times 25 credits) or fifty spotcredits. This is clearly a good play since you would have to do the impossible task of obtaining fifty bingo numbers to equal his input.

Chasing down the other 22 bingo numbers on this card is rather time consuming. A simpler method to obtain a bingo to reap the financial benefit of the previous play is to change the bingo game and play an Any Way bingo. (The accompanying table shows the relative difficulty of various types of bingo as played on a Bingo machine.) With this technique, you will certainly not need to obtain 22 more marks on the card to obtain a bingo. The financial input of the previous player is transferred to the new situation and you can begin collecting marks on the new card. The loss of the two previous spots marked on the old card is insignificant compared to the value derived from changing to another simpler type of bingo.

Changing to another type of bingo is unusual and I have used the technique relatively few times. However, the idea of changing bingos can be used at other times to obtain a desirable Bingo machine. Consider this situation. You are playing at a slot machine and you see some distance away another individual leave his Bingo machine. You leave your machine temporarily, probably setting some empty change containers on the seat. You then go to the vacated machine and see that it is worth playing and should best be played by changing to another type of bingo. You cannot play two machines at a noticeable distance apart. Therefore, you should immediately 'knock down' the vacated machine (generate an empty bingo card) and return to your current machine. That approach will prevent other individuals with comparable gaming savvy from realizing that the machine is of value. When you complete the machine with which you are currently involved, you will be more apt to find the vacated machine still available for play.

The last facet of Bingo that will be mentioned here is a feature called Instant Bingo Jackpot, which enables you to obtain the bonus payout in a single spin. The feature is designed so that if five bingo balls appear on the screen on a single spin, the machine immediately awards the bonus payout and then proceeds to a new bingo game. I have never experienced this rare event or know anyone who has.

Bingo machines are often played to completion of the bingo. The public understands bingo (or thinks it does) and individuals tend to play a bingo game to completion. Occasionally, people will tire, or run short of funds, or whatever. But more often on this machine than on many other games, individuals play to the end.

I will try to summarize for you the important part of all of the above information. Play to completion any fixed position bingo that is at least half done. Alternatively, determine the number of spotcredits of the previous player and decide if that number of spots additionally marked on the bingo card will result in a bingo. In relatively rare cases, consider changing to a different type of bingo game. Play in all cases should be at one credit per spin on one payline. Terminate play when a bingo is obtained.

Wait a minute! Isn't that the synopsis? This must be where you came in.

## Bingo Card Types

| | | | |
|---|---|---|---|
| Any Way | Any Vertical Line | Any Postage Stamp | Any Horizontal Line |
| Any Kite | Four Corners | Small Diamond | Small Picture Frame |
| Letter T | Plus Sign | Letter X | Large Diamond |
| Letter L | Letter N | Large Picture Frame | Cover All |

"Cards are in order of difficulty from easiest (Any Way) to the most difficult (Cover All)." is a quote from the information on Bingo machines. The statement is not correct for standard bingo.

# Blackjack

*Synopsis: This is not a banking game on most slot machines.*

Just what is blackjack doing in a book about advantageous slot machines? The reason that blackjack can properly be included in such a book is that in blackjack, good cards can in a sense be banked as the deck is depleted. In the standard game of blackjack, a player gains an advantage over the dealer by evaluating the cards as they are played (generally called card counting) and determining that the remaining cards in the deck(s) are favorable to the player. In other words, favorable cards can be banked by being a part of the cards in the dealer's possession that are still to be dealt.

However, there are plenty of very good books about blackjack and card counting, so we will not delve into card counting in this book. Also, although they do exist, there are relatively few slot machines offering blackjack that do not shuffle after each hand, thus eliminating the advantage that counting can give.

On a slot machine that offers blackjack, the usual procedure is to have the machine shuffle and deal from a single deck after every hand. In such a case, no banking operation occurs because the unused remainder of the deck is discarded (at least in the machine sense).

Most machines offering blackjack operate within these parameters: single deck with a shuffle after each hand. Most of these games cannot be beaten with long-run play because, for example, the machine does not pay 3-to-2 on a natural (21 in two cards), or doubling is significantly restricted, or some other facet of the game has somehow been altered.

However, there are a very few single-deck blackjack games with a shuffle after each hand that can be slowly beaten in the long run with extremely large amounts of error-free play. Sometimes the advantage comes about because of the use of a slot card and its associated benefits.

If, perchance, the casino is offering some sort of a deal for slot play and there are no advantageous slot machines in the establishment, then any player who wishes to take part in the casino offer may decide to play a slot machine offering a disadvantageous blackjack game. By playing such a game in preference to an ordinary slot machine, you would be able to estimate your average loss prior to play, something you could never do with a standard slot machine.

For whatever reason you may elect to play a single-deck blackjack game with shuffling after each hand, the most accurate basic strategy I have been able to glean from countless sources is given in the Appendix.

Because these tables are incredibly involved, The publisher, Arnold Snyder, suggested that this complex blackjack strategy be accompanied by a shorter, more easily remembered strategy. Consequently, there is a second strategy included which will do almost as well and is a lot easier on your cranium. Additionally, he suggested that with both strategies, insurance should never be obtained when offered.

# Blackout Poker

*Synopsis: Play, preferably alone, when the bonus for elimination of a group is over forty credits and the cards to be eliminated in that group are two or fewer low cards or three or fewer high cards. Terminate play when the desired bonus is no longer available.*

Blackout Poker is a form of video poker. Generally, this book does not deal with video poker in its many variations. But Blackout Poker is so much more of a banking game than a form of video poker that we will discuss the game in these pages.

Perhaps I should begin by saying that Blackout Poker was a form of video poker. I have not seen the game in any Las Vegas casino for some time, and there is the distinct possibility that the manufacturer has discontinued the distribution of this game. However, since there are areas of the country where casinos may still have this set of machines on the floor, it will be discussed in some detail and the reasons for its removal will be considered.

Blackout Poker involved a set of linked quarter slot machines. The set of machines could, of course, have been virtually any number, just as Flush Attack can include any number of machines. But five or six was the size of the sets of linked machines in the systems that I knew.

Above and in front of the set of machines was a large illuminated board with important information about the current status of the game in progress. The board had lights indicating each of the 52 cards of a standard deck. This set of lights was divided into two groups. One contained lights for the twenty cards: ten, jack, queen, king, and ace of each of the four suits. The second group contained the lights for the group of 32 cards, two through nine of each of the four suits.

Associated with each group was a bonus meter which was initially at zero but grew during the play of the machines. There was also a third bonus meter which functioned in a relationship with both groups. All three of these bonus meters grew during the general play of the set of machines.

The video poker game on all these machines was a version of Jacks or Better. One could play this Jacks or Better video poker on any of these machines in a manner similar to play on any other video poker machine. However, the pay schedule on this set of machines was rather poor, primarily because the payment for two pair was one credit per credit wagered.

Initially, the lights for all 52 cards were illuminated. The blackout process was begun by individuals playing at the machines. Their play caused two events to happen. First, their video poker play on the machine would cause the cards to be blackedout. A card was blackedout by being a winning part of a final hand that was a paying hand. That is: the final hand after the draw had to be a paying hand and only the cards that contributed to the win were blackedout, not necessarily the entire hand. This process slowly removed the illumination of the individual cards in the two groups by blacking them out, hence the name Blackout Poker.

The blackingout process continued until the final card of either group was blackedout. Then the entire set of twenty or 32 cards (or both simultaneously) was illuminated again and the process could repeat itself. Thus, the term blackingout also applies to the process of blackingout the final card of the group and is used interchangeably to refer to blackingout the group or groups.

Besides this blackout process, the video poker play of individuals at these machines also caused the amounts on three bonus meters to rise. The amounts on the three bonus meters were paid to the player as machine credits and associated with

1) blackingout the final card in group one, the cards ten through ace,
2) blackingout the final card in group two, the cards two through nine, and
3) blackingout the final cards in both groups, one and two, simultaneously.

As individuals played on the machines, all three of these bonus meters would slowly rise. The meters were strictly based on coin-in and winning or losing of the player(s) did not affect the meters' functioning.

Whenever group one or two was blackedout by a particular player, that player received the amount (in quarter increments) as a bonus on the credit meter of his machine. The machine then reset the bonus amount of that group to zero.

If perchance a player blackedout both groups one and two simultaneously, then the player would receive, in addition to the individual bonuses for groups one and two, the bonus amount on the third meter. The machine then reset the bonus amount of all three meters to zero.

This then is how a set of Blackout Poker machines functioned. Of course, to play this game one should have some knowledge of how to play this version of Jacks or Better.

After some time, the Blackout Poker machines were altered by the manufacturer so that the machines reset to a "random" amount of generally a few dollars instead of resetting to zero. This alteration was the result of observations that players avoided the set of machines when any one of the meters was at or near zero. This alteration did not affect how to advantageously play this game.

To play Blackout Poker profitably involved three distinct approaches. The first and least used approach involved winning the bonus associated with blackingout both groups simultaneously. To do this properly involved team play. A team of generally two or three individuals would wait until the bonus meter was over one hundred dollars. Then they would attempt to occupy the entire set of machines. This would involve each individual inserting some funds into the machines and feigning to play two machines each. If there was some problem in holding that many machines from other players, the team might resort to placing an out of order sticker over one or two of the machines. Also the teams tended to operate in the very late night or early morning to lessen customer interference.

The team would play to obtain a hand on one of the machines such that in the first five cards dealt there would be either two pair or a straight or a flush (containing cards or pairs of both groups). After accomplishing this feat (not a quick easy undertaking), the team would let this specially setup machine simply remain in its special state.

Using the other linked machines, the team would then try to structure the illuminated board so that the special machine could be played to obtain all three bonuses at once, but most importantly the large bonus for simultaneously blackingout both groups.

This technique is a profitable way to win at Blackout Poker, but is an extremely difficult procedure for an individual player to use alone. However, most of our readers are not into team play and so may find that information of little value. Also there is the possibility that if the casino personnel sensed that a group of individuals was artificially withholding machines from play by other customers, the entire team would be out the door.

A far more common way to win at a set of Blackout Poker machines would be for an individual to play under the proper conditions. The conditions are that one should only play when a bonus meter for a group is forty credits or higher.

Then, additionally, one should only play when the group with the bonus meter at forty credits or higher has two or fewer low (tens or less) cards remaining to be blackedout. If the bonus meter for a group is forty credits or higher and there are three or fewer high (jacks or higher) cards to be blackedout, the play should still, on average, be financially beneficial. This difference in the number of cards is because high cards function in the pay schedule as pairs whereas low cards do not. Even plays such as two high cards and one low card, or one high card and two low cards, are worth pursuing.

Individual play on a Blackout Poker machine should be terminated when there is no bonus for group one or group two which exceeds forty credits or the number of cards in the group requiring blackingout is too large.

It is obviously better to play Blackout Poker alone, but this will not always be the case. If the competition is slow-playing tourists who dwell seemingly endlessly over every hand, don't be concerned. With other competition, the game can be a real race to get the right cards.

It is extremely difficult to give any estimates about the profitability of playing Blackout Poker primarily because the profitability is linked very closely to a player's general skill at playing this version of Jacks or Better video poker. Certainly, skillful players can and will play profitably at levels below the forty credit boundary that has been promoted here.

As mentioned before, Blackout Poker was a form of video poker in the Las Vegas area. It is my opinion that the casinos which had this game tired of the noticeable intermittent team activity which occurred when the bonus meter for blackingout both groups was high. Having the entire set of machines tied up by as few as two individuals was more than a little irritating.

Besides this, the game may not have had a sufficient amount of additional play compared to other video poker machines to warrant its retention.

# Bonus 5 Line

*Synopsis: Never play.*

Bonus 5 Line is a game that can be found on Multi-Game machines. It is a banking game in which you must accumulate five symbols in order to receive five free spins at one credit per line. This is an abysmally poor reward for accumulating the five symbols. My experience with this game is that it is marginal even when four symbols have been accumulated and the next symbol is in one alinement. The machines are virtually never left in such a state and so it is generally not even worth the time and effort to check them. You would be financially better off to spend your time looking for lost coins on the floor.

# Bonus Bank

*Synopsis: Play when there are one or more blinking "HELD" symbols at a number of credits determined by the hold pattern. Terminate play when there are no blinking "HELD" symbols.*

Bonus Bank slot machines have gone through some evolution during their several months on the casino scene. One of these modifications has been to attempt to make it clear to the novice player that something has been banked. As the machines currently operate, when a Bonus Bank symbol lands on the payline and is not used to form a winning combination, the symbol itself is banked. An indicator above the reels blinks the word "HELD" to note that the symbol is banked. This blinking will continue until the symbol is actually used in a winning combination on the payline. Note that it is a blinking indicator light that indicates that a symbol is banked. When the indicator is a solid continuous light, the symbol has been used. Although somewhat unusual, it is possible to have two bonus bank symbols banked simultaneously.

The blinking indicator light also indicates the number of coins in play at the time the symbol was banked. The slot machine operates in such a manner that the symbol is banked at a particular number of coins played. Then in order to use the symbol, you must play the machine at the number of credits at which the symbol was banked, either one or two.

This is one of the causes of confusion for many tourists. Often you are playing a single credit per spin. Then if you bank a Bonus Bank symbol, you may decide, without reading the instructions, to play two credits per spin. The slot machine will then perform as an ordinary slot machine and will not give you the benefit of the banked symbol. The machine will only use the banked symbol when the proper number of coins is played.

Novice players often find Bonus Bank slot machines confusing to play. Consequently, the machines are frequently left in a desirable condition.

To advantageously play a Bonus Bank slot machine, you must locate a vacated machine on which a symbol is held, as indicated by the blinking indicator, and play at the appropriate number of credits until the banked symbol is used in a paying combination.

If you have any doubt about the value of finding a Bonus Bank with a banked symbol, let me relate an incident at the Golden Nugget. I was told that two individuals were waiting for a dollar Bonus Bank as a novice player departed. The two both tried to claim the machine as their own. Shoving turned into a full-fledged fist fight over the vacated machine. Almost needless to say, both individuals were expelled from the Golden Nugget on a permanent basis. The Golden Nugget management was not about to have such incidents occurring in its establishment and the Bonus Bank slot machines were removed the very next day.

# Bonus Spin

*Synopsis: Never play.*

Bonus Spin is a game that does have a banking process. During a special period that is brought about by alining three Bonus

41

Spin symbols on the payline, the visual screen will simulate the slot action of spinning a single reel repeatedly. Generally, numbers appear during this spinning and are accumulated as credits to be awarded at the end of this special period. Also during this spinning, various other symbols may appear and are banked. When five of any one type of symbol have occurred, you are given an award of credits depending on the type of symbol. Usually some of these other symbols have been banked by previous players and you are simply bringing the number of any banked symbol up to five in order to benefit by a payment of credits.

It may appear to be a good financial opportunity when you locate a Bonus Spin machine with what seems to be a sizable number of various symbols already banked in somewhat large numbers (three or four). However, our experience does not confirm this. The amount of play necessary to aline the three Bonus Spin symbols is generally so much that you will be a loser. The standard play in our experience appeared to drain away funds fairly rapidly while we continuously spun, hoping to make the alinement for the Bonus Spin.

# Boom

*Synopsis: Play at one credit per spin on exactly one line when thirty or more firecrackers are displayed. Terminate play when the firecracker row is eliminated.*

Boom is a game that, appropriate to its name, banks firecrackers. Firecrackers are earned by standard play on the slot machine. Whenever 25 credits are played on Boom, either one at a time or up to 45 per spin, a firecracker is added to the row of firecrackers displayed across the top of the video screen. Of course, if there are no firecrackers displayed, the machine will begin a row. A nice feature of Boom is that the firecrackers in the display, which can be as many as 49, do not have to be counted; instead the slot machine conveniently shows a count of the number of firecrackers in the row.

Firecrackers are banked into this row until the row contains fifty or more firecrackers, at which time the game will immediately transfer one credit for each firecracker to your credit meter and remove the entire row. It is actually possible to get a firecracker award of 51 credits by having almost fifty firecrackers, e.g. 49 plus twenty credits played toward the fiftieth, and then playing a sizable number of credits on the next spin, e.g. 45 credits, thus completing the requirements to earn the fiftieth and fifty-first firecrackers.

You can also obtain one credit for each accumulated firecracker if you obtain a scatter pay of two WILD MATCHES on the screen during the play of the game. Note that the two WILD MATCHES do not have to be on paylines.

To profitably play Boom, you should play one credit per line on exactly one line. Playing more lines or more credits per line simply benefits the casino. With this method of play, the game can be profitably played when there are 28 or more firecrackers in the row and play should be terminated when the row of firecrackers is eliminated. (See table p. 44.) However, note that if you don't hit a scatter pay of two WILD MATCHES, you may have to play 25 times 22 (the minimum setting suggested here), i.e. 550, spins in order to receive the firecracker bonus. This clearly can be a very time-consuming game to play.

Boom slot machines do have one feature that seems to be unique to them. On most slot machines, you must repeatedly press the play or spin button to continue to play. However, on a Boom machine, you can simply hold down the "PLAY 1 PER LINE" button to have repeated play. This, in turn, means that if the button is fastened down during play, the machine will virtually run itself, leaving both of your hands free. I personally use a small safety pin to wedge the button in the down position. You can easily play two or three adjacent machines with this technique and a minor amount of monitoring.

Until about a month before the manuscript of this book originally went to the publisher, I believed this feature on Boom machines was universal. At that time, I came across several Boom machines at various casinos in Las Vegas not possessing this lock-down feature. The button to play the machine had to be pressed repeatedly, making these Booms far less pleasant to play.

Boom machines are currently available in nickel and quarter denominations. With the nickel denomination, the profit per hour even playing on a lot of good machines is rather petty and the accumulation of slot points at five cents per spin is ludicrous. However, the game does provide a pleasant diversion that gives the edge to the knowledgeable player.

### Boom: Average Profit During Advantageous Periods

| Initial Number of Firecrackers | Average Profit in Credits | Initial Number of Firecrackers | Average Profit in Credits |
|---|---|---|---|
| 28 | 0.1 | 39 | 27.4 |
| 29 | 2.6 | 40 | 29.9 |
| 30 | 5.1 | 41 | 32.4 |
| 31 | 7.6 | 42 | 34.9 |
| 32 | 10.0 | 43 | 37.3 |
| 33 | 12.5 | 44 | 39.8 |
| 34 | 15.0 | 45 | 42.3 |
| 35 | 17.5 | 46 | 44.8 |
| 36 | 20.0 | 47 | 47.3 |
| 37 | 22.4 | 48 | 49.7 |
| 38 | 24.9 | 49 | 52.2 |

# Buccaneer Gold

*Synopsis: Play at one credit per spin when there are two or more daggers, except play at the maximum credits per spin during double-pay periods. Terminate play when there are five daggers to obtain.*

Buccaneer Gold is one of the games on the Odyssey machines. It plays a salty little jingle as you call the game onto the screen. This game has some interesting features, such as an occasional free spin and a more rare but predictable period of double pay on winning combinations. Of course, during these short periods of double pays, you should play rapidly and bet the maximum number of coins allowed. Because this short double- pay period may occur during your regular play, it is a good policy to be prepared with credits in the machine by using the bill acceptor rather than using the slower hand-feeding of coins.

The double-pay period is predictable in its arrival and occurs for a count of thirty when the Jolly Roger unfurls near the top of the course taken by a rope located on the left side of the screen. This rope is raised slowly during the regular play of Buccaneer Gold, eventually causing a flag to become visible and later to unfurl when reaching the top of its course. This double-pay period is a banked item on Buccaneer Gold. Although it is a banked item and can profitably be played on its own, I suggest you avoid that approach to this particular bonus for two reasons. First, the flag must be very high in its course for this play to be of significant value; and second, because although this bonus is of value, there is substantial volatility in the situation. That means you will generally spend some considerable time and funds playing to obtain, and unsuccessfully playing in, these double-pay periods before winning enough to be ahead.

However, the double-pay period is definitely worth playing aggressively when incorporated into play for the other banked item on Buccaneer Gold (as will be mentioned below). You can simply examine Buccaneer Gold machines in a standard manner looking for the proper number of daggers but additionally check to see the position of the flag. If it is high enough (that means very high), the machine can be profitably played until the special pay period is over. Then the machine's status should be reexamined because you may receive additional daggers during this play.

The second banking feature of Buccaneer Gold involves the collection of daggers. After collecting five daggers which are displayed in the lower right corner as they are obtained, you are permitted to fire a cannon to blow up a treasure chest with a ricocheting cannon ball. The contents of this chest are awarded to you as a bonus.

During the awarding of a dagger, a crew member appears and encourages you to continue to the bonus round. This causes many novice players to remain at their machines and play till the bonus is received. Consequently, the finding of desirable Buccaneer Gold machines is somewhat reduced.

It is, on average, financially beneficial to you to play Buccaneer Gold after two or more daggers have been obtained. Generally, ten credits will be required to obtain a dagger; and, on average, the chest will contain 39.7 credits. You should (except for double-pay periods) play one credit per spin until the treasure chest is opened. The table below shows the average profit based on the initial number of daggers.

**Buccaneer Gold: Average Profit During Advantageous Periods**

| Number of Daggers | Average Profit in Credits |
|:---:|:---:|
| 2 | 9.7 |
| 3 | 19.7 |
| 4 | 29.7 |

# Buccaneer Gold (Max Bet Version)

*Synopsis: Play at three credits per spin when there are three or more daggers, and play as rapidly as possible during double-pay periods. Terminate play when there are five daggers to obtain.*

Buccaneer Gold as described above has been modified, along with several other games on the Odyssey machines. In the case of Buccaneer Gold, the game has been altered so that you must play three coins, maximum wager, in attempting to obtain the daggers necessary to reach the bonus event of blowing up a treasure chest with a ricocheting cannon ball.

As a result of this change, playing one or two coins does not alter the number of daggers. Additionally, the pay schedule is such that those players who play a third coin are generally not receiving any extra pay for their additional coin. These players tend to realize this fact and so either continue to play the machine through to the bonus round or revert to playing only one or two credits.

Since you must wager three coins per spin to win the bonus and since the pay schedule has been significantly modified, you will find it more expensive to obtain a dagger. The cost of obtaining a dagger seems to average 34.5 credits. The bonus obtained from the treasure chest averages 89.9 credits. These figures determine the proper play of this version of Buccaneer Gold.

To advantageously play this newer version of Buccaneer Gold, you must locate a machine which has three or more daggers and then play at three coins per spin until the treasure chest is opened. The table below gives the average profit in credits based on the initial number of daggers. You will, with continued play, experience similar results, but it should be mentioned that this version of Buccaneer Gold appears to have greater volatility. That is, the losses and wins both tend to be greater, with the net effect that they average to values near to those described in the table.

The other banking feature, the double-pay period, is as described in the previous chapter. However, the pay schedule on this version of Buccaneer Gold has been significantly modified; as a result, this feature should only be played in conjunction with the usual banking of the daggers and not on its own. The doubling effect is to some extent negated by most of the pay schedule not increasing proportionately as you change from a two-coin to a three-coin wager. As usual, during this double-pay period, the play should still be as rapid as possible.

### Buccaneer Gold (Max Bet Version)
### Average Profit During Advantageous Periods

| Number of Daggers | Average Profit in Credits |
|---|---|
| 3 | 20.9 |
| 4 | 55.4 |

# Build Your Bonus

*Synopsis: Play at one credit per spin when the ten valued currency has a single puzzle piece undone or when the 25, 100 or 200 puzzles require two or fewer pieces for completion. Terminate play when the bonus is obtained.*

Build Your Bonus is very difficult to find and seems to be a rather unpopular game. The machines I have seen have all been one dollar denomination and that may contribute to the lack of play the game receives.

On the machines I have seen, there are three facsimiles of paper currency displayed on a visual. The three pieces are all structured as jigsaw puzzles. Each puzzle is composed of 24 pieces in a three by eight pattern. Four central pieces in each puzzle are already in place and display the value (in credits) of the particular piece of currency. Obtaining the other twenty pieces of any of the jigsaw will award the numerical value on the completed currency

A piece of the puzzle is in place by being highlighted and definitely brighter.

Additional pieces of the puzzle are obtained during standard slot play.

The three bills on the machines I have seen had either the values of 2, 10, and 200 or 10, 25, and 100.

With this structure of bill values, I would suggest playing for the ten values only when a single piece remains to be filled in that puzzle. Play for the 25, 100 or 200 should be limited to situations where two or fewer pieces are needed for completion of one of those puzzles. And finally, never play to complete the jigsaw puzzle with the two on the paper currency.

Based on my data, these jigsaw puzzles must be so near to completion that generally the puzzle is not left undone by the previous player.

Play is at one credit per spin and should be terminated with the winning of the bonus.

# Chuck Wagons

*Synopsis: Play the maximum credits per spin when at least 21 miles of the seventy miles needed to reach the bonus area by Your Wagon are completed, and the distance remaining for Your Wagon to reach the bonus area is less than or equal to three-quarters of the distance remaining to be traversed by Their Wagon to reach the finish line. Terminate play when the mileage indicators return to zero or it becomes obvious that Your Wagon will not reach the bonus area before Their Wagon reaches the finish line.*

Chuck Wagons is a game quite similar to Empire, Isle of Pearls, and Spacequest in that you can advantageously play the slot machine when a figure (a horse drawn wagon in Chuck Wagons) is half or more of the distance to the bonus area (called the Bonus Zone) while a third or less of the allotted time has elapsed.

However, Chuck Wagons does not have a standard timer like the timing device used in these other games. Instead, this game has a competing wagon (labeled Their Wagon) which moves with every play of the slot machine. Instead of you trying to "beat the clock" by moving Your Wagon a certain distance in a certain amount of time, you must move Your Wagon that distance before the competing wagon operated by the slot machine goes a specified distance to the finish line. Basically, this competing wagon acts as the timing device in Chuck Wagons. So, in essence, the situation is equivalent to the systems in the other games; consequently, the play of Chuck Wagons is very similar to the play of these other games.

In Chuck Wagons, you are attempting to move Your Wagon to the bonus area for a bonus of 10, 15, or 25 credits. To be a winner, you must move your wagon into the bonus area before Their Wagon reaches the finish line. This competing wagon moves with every spin of the reels and functions as a timing device, while your wagon only moves when an ADVANCE! symbol is on the payline. The distance moved by Their Wagon is such that you are assured 25 slot plays or spins before the game is terminated by Their Wagon reaching the finish line.

To advantageously play Chuck Wagons, you need to locate a machine on which Your Wagon has completed at least 21 miles of the seventy miles needed to reach the bonus area. So if less than 21 miles have been completed by Your Wagon, avoid the machine. Actually, 21 (or 24 or 27) miles is a very weak play because there is still much of the distance to be completed to reach the bonus area at seventy miles.

The reason for pointing out this 21-mile criterion is that you can easily use it to determine at a glance that many machines are not favorable for continued play.

Additionally, for a Chuck Wagons slot machine to be, on average, of value to play, the number of miles remaining to be traversed to reach the bonus area by Their Wagon should, when beginning your slot play, be at least 1.33 times the number of miles remaining to be traversed by Your Wagon. Thus, if there are 34 miles remaining to be traversed by Your Wagon (roughly the position halfway to the bonus area), Their Wagon should have at least 45 miles to go to the finish line.

Since 1.33 is extremely close to the fraction 4/3, you may wish instead to use this fraction for "in the head" calculations. So, for the halfway position mentioned above, using the factor 4/3, you would again want to have at least 45 miles remaining for Their Wagon to reach the finish line.

An equivalent alternative to the above is that the distance remaining for Your Wagon to reach the bonus area must be less than or equal to three-quarters of the distance remaining for Their Wagon to reach the finish line. If you find this statement more comprehensible (and many prefer fractions of less than one to those larger than one), then use it appropriately.

Such machines can be found occasionally. Having located an appropriate Chuck Wagons machine, you must move Your Wagon as quickly as possible to the bonus area. Consequently, play should be at maximum coins per spin, which will move Your Wagon three miles times the number of credits played on that spin for each ADVANCE! symbol on the payline. There are a few minor exceptions to this "play at maximum coins" rule, but they are usually clear in the particular situations and also can be ignored without significant financial loss.

Play should be terminated when the mileage indicators return to zero or it becomes obvious that Your Wagon cannot reach the bonus area before Their Wagon reaches the finish line.

# Diamond Thief

*Synopsis: With five diamonds or fewer needed to finish filling the valise, play the machine. The number of credits to play per spin is dependent on the layout, but you can always interminably play one credit per spin. Terminate play after the valise is filled.*

When Diamond Thief was first introduced, the game, at first glance, seemed quite similar to the then popular Wild Cherry Pie. Similar! It appeared to be exactly the same game only there were diamonds instead of cherries and a valise (or case) instead of a pie shell; and instead of a basket, the game used a jewel box.

Well, it may have appeared to be the same game but it certainly wasn't. In some major respects, Diamond Thief departed radically from Wild Cherry Pie. Some short time later, Wild Cherry Pie was remade into Wild Cherry Bonus Pie which is, except for cosmetics, basically Diamond Thief.

Diamond Thief, like the other games, is so difficult to explain that by the time one completes the instructions, the reader is usually totally confused. With that in mind, here goes.

The Diamond Thief machine has three reels. As on most modern slot machines, the areas above and below the payline are visible to the slot player. Therefore, each of the three reels has three areas that you can clearly see: the space on the payline, the space above the payline, and the space below the payline.

Since there are three spaces on each reel that can be seen and there are three reels, there are nine areas visible. These nine areas correspond to the nine sections of a valise (the machine uses the term case) that is displayed above the reels. During the play of the Diamond Thief machine, diamonds are slowly added to the sections until all the sections are filled with diamonds. Six diamonds are required to fill each of the nine sections of the valise.

When a diamond thief symbol appears on the reels in one of the nine visible locations, the symbol functions in two distinct ways. First, it acts as a wild symbol and as though it were on the payline functioning in standard slot pays. Secondly, the symbol transfers into the corresponding section of the valise display a number of diamonds equal to the number of credits wagered. However, if the section of the valise corresponding to the location of the diamond thief symbol on the reels is already filled with six diamonds, then the diamonds are instead transferred to a smaller valise (also called small jewel case) located to the left side of the screen.

Additionally, if the section of the smaller valise corresponding to the location of the diamond thief symbol on the reels is also already filled with six diamonds, then the diamond award is doubled and added to the bonus meter which is located above the small valise. The number on the bonus meter is also referred to as the jewel box value since the number is displayed on top of a jewel box.

The complete filling of the large valise with 54 diamonds ends the game. At that time, the amount on the bonus meter is added to a bonus jewel case pay and the total is awarded on the machine's credit meter. The bonus jewel case pay is a value between 25 and 500 credits. Another way of saying all this is: on completion of filling the large valise, a bonus amount of 25 to 500 credits plus the jewel box value (bonus meter) is awarded on the credit meter.

The large valise is then replaced by the small valise, which is enlarged to fill the space taken by the former large valise and a new empty small valise appears. The bonus meter is reset to zero. The game is then ready to be played again.

The manufacturer's purpose in having the small valise replace the large valise is undoubtedly to encourage players to continue playing and also to avoid discouraging new potential players who approach the game. Studies have shown that slot players are often dissuaded from playing on slot machines which are clearly in a starting position. The replacement of the large valise by the small valise tends to mask this reality by displaying a valise which is only very rarely totally empty.

Clearly, diamonds are the item that is banked in this game. However, diamonds are handled in so many different ways that the game is difficult to analyze. Trying to analyze Diamond Thief to predict the average value of a Diamond Thief machine based on the initial number of empty spots in the valise proved to be clumsy.

From the data I have obtained, it appears that a Diamond Thief can, on average, be profitably played when there are seven or fewer spots remaining to be filled in the large valise. The size of the bonus meter is generally relatively unimportant compared to the bonus jewel case pay which is between 25 and 500 credits. If the bonus jewel case pay is large, you will usually be a winner; if not, you will be behind financially for having played the game.

You should be cautious when deciding to play Diamond Thief because your success will be very dependent on the unknown bonus jewel case pay.

However, the number seven should generally not be used as a guide with this game. If you were to locate a game with seven diamonds needed that had just been vacated by a novice, it would, on average, be a marginally positive play. Let us assume that you played this machine through the bonus round and the new replacement valise then possessed six empty spots needing diamonds. This new valise is not a play which, on average, will be of positive value, even though the rule involving seven blindly says play some more. Thus, the advice had to be modified to accommodate this situation.

Consequently, the rule should better read: Diamond Thief can, on average, be profitably played when there are five or fewer spots remaining to be filled in the large valise. Thus, if you play through the bonus round and have a new valise with six diamonds needed, terminate play.

The best method to play a Diamond Thief slot machine can be slightly confusing. The maximum number of credits that can be played on the Diamond Thief machine is two. If the section of the large valise needing the most diamonds requires six, five, four, three, or two diamonds, then play two credits per spin. If, however, the section of the valise needing the most diamonds needs only one diamond, then play only one credit per spin.

It is probably minutely more profitable, on average, to play one credit per spin all the way through each Diamond Thief game. I have not checked this; but because I have found other banking slot machines function in this manner, I believe the advice to be true. This wagering approach (one credit per spin) can be incredibly lengthy timewise and boring, but generally there is a stability in playing one credit in comparison to playing two. Playing more than one credit per spin will save considerable time but will generally generate greater financial swings.

Play should then be terminated on a Diamond Thief slot machine when the large valise is filled.

## Double Bonus

*Synopsis: On machines with one or more DB symbols, hand feed up to ten coins, automatically triggering the machine to play and use one DB symbol. Terminate play when no DB symbols are available for use.*

Double Bonus is as close to finding money as it gets. If you find a Double Bonus machine worth playing, then you will absolutely positively win.

Double Bonus is a game on some slot machines. I have never seen this game by itself on a slot machine. The game is, in my experience, always in a five cent denomination.

During the regular play of Double Bonus, a player will occasionally receive small upright rectangles that contain the letters D and B. The D is in a cursive style, $\mathcal{D}$, while the B is in an outline format, B. Together, they will appear as below.

There can be at most ten such symbols on the screen at one time and all will be located toward the left side of the screen below the video reels. These symbols are the banked item.

The previous player will have obtained these symbols. Two of these symbols are banked when three sevens occur in any position in the first three columns, reading left to right, of the three paylines. Similarly, five of these symbols are banked when four sevens occur in any position in the first four columns of the three paylines. Ten of these symbols are banked when five sevens occur in any position on the five reels. The exact method of winning these symbols is information of little interest to us, since it is the previous player who banks these and not one of our enlightened readers. Suffice it to say that the previous player has received some of these symbols in one lucky spin as a payment for a certain scatter award. Each of these DB symbols entitles the player to a spin at the same amount wagered on the previous spin. The DB symbols must be used immediately on the following spins. With each spin, a symbol is removed electronically from the video screen. The bonus ends with the use of the final displayed symbol.

There are several special features attached to these spins. First, the spins must be paid for. The bonus spins are not free; you must continue to add funds to the slot machine or use credits. Second, winning paylines during these spins are paid at double the usual rate. And third, all losing paylines are paid double the amount wagered on those paylines. This last feature makes it impossible to lose during these bonus spins.

Why would anyone leave a machine with any of these symbols unused? Conceivably, the casino customer was out of funds just at that particular moment and couldn't use the accrued symbols. That, of course, seems like an extremely unlikely scenario.

More likely is that the customer didn't understand the symbols and their function. As a general rule, the number of symbols that are deserted appears to be the number of symbols won on the immediately preceding spin.

Another possibility is that the customer, especially using credits, attempts to change the size of his bet. Being unable to do so, he senses a problem, terminates his play, cashes out, and departs from the machine.

Whatever his motivation, on finding a machine with one or more DB symbols in the lower left section of the screen below the video reels, you should play until these are no longer present. If it is unclear just how many credits to wager in the situation (it would be unusual that it was not readily decipherable), simply put a dollar into the machine and cash out the twenty credits of funds. Then hand feed the coins one at a time into the machine. On reaching the proper number, the number of coins bet during the winning of the DB symbols, the machine will automatically play and use one of the DB symbols. Terminate your play when no DB symbols are available for such use.

Finding Double Bonus games with DB symbols unused is somewhat unusual but certainly not a rare event. In their own right, these games are not worth checking in order to locate DB symbols to obtain the bonus spins. However, commonly, this Double Bonus is on slot machines that have other games which are worth examining. Thus, it is relatively easy to check this game while checking the other game or games on the particular slot machine.

# Double Diamond Mine

*Synopsis: Play at one credit per spin on machines which have nine diamonds in one shaft, or eight diamonds in each of two shafts, or seven or more diamonds in each of the three shafts. Terminate play when the machine does not meet any of the above conditions.*

Double Diamond Mine is basically quite close to an ordinary slot machine. The slight difference is that each of the three reels contains some diamond symbols. These symbols do nothing as far as the pay table is concerned and alining three diamonds on the payline will not in any direct way earn you additional credits.

Instead, a diamond or diamonds appearing on the payline will trigger the slot machine to drop a number of diamonds, equal to the number of credits wagered, into the corresponding mine shaft(s) on the display above the three reels. When any mine shaft is filled with a total of ten diamonds, the shaft is emptied of diamonds and you receive ten credits. Clearly, the items that are banked in Double Diamond Mine are the diamonds in the mine shafts.

The proper play of a Double Diamond Mine is to play one credit per spin on any machine which has nine diamonds in any one of its shafts. It is also profitable to play at the rate of one credit per spin any of these machines that have two shafts containing eight diamonds each. You can also profitably play any Double Diamond Mine that has three shafts each containing at least seven diamonds, and again this is at the rate of one credit per spin. Play should be terminated when the slot machine does not satisfy the above conditions.

The above rule tends to be on the conservative side. What is interesting is that sometimes a machine which has several shafts with sizable numbers of diamonds will become a poor play before all of its shafts are emptied. Consider, for example, a machine that has three shafts of seven diamonds each. This machine is a good play. If perchance one of the shafts is emptied by fortuitous play before any diamonds are obtained in either of the other shafts, then with only two mine shafts of seven each, play on the machine should be stopped and the other mine shafts not emptied.

Generally, it will cost somewhat more than one credit to obtain a diamond. But, of course, the diamond will not necessarily be in the shaft that you want. Good luck with this machine, and here's hoping that someone gives you a good shaft.

# Empire

*Synopsis: Play three credits per spin when 49 floors or fewer remain to be climbed to reach the first bonus level, and the amount of time in seconds remaining is at least double the number of floors remaining to be climbed to reach the first bonus level. Ter-*

*minate play when King is grounded or it becomes obvious that King will not reach the bonus area before time expires.*

Empire is a game which depicts the part of the movie, King Kong, in which the Empire State Building is scaled. In the Empire slot machine, "King" needs to climb at least seventy floors in one minute and forty seconds (one hundred seconds) or 25 spins, whichever comes second, in order for you to be a winner. Play is such that each CLIMB! symbol on the payline moves King three floors times the number of credits wagered: one, two, or three. The machine displays a counter that informs you how many floors King has climbed and a timer that shows the amount of time remaining for the climb to be completed.

King must climb at least seventy floors for you to receive a bonus. But if King is exceptionally energetic and climbs ninety floors or 110 floors, you will obtain, instead of ten credits, a higher reward of 15 or 25 credits respectively at the completion of King's climb.

I have never observed King to use the hundred seconds without using the minimum of 25 spins, so the 25 spins are generally not a factor in determining if an Empire slot machine is valuable to play.

This slot machine does have two significant pieces of information on its display. One is the number of floors that King has already climbed, and the other is the amount of time of the initial hundred seconds remaining for King to complete his climb. These two pieces of information can be used to determine if a particular machine is, on average, valuable to play.

First, in order for an Empire slot machine to be, on average, of value to play, the amount of time remaining to be played should, at the beginning of your slot play, be at least double the number of floors remaining to be climbed. Thus, if there are 34 floors remaining to be climbed (roughly the half-way position to the first bonus level), you should have 68 seconds, i.e. one minute and eight seconds, remaining on the timer.

There are small anomalies to this rule, of course, because of the discrete nature of the timing device and the floor count. Time, which is always continuous, is a discrete item on these machines and seems repeatedly to be a multiple of four seconds, while the number of floors is definitely discrete but is always a multiple of three. Thus, there are small oddities such as if King has completed 63 floors and seven remain to ascend, then if 12 seconds remain, the game is favorable to you. The rule about the ratio of time and floors remaining to ascend has some minor flexibility, especially near the end of the game. Clearly, the rule is not carved in stone but should generally serve you well.

A consequence of this rule is that for an Empire slot machine to be, on average, valuable to play, there must be 49 floors or fewer remaining to be climbed to reach the first bonus level. The slot machine does not tell you that information directly. The machine displays how many floors King has already climbed. Consequently, the number of floors already climbed must be at least 21. Actually, 21 (or 24 or 27) is a very weak play because there is still much of the building to be scaled.

Play on an Empire machine that meets the above requirements should be at the maximum number of credits permitted per spin. It is imperative to move King as much as possible with each CLIMB! symbol. There are a few anomalies where it is unnecessary to wager the maximum of three credits per spin. For example, if you have moved King 69 floors and there are only a few seconds remaining, then you should wager only one credit per spin. However, these anomalies occur seldom enough that you can ignore them at comparatively little cost.

Play on an Empire slot machine should be terminated when King is grounded and the machine resets for another climb, or if it becomes obvious that King cannot complete the climb before the allotted time elapses. The Empire machine is difficult to find in a condition which is profitable to play because most slot players only leave when it is obvious that King will not complete his climb within the designated time allotment.

Now if you've read the above material superficially and not given a lot of thought to the matter, then you probably missed an error in the situation. I believe that even the manufacturer of this machine did not pause to consider the dilemma. King's counter starts at zero when King is on the ground. But ground level is called the first floor. So if King climbs one floor, he is on the second floor; similarly, if King climbs seven~~t~~ floors, he is on the seventy-first floor. The only way to cope with this is to claim that at this particular building, the ground floor is called the zero-eth floor and the floor commonly called the second floor is called the first, etc. This is the type of problem and inconsistency with which individuals who write about slot machines have to contend.

# Empire (Enlarged Bonus)

*Synopsis: Play maximum credits per spin when the number of floors remaining to climb is less than half the number of seconds remaining for climbing. Terminate play when the distance counter resets to zero.*

Empire slot machines have gone through a considerable evolution. This version was just one small step in a series of machines. In this step, the very noticeable difference was that the bonuses were significantly increased from the previous levels of 10, 15, and 25 to new and higher levels of 20, 40, and 250.

Now the casinos weren't suddenly going to start giving away money, so a compensating factor was introduced in order to make these slot machines function profitably for the casinos. This compensating factor was a reduction of the amount of time available to reach the bonuses. The time allotted was significantly reduced from two minutes to one minute and 24 seconds or, as the machine displays this, 1:24. No matter how it's written, you have only 84 seconds in which to obtain a bonus.

Let me assure you that having only 84 seconds instead of 120 seconds has a huge impact on obtaining a bonus. For all practical purposes, this machine is worthless to look for in order to get a valuable play.

First and foremost, I found that this version of Empire was rarely left in a valuable state. This was, in part, because individuals didn't leave machines at which they perceived that they were doing well, but, I believe, moreso because the machines did not get into a valuable condition nearly as often.

Another occurrence, but of less importance, was that there was much more variability in the results of play on these machines. This type of Empire had much larger wins but additionally had many more losing sessions. This, I believe, contributed to its unpopularity and eventual removal from several casinos.

The bright side of this version of Empire is that the rules which determine if this machine will be valuable to play are exactly the same as previously. In other words, in order to, on average, profitably play this version of Empire, you should locate a machine on which the number of floors remaining to be climbed to the first bonus is less than half the number of seconds remaining for climbing. This will put you into a relatively strong position to receive a bonus. Then you must play maximum credits per spin in order to quickly move King to this bonus level. Play should be terminated immediately when the counter resets to the initial setting of zero floors climbed.

This strategy is effective to profitably play this version of Empire. However, you will have difficulty finding machines satisfying these conditions. In fact, you'll have so much trouble that you will probably stop looking for good plays on this particular model of Empire.

# Empire Deluxe

*Synopsis: Play maximum credits per spin when the number of floors remaining to climb is less than half the number of seconds remaining. Terminate play when the distance counter resets to zero or it becomes obvious that King will not reach the bonus area before time expires.*

Empire Deluxe is one in a series of Empire slot machines which have an assortment of variations. These Empire machines, to my knowledge, are still evolving and continually being remade. In this version, two major differences were introduced.

One was that the bonuses were increased from the previous levels of 10, 15, and 25 to new and higher levels of 20, 40, and 100. The second was that the time allotted to reach the bonuses was reduced to one minute and 28 seconds for a total of 88 seconds.

Reducing the amount of time radically affected reaching the bonus levels. The Climb symbols had to be hit repeatedly and definitely with max coins wagered. There wasn't much leeway for missing Climb symbols.

But from our standpoint, things don't seem to have changed much. When to play Empire Deluxe is very much like when to play an ordinary Empire. In order to, on average, profitably play Empire Deluxe, you should locate a machine on which the number of floors remaining to be climbed to the first bonus is less than half the number of seconds remaining for climbing. This will put you into a relatively strong position to receive a bonus. Then you must play maximum credits per spin in order to quickly move King to the bonus levels. Play should be terminated immediately when the counter resets to the initial setting of zero floors climbed or it becomes obvious that King will not reach the bonus area before time expires.

This strategy is effective to profitably play Empire Deluxe. However, these machines have disappeared as other versions of Empire have come on the gaming scene. Thus, besides having difficulty locating Empire Deluxe slot machines satisfying these conditions, you will have trouble even finding Empire Deluxe. In fact, you'll have so much trouble that you will probably stop looking for good plays on Empire Deluxe.

# Empire King

*Synopsis: Play maximum credits per spin when the number of floors remaining to climb is less than half the number of seconds remaining for climbing. Terminate play when the distance counter resets to zero.*

Empire King is yet another game similar to the rest of the Empire series which all involve "King" climbing the outside of a skyscraper. However, this version of the game involves reaching only one bonus level, which is called the Bonus Area. Any number of floors of 90 or over is considered to be a part of that area; King's reaching the ninetieth floor will automatically begin the bonus round without requiring you to exhaust the remainder of the two minutes of climbing time as supplied on other machines in the series to reach higher bonus levels.

In Empire King, there are two ways for King to reach the bonus area and receive the bonus. One is for you to be lucky enough to have the Empire King symbol land on the payline when a maximum bet of three credits has been made. The appearance of this symbol will immediately transport King to the bonus area above floor 89. The bonus is then awarded.

The second and commonest way for King to reach floor 90 or higher is by more slowly scaling the outside of the building. This is done by being fortunate enough to have a Climb symbol land on the payline. When this occurs, King will move upward by a number of floors equal to three times the number of coins wagered on that particular spin for each symbol. King will thus move at most 27 floors on a spin if the incredible outcome should be three Climb symbols on the payline while three coins were wagered.

The bonus given on Empire King is a random amount which will range from ten to 1000 credits. Specifically, the bonus in credits will be one of the numbers 10, 15, 20, 25, 35, 40, 50, 75, 100, 250, 500, or 1000. Commonly, the bonus received is 35 credits; and, naturally enough, the average of all bonuses received is around 35 credits. Bonuses beyond 100 are definitely rarities.

In order to, on average, profitably play Empire King, you should locate a machine on which the number of floors remaining to be climbed is less than half the number of seconds remaining for climbing. This will put you into a relatively strong position to receive the bonus. Then you must play maximum credits per spin in order to quickly move King to the Bonus Area.

Play should be terminated immediately when the counters reset to the initial setting of two minutes and zero floors climbed.

It is not common to find Empire Kings left in a valuable state. Novice players often seem to 'get it right' about when to give up on these machines.

# Fireworks

*Synopsis: Because of variability and time considerations, avoid play. On machines with a bonus of at least one hundred for each question mark remaining, play one credit per spin. Terminate play when the bonus is received.*

Fireworks is, in my opinion, an extremely poor game to play. This is because the game is extremely volatile or variable. This variability is a general feature of the machine and not simply a function of attempting to obtain the bonus.

During the play of Fireworks, there seem to be very few good size pays and also a serious shortage of minor payouts. The valuable pays are definitely few and far between. Thus, for many spins in a row, you are simply having your pocketbook emptied. This has made the machine relatively unpopular with the public.

The bonus in Fireworks is a number of credits equal to the number clearly displayed on the screen. This number can increase slightly during your play. The bonus is obtained by removing question marks from a rectangle also clearly visible on the video screen. The process of removing these question marks is slow and seems excruciatingly slow as you are losing repeatedly with the general play on the Fireworks machine.

The proper play to obtain the bonus is one credit per spin on one payline. The bonus is financially worth pursuing if the number displayed on the screen is at least one hundred for each question mark remaining.

All the Fireworks machines that I have experienced have had only one or two question marks remaining to be removed. There can be more question marks, but then the number for the bonus is rarely sufficiently high from the previous play of other casino customers.

In part because of the high variance, I suggest you avoid play on Fireworks. Another reason for avoiding play on this machine is that Fireworks usually requires some sizable amount of time to obtain the bonus. Maybe my major dislike of Fireworks is that I never associated its play with fun.

# fishin' for Cash

*Synopsis: Play at one credit per spin on machines which have nine fish in one stack, or eight fish in each of two stacks, or seven or more fish in each of the three stacks. Terminate play when the machine does not meet any of the above conditions.*

An old game by a new name, fishin' for Cash, has the problem that if you put the name at the start of the sentence, there is a quandary of whether to capitalize the first letter of the sentence since the initial letter of the name is not capitalized by the manufacturer.

The visual on this screen has three fisherpersons (Is this non-sexist terminology getting out of hand?) who have cast their lines into the water. They are associated with the three corresponding reels on the slot machine.

Whenever a fish lands on the payline, the appropriate figure reels in the fish, which is then cast onto a corresponding stack at the pier to the rear. Actually, the figure lands a number of fish equal to the number of credits wagered on that spin, either one or two. The fish continue to be caught during standard slot play, whenever one or more fish land on the payline. Whenever any of the individuals on the visual has caught the limit of ten fish, the individual takes his rod and fish and departs from the screen, only to be replaced by a new and different fisherperson who has yet to catch the limit of ten fish. This new fisherperson may begin with a fish since the last play may have involved a fish landing on the payline while two credits were wagered, and that fisherperson already had nine fish accumulated on his stack. During the departure and replacement of the fisherperson, the slot player is awarded a bonus of ten credits (one credit per fish).

This game is extremely similar to Double Diamond Mine. Basically, fishin' for Cash banks fish in stacks as compared to Double Diamond Mine, which banks diamonds in the mine shafts.

A method to profit from a fishin' for Cash is to play one credit per spin on any machine which has nine fish in any one of the stacks. This can be enlarged upon by adding that it is also profitable to play at the rate of one credit per spin any fishin' for Cash machines that have two stacks containing eight fish each. And continuing from that statement, you can also, on average, profitably play any fishin' for Cash that has three stacks each containing at least seven fish, again at the rate of one credit per spin.

Play should be terminated when the fishin' for Cash slot machine does not satisfy any of the above conditions

# Flush Attack

*Synopsis: Play at maximum credits per hand during Flush Attack mode. Terminate play with the ending of Flush Attack mode.*

Flush Attack is a form of video poker. This text does not deal with video poker, which is an area of gaming all to itself. Actually, any video poker machine can be turned into a banking machine simply by connecting it to a progressive meter. Then if the progressive jackpot reaches some specified level, the video poker machine becomes, on average, valuable to play. This level could be readily calculated for any video poker game in a jurisdiction such as Nevada which requires cards to be dealt randomly.

Incorporating information about video poker machines with such a possible type of banking feature into this text would require this book to become something is was never meant to be: a vast collection of video poker strategies. However, a few video poker machines are so designed that they function more as banking games than as video poker machines. One of these games is Flush Attack.

In Flush Attack, the item that is banked is flushes. The system keeps track of how many flushes have occurred. On approaching a machine, you will have no idea how many flushes have already occurred in the system. There is no count displayed. When the designated number of flushes occurs (three, four, or sometimes five) the system shifts into what is called Flush Attack mode. During this Flush Attack mode, the next common flush (not a straight or royal flush) that is obtained by a player is paid 100 credits or 125 credits (depending on the system) for a five-credit wager.

In the above paragraph, we talked about a system. Let us now clarify that concept for this game. Some Flush Attack machines are unlinked. That is, each machine is totally independent of all other machines. The system as described above is all contained in the single machine. With an unlinked machine, the player is simply playing a version of video poker with an interesting anomaly.

Our primary concern in this chapter about Flush Attack involves linked machines. With linked machines, the system counts the flushes of all the connected machines in the system, and when the designated number of flushes occurs, the entire system, including all machines, enters Flush Attack mode. The next machine to have a common flush (not a straight or royal flush) after the draw is awarded the extravagant bonus as credits.

The most lucrative manner of playing Flush Attack is to locate a set of linked Flush Attack machines. Assuming the other machines in the system are occupied by playing and paying customers, you are advised to simply patiently wait until the play of the other Flush Attack participants initiates the Flush Attack mode for all the machines. The system always clearly indicates the initiation and presence of Flush Attack mode by prominently displaying the words FLUSH ATTACK across the video screen. During this relatively short interval, you should play rapidly at maximum credits per hand to obtain the next common flush.

Then when Flush Attack mode ends, terminate play until the system reenters Flush Attack mode.

There is an interesting facet to the banking feature on Flush Attack. When playing at a machine in Flush Attack mode, you may not derive any benefit from the banked item. Generally, on other banking games, you play until some bonus is personally received. However, on a Flush Attack machine, the bonus of an extra large payment for a common flush is not guaranteed to any particular player.

You can learn a special strategy to play Flush Attack. Actually, there are really two strategies for Flush Attack: one for play during standard times and another for the period when Flush Attack mode is present. Since you are advised to play only during Flush Attack mode, one strategy would suffice. However, even learning the correct and proper strategy for that situation is unnecessary.

The simplest strategy that will, in my experience, "get the money" is as follows. Save any paying hand dealt. This, of course, means save the paying portion of the dealt cards and then complete the draw. For example, if you receive three jacks, an eight, and a five, hold only the paying portion of the hand, which in this case is the three jacks. Then draw two additional cards. A single exception to the above is to save four to a flush, straight flush, or royal flush in preference to a paying pair.

If you have no paying combination, you should hold as many same-suited cards as possible (two, three, or four) with the proviso that if you have a choice between two cards to a flush in two different suits, you should hold the set of two that has the most high cards (jack, queen, king, ace). Then complete the draw.

This strategy, which is incredibly poor and yet easy to remember, will win money if used only during Flush Attack mode.

I should qualify the above by elaborating that my wife and I have only played on sets of linked machines which were few in number, sometimes as few as three. Also, speed is extremely important during Flush Attack mode. And finally, I believe that in many incidents our opposition consisted of totally untutored individuals. Since you will probably play under similar conditions, hopefully your results will also be favorable.

# Fort Knox

*Synopsis: Play at one credit per spin when there are four or more obtained digits in the combination. Terminate play when a new combination is created.*

Fort Knox is one of the games on the Odyssey machines. It comes in three varieties: 3-Reel with Bonus, Buy-a-Pay with Bonus, and Triple Jackpot with Bonus. However, all of these are very much the same as far as their play is concerned.

The play of the Fort Knox machines is like a standard slot machine (in video form) with three spinning reels. Additionally, you are accumulating the digits of the combination to open the vault and receive the funds in one of the three safe deposit boxes. It seems on average to take over twenty spins to obtain each digit.

The item that is banked in Fort Knox is the obtained digits of the vault combination. In order for the Fort Knox machine to be favorable on average for you to play, four or more of the digits should have been obtained previously. Play should be terminated on Fort Knox when the safe deposit box is opened and a new combination created.

The cost of obtaining each new digit is on average slightly under 4.8 credits and the bonus in the safe deposit box averages 37 credits. These figures are based on play of one credit per spin. It is not recommended that you play more than one credit per spin even though some of the Fort Knox games, notably Buy-a-Pay with Bonus, encourage the play of additional credits.

A minor calculation will show that Fort Knox machines can, on average, be profitably played when only three numbers in the combination have been obtained. This is technically correct;

however, the majority of such plays will be negative financial experiences with an occasional large win balancing the losing plays. Unless you are playing often at this level, it is better to use your time to locate more profitable machines.

### Fort Knox: Average Profit During Advantageous Periods

| Average Number of Digits | Profit in Credits |
|---|---|
| 3 | 3.3 |
| 4 | 8.2 |
| 5 | 13.0 |
| 6 | 17.8 |
| 7 | 22.7 |
| 8 | 27.5 |
| 9 | 32.4 |

# Fort Knox (Max Bet Version)

*Synopsis: Play at three credits per spin if there are four or more obtained digits in the combination. Terminate play when a new combination is created.*

Fort Knox as described above has been modified, along with several other games on the Odyssey machines. In the case of Fort Knox, the game has been altered so that you must play maximum coins, in this case three, in attempting to obtain the digits of the combination leading to the bonus event of opening the vault.

As a result of this change, individuals playing one or two coins do not alter the number of combination digits already obtained. Another feature incorporated into this version involves the pay schedule; players who play a third coin are generally not receiving any extra pay for their additional coin. These players tend to realize this fact and so either continue to play the machine through to the bonus round or revert to playing one or two credits.

Accumulating digits of the combination to open the vault and receive the funds in one of the three safe deposit boxes is as before, except that the machine is now programed to only activate the system for obtaining another digit when a wager of maximum coins is made by the slot player. Wagers of one or two credits will cause the machine to perform only as a standard slot machine in video form.

However, the manufacturers of Odyssey have added an unusual feature to this newer version of Fort Knox. If you touch the screen of the Odyssey in the usual manner to call this version of Fort Knox, the game will appear but with the current digits of the combination hidden. So you will not know how many of the digits in the combination have already been obtained. It appears that you cannot know how many of the digits in the combination have been obtained without playing the machine at least once at the level of the maximum wager. So, in other words, it seems as if you must insert three coins and play once in order to see how many digits of the combination have already been obtained.

Let us assume that you decide to play three credits for one spin on a Fort Knox machine just to see how many digits have already been obtained. If the machine has a five percent hold, this means that you are on average paying five percent of three credits or fifteen percent of one credit to determine the number of obtained digits. If the credits are each worth 25¢ (or one dollar), then you are on average paying 3.75¢ (or 15¢) to obtain the desired information.

Casinos and slot manufacturers both love people who will spend that type of money for what will generally turn out to be worthless information. My advice is to not be one of those people. Actually, this type of tactic reminds me of a trick that youngsters used to play on each other. It went something like this: "I'll show you what I have in my hand for a nickel." (Sometimes this was negotiable down to as low as a single penny.) Then after making said payment, one learned that the item in the individual's hand was a stone, a blade of grass, hot air, or some other equally worthless item.

Of course, this same tactic is now being made available on the corporate level for gullible adult gamblers. I sincerely hope you've learned by now to avoid this offer.

Surprisingly, it is at times possible to obtain the desired information and yet avoid paying this ridiculous fee. If a coin (one is sufficient) or paper bill is inserted into the Odyssey machine when the machine is in the "game selection" mode and then this version of Fort Knox is called to the screen, the Odyssey machine will reveal the Fort Knox game in its entirety if the previous player has wagered three credits per spin on his last play. Thus, the condition of the Fort Knox game will be revealed and the funds can be cashed out of the machine. If the previous player has not wagered three credits per spin on his last play, the machine may or may not give you a momentary glance at the obtained digits. This final case is uncertain. Nonetheless, you can cash out your funds and have spent nothing.

Alternatively, if you are playing any other game on an Odyssey machine and, during the play of the other game, pause to call the Fort Knox game onto the screen, the desired information will appear. Then you can return to the game you were playing without ill effect. An alternative to inserting coins or bills is to sit down at an Odyssey machine that someone has just played and vacated and call the Fort Knox game to the screen. The game will appear with the information about the digits of the combination. This can only be done once and must be done almost immediately after the departure of the other player. Generally, never play even once simply to learn the information.

Other than the requirement to play maximum coins to obtain the digits of the combination and thus the bonus, the entire modification of the play of Fort Knox is such that a knowledgeable individual still plays Fort Knox when four digits of the combination have already been obtained. Play is as usual terminated when the bonus is obtained and a new combination created.

On this version of Fort Knox, safe deposit boxes will generally be larger than they are on the other versions. This in part compensates for the extra expenditure. This version also has greater variability. That is, the losses and wins both tend to be greater than in the other versions, but the net effect is that the profits, at any particular number of obtained combination digits, average to values larger than those of the other versions of Fort Knox.

# French Dough

*Synopsis: Play at one credit per spin on machines which have nine loaves of bread in one window section, or eight loaves in each of two window sections, or seven or more loaves in each of the three window sections. Terminate play when the machine does not meet any of the above conditions.*

French Dough really isn't a new game. It's simply a remake of Double Diamond Mine that has been altered appropriately for Paris.

In this version of the game, you accumulate loaves of bread instead of diamonds. The loaves of bread are neatly stacked in three sections of the front window of the bakery. Each of the three window sections corresponds to one of the three reels on the slot machine. Loaves of bread are accumulated by a loaf of bread landing on the payline. When this occurs, a number of loaves equal to the number of credits wagered on that spin is added to the corresponding window pane of the bakery for each loaf appearing on the payline. When ten loaves have accumulated in any window area, a cyclist arrives, loads the loaves, and while the baker sings a little ditty, rides away and transfers to the credit meter one credit for each of the ten loaves.

If you think this computer routine on French Dough is a little cutesy, Paris, at busy times, also has a real cyclist selling bread as he pedals around various parts of the casino property. The cyclist does not go between the slot machines as part of his sales route. Most such aisles aren't wide enough to accommodate that.

To profitably play French Dough, you can use a strategy like that of Double Diamond Mine. Simply play one credit per spin on machines which have nine loaves of bread in one window section, or eight loaves in each of two window sections, or seven or more loaves in each of the three window sections. Then terminate your play when the machine does not meet any of the above conditions.

There are lower machine settings that can be played profitably on French Dough, such as 8 loaves in one window section, 7 loaves in another window section, and 6 loaves in the remaining window. This is also a profitable play. However, as one begins to play at lower machine settings, the profit generated becomes very marginal. It also becomes awkward and of little additional value to remember more complicated rules.

With the above rules, you will definitely be getting dough out of French Dough machines.

# Greased Lightning

*Synopsis: Play maximum credits per spin when distance remaining for Your Car to reach the bonus area is less than or equal to 3/4 the distance remaining to be traversed by Their Car to reach the finish line. Terminate play when the mileage indicators return to zero or it becomes obvious that Your Car will not reach the bonus area before Their Car reaches the finish line.*

Greased Lightning is another racing game. This one is a variation of Chuck Wagons. The horse drawn wagons of Chuck Wagons have been replaced with miniature souped-up '57 Chevys.

In Greased Lightning, the player is attempting to move his car (labeled Your Car) to the bonus area for a bonus of ten, fifteen, or 25 credits before the competing car (labeled Their Car) reaches the finish line.

This competing car, operated by the slot machine, moves with every spin of the reels and functions as a timing device, while the player's car only moves when an ADVANCE! symbol is on the payline. The distance moved by Their Car is generally three miles per spin.

For a Greased Lightning slot machine to be, on average, of value to play, the number of miles remaining to be traversed to reach the bonus area by Their Car should, when you begin, be at least 1.33 times the number of miles remaining to be traversed by Your Car to reach the bonus area. Thus, if there are 34 miles (roughly the position halfway to the bonus area) remaining to be traversed by Your Car, Their Car should have at least 45 miles to go to the finish line.

Since 1.33 is extremely close to the fraction 4/3, you may wish instead to use this fraction for "in the head" calculations. So for the roughly halfway position mentioned above, using the factor 4/3, you would again want to have at least 45 miles remaining for Their Car to reach the finish line.

An equivalent alternative to the above is that the distance remaining for Your Car to reach the bonus area must be less than or equal to 3/4 of the distance remaining for Their Car to reach the finish line. If you find this statement more comprehensible (and many prefer fractions less than one to those larger than one), then use it appropriately.

Such Greased Lightning slot machines can be found occasionally. Having located an appropriate Greased Lightning, it is necessary during the play of the slot machine to move Your Car as quickly as possible to the bonus area. If play is at a single credit per spin, Their Car will easily outdistance Your Car. Consequently, play should be at maximum coins per spin, which will move Your Car three miles times the number of credits played on that spin for each ADVANCE! symbol on the payline. There are a few minor exceptions to this "play at maximum coins" rule, but they are usually clear in the particular situations and also can be ignored without significant financial loss.

Play should be terminated when the mileage indicators return to zero or it becomes obvious that Your Car cannot reach the bonus area before Their Car reaches the finish line.

# Isle of Pearls

*Synopsis: Play three credits per spin when 49 feet or fewer remain to be descended to reach the first bonus level, and the amount of time in seconds remaining is at least double the number of feet remaining to be descended to reach the first bonus level. Terminate play when the dive is completed or it becomes obvious that the diver will not reach the initial bonus level before time expires.*

Isle of Pearls is a game which is simply an Empire slot machine turned upside down. Well, not exactly. The difference between an Empire slot machine in which King climbs and an Isle of Pearls slot machine in which a diver descends is only a matter of direction. Isle of Pearls is for people who like to go down.

In an Isle of Pearls slot machine, the diver needs to descend at least seventy feet in one minute and forty seconds (one hundred seconds) or 25 spins, whichever comes second, in order for you to win a bonus. Play is such that each DIVE! symbol on the payline moves the diver three feet times the number of credits wagered: one, two, or three. The machine displays a counter that informs you of the depth that the diver has attained and a timer that shows the amount of time remaining in which to complete the dive.

The diver's descent must be at least seventy feet for you to receive a bonus. But if the diver is exceptionally energetic and reaches additional specified depths of ninety feet or 110 feet, you will receive instead of a bonus of ten credits, a higher reward of 15 or 25 credits respectively at the completion of the dive.

I have never observed the diver to use the hundred seconds without using the minimum of 25 spins, so the 25 spins are generally not a factor in determining if an Isle of Pearls slot machine is valuable to play.

This slot machine does have two significant pieces of information on its display. One is the number of feet that the diver has already accomplished, and the other is the amount of the initial hundred seconds remaining for the diver to complete his dive. These two pieces of information can be used to determine if a particular machine is, on average, of value to play.

First, in order for an Isle of Pearls slot machine to be valuable to play, the amount of time remaining to be played should, at the beginning of your slot play, be at least double the number of feet remaining to be descended. Thus, if there are 34 feet remaining to be descended (roughly the half-way position to the first bonus level), you should have 68 seconds, i.e. one minute and eight seconds, remaining on the timer.

There are small anomalies to this rule, of course, because of the discrete nature of the timing device and the depth measurement. Time, which is always continuous, is a discrete item on these machines and seems repeatedly to be a multiple of four seconds, while the depth in feet is always an integer and a multiple of three, thus a discrete item. Thus, there are small oddities such as if the diver has completed 63 feet and seven remain to descend, then if 12 seconds remain, the game is favorable. The rule about the ratio of time and feet remaining to descend has some flexibility, especially near the end of the game. The rule is not carved in stone but should generally serve you well.

A consequence of this rule is that for an Isle of Pearls slot machine to be, on average, valuable to play, there must be 49 feet or fewer remaining to be descended to reach the first bonus level (seventy feet). The slot machine does not tell you that information directly. The machine displays how many feet the diver has already descended. Consequently, the number of feet already descended must be at least 21. Actually, 21, 24, and 27 feet are very weak plays because there is still much of the distance to be descended.

Play on an Isle of Pearls machine that meets the above requirements should be at the maximum number of credits permitted per spin. It is imperative to move the diver as much as possible with each DIVE! symbol. There are a few anomalies where it is unnecessary to wager the maximum of three credits per spin. For example, if you have moved the diver 69 feet and there are only a few seconds remaining, then you should wager only one credit per spin. However, these anomalies occur seldom enough that you can ignore them at comparatively little cost.

An Isle of Pearls machine is difficult to find in a condition which is profitable to play because most slot players only leave when it is obvious that the diver will not complete his descent within the designated time allotment.

# Jewel in the Crown

*Synopsis: Play max credits per spin when there are two jewels in any row labeled 25, 100, or 1000. Terminate play when any row of three jewels is obtained.*

At the time of its introduction, Jewel in the Crown was a game unlike any other banking machine. As one would expect from its name, the game banks jewels. The jewels come in five assorted colors with a number associated with each color. The five numbers are: 5, 10, 25, 100, and 1000.

When in the course of standard play at max bet on Jewel in the Crown, you accumulate three jewels of the same color, you will receive on the credit meter the number of credits associated with that color. The other accumulated jewels at that time are of no value.

Jewels are obtained by two methods. The most common method is to have them appear on a payline with maximum coins bet. Machines I have seen have only one payline and the maximum wager is either two or three credits per spin. Each jewel on a payline will generate a corresponding banked jewel. If, perchance, more than one jewel lands on a payline, then the appropriate number and color of jewels appearing will be banked.

You may think it is significant whether the maximum bet is two or three. Having three as the max bet does create greater variance in individual machine results and you will experience greater financial swings. However, the long run results are about the same. In other words, the results, on average, will be about the same. This appears to be the case because on the machines where the max bet is three, jewels are awarded more frequently than jewels are awarded on machines with a max bet of two.

The other method of obtaining jewels is through the start-up award. After each awarding of a bonus for collecting three jewels of a particular color, the machine will, on the next play at maximum coins or credits, reset the jewels to a random position. Just what is involved in the manufacturer's use of the word random is unclear. Certainly, all possible resettings do not appear to be equally likely. The primary purpose of this start-up award is, in my opinion, to encourage players to remain at their machines after receiving an award for obtaining three jewels of the same color. It is well known that even novice players often avoid playing games at slot machines on which it is clear that the player must begin from a zero or null position.

As a result of this start-up award, a number of illuminated jewels on the front panel does not mean that any person has played that particular Jewel in the Crown more than once since the last bonus.

My limited observations at Jewel in the Crown indicate that the "random" resetting is not worth investing an extra wager to see.

As a practical matter for those readers who have not seen a Jewel in the Crown machine, let me describe the machine further. A Jewel in the Crown machine has five rows across its front panel. Each of these rows has three jewels in a darkened format of a particular color and with an associated number. Whenever a jewel is obtained on a payline, a corresponding jewel is illuminated on the front panel of the slot machine. When all three jewels of any color are illuminated, a bonus is awarded to the player. The size of the bonus is a number of credits equal to the number associated with the particular color.

It is actually possible to win two awards by completing two rows simultaneously on the same spin. This is definitely a rarity.

After the awarding of the bonus for completing a set of three same colored jewels, the machine, as mentioned above, resets some amount of jewels to a "random" position by illuminating them on the front panel.

For a Jewel in the Crown slot machine to be advantageous to play, the number of jewels in any of the 25, 100, or 1000 rows should be two. If you locate such a machine, hopefully the 5 or 10 row will not also contain two jewels, because you will often suffer a net loss by getting one of these rows instead of completing the higher valued row.

Nonetheless, the rule is still the same; that is: for a Jewel in the Crown slot machine to be advantageous to play, the number of jewels in either the 25, 100, or 1000 row should be two.

Play should be terminated when any row of three jewels is obtained. I do not recommend playing an extra spin just to see the positions of the jewels when the machine resets. Invariably, you will be disappointed.

# Jungle King

*Synopsis: Play three credits per spin when the amount of time in seconds remaining is at least double the number of feet remaining to be climbed to reach the first bonus level. Terminate play when the machine resets for another climb or it becomes obvious that the Jungle King will not reach the bonus area before time expires.*

Jungle King is another one of those games where a player has to move some figure a minimum of seventy units in one minute and forty seconds in order to receive a bonus, the minimum of which is ten credits.

On the Jungle King slot machine, the Jungle King (also called Jungle Man) needs to climb up a vine at least seventy feet in one minute and forty seconds (one hundred seconds) or 25 spins, whichever comes second, in order for the player to receive a bonus. The purpose of this treatment of one hundred seconds or a minimum of 25 spins is unclear since each spin seems to require four seconds.

Play is such that each CLIMB! symbol on the payline moves Jungle King three feet times the number of credits wagered: one, two, or three. The machine displays a counter that informs the player the height Jungle King has attained and a timer that shows the amount of time remaining in which to climb. The timer seems somewhat ludicrous in that it invariably uses four seconds per spin no matter how rapidly or slowly one attempts to play.

The Jungle King's climb up the vine must reach at least seventy feet for you to receive a bonus. But if Jungle King instead climbs to ninety feet or 110 feet, you will obtain the higher reward of 15 or 25 credits respectively, at the completion of the climb.

This slot machine does have two significant pieces of information on its display. One is the number of feet that Jungle King has already climbed and the other is the amount of time of the initial one hundred seconds remaining for Jungle King to complete his climb. These two pieces of information are used to determine if a particular machine is, on average, valuable to play.

In order for a Jungle King slot machine to be, on average, of value to play, the amount of time remaining to be played should, when you begin, be at least double the number of feet remaining to be climbed to reach the first bonus level. Thus, if there are 34 feet remaining to be climbed (roughly the halfway position to the first bonus level), you should have 68 seconds, i.e. one minute and eight seconds, remaining on the timer.

Play on a Jungle King that meets the above requirements should be at the maximum number of credits permitted per spin. It is imperative to move the Jungle King as much as possible with each CLIMB! symbol. There are a few anomalies where it is needless to wager the maximum of three credits per spin. For example, if you have moved the Jungle King 69 feet and there are only a few seconds (say four or eight) remaining, then you should wager only one credit on the final spin(s). However, these anomalies occur seldom enough that you can ignore them at comparatively little cost.

Play on a Jungle King slot machine should be terminated when the machine resets for another climb or if it becomes obvious that the Jungle King cannot complete the seventy foot requirement before the allotted time elapses.

Jungle King is difficult to find in a condition which is profitable to play because most slot players only leave when it is blatantly obvious that the seventy foot requirement will not be completed within the designated time allotment.

# Jungle King (Enlarged Bonus)

*Synopsis: Play maximum credits per spin when the number of feet remaining to travel is less than half the number of seconds remaining. Terminate play when the distance counter resets to zero.*

Jungle King has been remade. This version is like Empire (Enlarged Bonus) and, with minor word changes, the information below is exactly like the material in Empire (Enlarged Bonus). However, it was felt that each game should have its own description.

This version of Jungle King is basically like the previous version except that the bonuses and time allotments have been changed. Looking at the machine, the most noticeable difference is that the bonuses were significantly increased from the previous levels of 10, 15, and 25 to new and higher levels of 20, 40, and 250.

Now the casinos weren't suddenly going to start giving away money with these higher bonuses; to compensate a new time allotment was introduced in order to make these slot machines function profitably for the casinos. The amount of time available to reach the bonus levels was changed. The time allotted was significantly reduced from two minutes to one minute and 24 seconds or, as the machine displays this, 1:24. No matter how it's written, you have only 84 seconds in which to obtain a bonus.

Let me assure you that having only 84 seconds instead of 120 seconds has a huge impact on obtaining a bonus. For all practical purposes, this machine is worthless to look for in order to get a valuable play.

First and foremost, I found that this version of Jungle King was rarely left in a valuable state. This was, in part, because individuals didn't leave machines at which they perceived that they were doing well, but, I believe, moreso because the machines did not get into a valuable condition nearly as often.

Another occurrence, but of less importance, was that there was much more variability in the results of play on these machines. This type of Jungle King had much larger wins but additionally had many more losing sessions. This, I believe, contributed to its unpopularity and eventual removal from several casinos.

The bright side of this version of Jungle King is that the rules which determine if this machine will be valuable to play are exactly the same as previously. In other words, in order to, on average, profitably play this version of Jungle King, you should locate a machine on which the number of feet remaining to be climbed to the first bonus is less than half the number of seconds remaining for climbing. This will put you into a relatively strong position to receive a bonus. Then you must play maximum credits per spin in order to quickly move Jungle King to the bonus level. Play should be terminated immediately when the counter resets to the initial setting of zero feet traveled.

This strategy is effective to profitably play this version of Jungle King. However, you will have difficulty finding machines satisfying these conditions. In fact, you'll have so much trouble that you will probably stop looking for good plays on this particular type of Jungle King.

# Jungle King (Random Bonus)

*Synopsis: Play maximum credits per spin when the number of feet remaining to climb is less than half the number of seconds remaining. Terminate play when the distance counter resets to zero.*

Jungle King has been remade again. Some of these games seem like automobiles with a new model each year. This version is like Empire King in which the bonus award is a random amount of from ten to 1000 credits. With minor word changes, the information below is exactly like the material in Empire King. However, it was felt that each game should have its own description.

All Jungle King games involve Jungle King traveling up a vine. This version of the game involves reaching only one bonus level, which is called the Bonus Area. Traveling any number of feet of 90 or over within the two minute time frame is considered to have placed Jungle King in the Bonus Area. Jungle King's reaching the Bonus Area will automatically begin the bonus round without requiring you to exhaust the remainder of the two minutes of time as is supplied on other machines in the series to reach higher bonus levels.

In this version of Jungle King, there are two ways for Jungle King to reach the Bonus Area and receive the bonus. One is for you to be lucky enough to have the special Jungle King symbol land on the payline when a maximum bet of three credits has been made. The appearance of this symbol will immediately transport Jungle King to the Bonus Area. The bonus is then awarded.

The second and commonest way for Jungle King to reach the 90 foot level or higher is by traversing the 90 foot distance in smaller increments. This is done by being fortunate enough to have a Climb symbol land on the payline. When this occurs, Jungle King will move upward by a number of feet equal to three times the number of coins wagered on that particular spin for each Climb symbol. Jungle King will thus move at most 27 feet on a spin if the incredible outcome should be three Climb symbols on the payline while three coins were wagered.

The bonus given on this version of Jungle King is a random amount which will range from ten to 1000 credits. Specifically, the bonus in credits will be one of the numbers 10, 15, 20, 25, 35, 40, 50, 75, 100, 250, 500, or 1000. Commonly, the bonus received is 35 credits; and, naturally enough, the average of all bonuses received is around 35 credits. Bonuses beyond 100 are definitely rarities.

In order to, on average, profitably play Jungle King, you should locate a machine on which the number of feet remaining to be traversed is less than half the number of seconds remaining for travel. This will put you into a relatively strong position to receive the bonus. Then you must play maximum credits per spin in order to quickly move Jungle King to the Bonus Area. Play should be terminated immediately when the distance counter resets to the initial setting of zero feet traveled.

It is not common to find this version of Jungle King left in a valuable state. Novice players often seem to 'get it right' about when to give up on these machines.

# Kool Kat

*Synopsis: Play at one credit per spin on any machine with a crown on the Kool Kat's head. Similarly play when any pile equals or ex-*

*ceeds 99, or two piles each have 75 or more, or all piles exceed 51. Terminate play when none of these conditions exist.*

This machine displays three piles of hats on its visual. The number of hats in each pile does not have to be counted because the designer and manufacturer were nice enough to have the number of hats in each pile conveniently displayed below the pile. There are always three piles of hats during the game, with each pile having at least three hats.

The banked item is the number of hats in each pile. During a bonus round, one credit is awarded for each hat in the particular pile eliminated during that bonus round.

The following discussion assumes play at one credit per spin, which is believed to be the most financially advantageous method to play Kool Kat in pursuit of the bonus.

The piles of hats all begin at three (not simultaneously); and whenever a Kool Kat symbol appears on the payline, three hats are added to the pile which corresponds to that reel. (Technically, the machine adds a number of hats equal to three times the number of coins bet; but we are assuming three in this entire discussion.) As the piles grow, the hats are naturally compressed somewhat to prevent them from growing beyond the visual. The hats in the piles are always in multiples of three, so you will never see a pile with forty hats unless the machine is malfunctioning.

Because each banked hat is ultimately worth one credit, the banking of hats is a sort of machine pay even though it does not appear on the pay schedule.

Because three hats (three credits) can be banked for the play of a single credit, the machine is generally paying rather poorly as far as the novice customer is concerned. This causes many customers to quickly lose interest in the game.

In order to receive a bonus, a crown must appear. The crown will appear on the visual on the head of the Kool Kat seated at a table. The timing of this arrival of the crown is seemingly random, with no apparent way (such as playing more credits) to induce the appearance of the crown sooner.

When the crown appears, it will remain on the Kool Kat's head until it is used to obtain a bonus. After its appearance, the next Kool Kat symbol on the payline will trigger the associated pile of hats to be eliminated With this elimination, you will see the Kool Kat dance a little jig with a female cat. Then you will be awarded on the credit meter one credit per hat for each hat in the pile. The machine will then begin another pile with three hats in the same location.

There are two strategies for profitably playing Kool Kat slot machines. The first is to only play these machines when there is already a crown on the Kool Kat's head. Playing at one credit per spin and terminating play when a bonus is received will assuredly, on average, win some money.

This idiotically simple strategy will have the definite result that you are not playing many Kool Kats since machines are rarely found in that state.

The second strategy which will win funds is as follows. Play any Kool Kat slot machine where any pile equals or exceeds 100 (99) hats. Then also play any machine where there are two or more piles with 75 hats each. And finally, play any machine where all three piles of hats equal or exceed fifty (51). The numbers in parentheses are included to remind you that the exact numbers of 50 and 100 do not occur on the Kool Kat machine, but only numbers which are multiples of three. (Readers find it easier to remember 50, 75, and 100 rather than 51, 75, and 99,) As mentioned above, play should be at one credit per spin. Play should be terminated when a machine does not meet any of the above criteria.

The above recommendations should serve you well. I should mention that the information is not all derived from direct play. First, my wife and I have only played on machines that had a single large pile of hats. The figure of 100 (99) is somewhat on the high side. It is a 'good' number to use for profitable play. However, the second and third parts of the above rule are not the result of direct play.

In all the machines that we have examined, we have never played a Kool Kat where two piles or three piles were, in addition to being reasonable sizes, roughly of equal sizes and the largest. Those two parts of the above rules are inferred and the result of other than direct observation and play. Nonetheless, those parts of the rule should, on average, prove profitable if followed.

A final comment about Kool Kat is in order. When playing this machine, you will notice that there is only one payline. However, you will be able to see both above and below the payline on all three reels. If you notice the combinations of symbols that appear on these two non-paylines, you will repeatedly observe winning combinations far in excess of what is happening on the single payline. This phenomenon of winning combinations on non-paying lines is, of course, not due to chance and illustrates the attempts of manufacturers to lure customers to and retain them at machines by repeatedly giving the sensation of a near miss.

This phenomenon also occurred on Piggy Bankin' slot machines with the comparatively often alinement above the single payline of three pigs, the top award on that pay schedule. What is different about Kool Kat in this regard is that the appearance of winning combinations on non-paylines is far more pronounced and is definitely noticeable.

In our experience, a Kool Kat slot machine is generally tight in its standard play. The sensation of coming close may have some mental appeal; but on slot machines' paytables, a miss is a miss.

# Krazy Keno

*Synopsis: Avoid play even when the special ball is next in the tube.*

Krazy Keno is a game found on many of the Odyssey slot machines and can be played advantageously under certain conditions. This game, however, has been disappearing recently in preference to other games appearing on the Odyssey displays.

By playing one dollar, four credits, when the next ball in the tube is a bonus ball, you will have an advantage ranging from 1%

to over 35% depending on your selection of two through ten spots. (The one spot is never advantageous.)

Because of the qualities of the game of keno, i.e. losing upwards of 75% of the games while waiting for a rare large win, it is suggested that you play only a three-spot (nearly 11% edge) under the above conditions. Even then, you will have to be very lucky or play for hundreds of games to be ahead financially. Consequently, Krazy Keno is generally not recommended except to those willing to spend extreme amounts of time looking for machines fitting the necessary conditions and enduring the repeated losses incurred while waiting for the large wins.

The table below gives the expected values during advantageous periods. These are the theoretical values that would result from repeated play, technically an infinite amount of play. In practice, the results are usually negative and require relatively rare events to make the results positive.

### Krazy Keno: Expected Values During Advantageous Periods

| Number of Spots Selected | Expected Value per $1 Wager | Number of Spots Selected | Expected Value per $1 Wager |
|---|---|---|---|
| 1 | 0.8250 | 6 | 1.2325 |
| 2 | 1.0101 | 7 | 1.2622 |
| 3 | 1.1086 | 8 | 1.3214 |
| 4 | 1.1212 | 9 | 1.3380 |
| 5 | 1.2292 | 10 | 1.3508 |

*Do not be deceived by the entries in the above listing. Exceptional amounts of play will be necessary to achieve these results.*

# Lady of Fortune

*Synopsis: Play at one credit per spin when there are five or more highlighted letter/symbols. Terminate play when there are 12 letter/symbols to obtain.*

Welcome, Mortal, to the world of the occult! Or, at least in the world of slot machines, this game is currently as close as it gets. With a gypsy that resembles a manikin, a crystal ball with clear legible messages, and zodiac symbols, you can be entertained for quite a while, with a message on almost every spin. This standard play is followed by a bonus round, which is a trip into weird, beginning with the gypsy separating into several distinct pieces.

The Lady of Fortune will turn out to be the Lady of Misfortune if you try to play this game from its initial state. In order to have the long-run advantage in this particular game, you have to pick up the play where some other player has conveniently left off.

In Lady of Fortune, the items that are banked are the letters and symbols in +BONUSxROUND. These 12 letters and symbols appear one at a time in the crystal ball, and you must obtain each in its turn as the ball indicates. On completion of that task, the programing carries you to another dimension in which you will obtain your reward by placing your palm against the video screen and making contact with the female in the Realm of Fortune.

This female will urge you to continue on to obtain even greater wealth, but don't fall for that old line. Take the money and run or at least walk to the change booth.

Lady of Fortune is, on average, advantageous to play at one credit per spin if five or more of the letter/symbols have previously been collected and thus highlighted. Play should be terminated when the machine resets and there are 12 letter/symbols to collect. The cost of collecting each letter/symbol is about 5.3 credits and the bonus averages roughly 42 credits. (See table page 90.)

Commonly, professionals avoid playing Lady of Fortune machines when only five letter/symbols are highlighted, partly because the machines can be time-consuming to complete by getting the remainder of the letter/symbols and playing the bonus round.

**Lady of Fortune: Average Profit During Advantageous Periods**

| Number of Letter/Symbols | Average Profit in Credits |
|:---:|:---:|
| 5 | 5.0 |
| 6 | 10.3 |
| 7 | 15.7 |
| 8 | 21.0 |
| 9 | 26.4 |
| 10 | 31.7 |
| 11 | 37.0 |

# Lady of Fortune (Max Bet Version)

*Synopsis: Play at three credits per spin when there are five or more highlighted letter/symbols. Terminate play when there are 12 letter/symbols to obtain.*

Welcome again, Mortal.

Lady of Fortune as described above has been modified, along with several other games on the Odyssey machines. In the case of Lady of Fortune, the game has been altered so that you must play three coins, the maximum wager, in attempting to obtain the letter/symbols necessary to reach the bonus event of placing your hand on the screen and making contact with the female in the Realm of Fortune.

As a result of this change, playing one or two coins does not alter the number of obtained letter/symbols. Additionally, the pay schedule is such that those players who play a third coin are generally not receiving any extra pay for their additional coin. These players usually realize this fact and so either continue to play the machine through to the bonus round or revert to playing one or two credits.

So to obtain the bonus, you must wager three coins per spin. (There are Lady of Fortune machines where the maximum wager is two credits per spin.) Other than the requirement to play maximum coins, the entire modification of Lady of Fortune is such that a knowledgeable individual plays the max bet version of Lady of Fortune in the same manner as before, i.e. when five letter/symbols have already been obtained and thus highlighted. Bonuses will tend to be much larger than they were in the previous version, averaging 119 credits, and this tends to compensate for the expenditure of the extra coinage. The cost of getting a letter/symbol averages 16.4 credits.

This max bet version of Lady of Fortune has greater volatility. That is, the losses and wins both tend to be greater with the net effect that they will average to the values given in the table on page 50. It appears that the letter/symbols are easier to obtain in this version of Lady of Fortune and inexperienced players do not tire as easily and terminate their play. Therefore, fewer of these machines are left available for play by knowledgeable players.

Okay, Mortal, now you're ready!

### Lady of Fortune (Max Bet Version)
### Average Profit During Advantageous Periods

| Number of Letter/Symbols | Average Profit in Credits |
|---|---|
| 5 | 3.7 |
| 6 | 20.2 |
| 7 | 36.7 |
| 8 | 53.2 |
| 9 | 69.6 |
| 10 | 86.1 |
| 11 | 102.6 |

# Lost City Adventure

*Synopsis: Play three credits per spin when five or more diamonds are displayed on the screen, terminating play when the bonus round is completed.*

Lost City Adventure is a game that, to my knowledge, only comes in a nickel denomination. I first noticed this game at Sunset Casino in Henderson, a suburb of Las Vegas.

Lost City Adventure plays like many other video slot machines having pays for various four reel combinations, a wild symbol (Major Money himself), and a scatter award. The game also has a bonus round, which is referred to as Major Money's Lost City Adventure.

The bonus round is reached by completing a jigsaw puzzle through the obtaining of icons with their appearance on the fifth reel and on a winning payline. The value of the bonus round is affected by the number of diamonds obtained during the regular previous play.

If the above paragraph sounds stupidly involved, that's only because it is.

First, let's examine the completion of the jigsaw puzzle. The first four reels of this video slot machine pay for certain winning combinations and pay left to right or right to left on these four reels. There is a fifth reel on the right that also spins and has only icons. Each time there is a winning combination on any wagered payline, the icon associated with that payline is removed from the jigsaw puzzle. The item that is removed from the jigsaw puzzle is technically a rectangle with only that icon written on it.

In a sense, this jigsaw puzzle is not a matter of putting various pieces in their proper place but rather a matter of removing pieces from a layout to reveal what is underneath. What is revealed underneath is of no significance to playing the game, to my knowledge. Nonetheless, the puzzle has fifteen icons and associated rectangular pieces in a three by five pattern. The removal of the final jigsaw piece triggers the bonus, which is referred to as Major Money's Lost City Adventure.

That, in a nutshell, is the jigsaw part of this game.

Let us now examine the value of the bonus round. It is really unnecessary to go into the details of this mini-cartoon that will flow across the screen of the slot machine. Simply be assured that you are seeing cartooning presented as a version of slot action. This is a little hard for me to believe but there is actually cartoon action on this slot machine's screen.

At this point, I should mention that there are two items banked in this game. One is the removal of the rectangular pieces with icons (or the associated revealing of the area underneath) and the other item is a collection of diamonds located in the upper left corner of the screen.

Since we have already discussed the jigsaw quality of this game, we will now explain the functioning of the diamonds. The amount received during the bonus round is multiplied by the number of diamonds that have been collected during the regular play of Lost City Adventure. Since the number of diamonds may be as high as fifteen, this can clearly have a substantial impact on the profitability of a machine. The minimum number of diamonds a player will have at the bonus round is one.

Diamonds are collected during regular play by a method involving the collection of points. Whenever an icon on a winning payline can be used in the puzzle, you are awarded a number of points equal to the amount wagered on that particular payline. These points are displayed on the screen in a square box in the upper left corner near the location of the diamonds that have been collected, if any have already been collected. Whenever fifteen points have been awarded, the machine converts the points into a diamond. Thus, the number of diamonds grows as the game progresses.

To my knowledge, the most profitable manner, on average, to play Lost City Adventure is to ignore the number of pieces remaining to be obtained in the puzzle. This is because the pieces are relatively easy to obtain when the puzzle is several pieces from completion. The pieces become progressively more difficult to obtain, with the last piece being the most difficult.

What should not be ignored is the number of diamonds that have been previously collected. These are extremely important because of their multiplying of the bonus round award. Since I advocate that you play three credits per spin, one credit on each of the three paylines, you should not expect the number of diamonds to increase by more than one during play. In fact, you can, if you so desire, determine the number of diamonds that you will have at the bonus round by adding one point per remaining puzzle piece to the current total of points and diamonds.

To, on average, profitably play Lost City Adventure, there should be at least five diamonds already collected by the previous player(s). Then play should proceed at the rate of three credits per spin until the bonus round is completed.

# Merlin

*Synopsis: Play three credits per spin when fifty feet or fewer remain to be traversed to reach the first bonus level and the amount of time in seconds remaining is at least double the number of feet remaining to be traversed to reach the bonus area. Terminate play when the distance counter resets to zero or it becomes obvious that Merlin will not reach the bonus area before time expires.*

Merlin is another one of those games where you must move a small figure at least seventy units in one minute and forty seconds. This is nothing but the same game as Empire, Isle of Pearls, Jungle King, and Spacequest. There are a few word changes, a different figure, a varied backdrop, and the same mathematics in all these games. So if the advice sounds the same as before, don't be surprised.

Merlin is a game which depicts the magician moving toward a castle in the background. The display shows a winding trail, but Merlin bee lines it and one is uncertain if he is supposed to be traveling on the trail or somehow magically ascending. Whichever, Merlin needs to move at least seventy feet in one minute and forty seconds (one hundred seconds) or 25 spins, whichever comes second, in order for the player to obtain one of the bonuses, the minimum of which is ten credits. If Merlin performs exceptionally and moves ninety to 109 feet, or 110 feet or more, you will obtain instead of ten credits, a higher award of 15 or 25 credits respectively, at the completion of Merlin's trip. What seventy or ninety or 110 feet has to do with the castle and trail in the background is never clear. Don't let this detail bother you as player, because all the casino and manufacturer really want is the player to mindlessly drop money into the machine.

Play on Merlin is such that each ADVANCE symbol on the payline moves Merlin three feet times the number of credits wagered: one, two, or three. The machine displays a counter that informs you how many feet Merlin has moved and a timer that shows the amount of time remaining for Merlin to complete his movement. The timer, which seemingly should only run during the actual spinning and pay periods, appears to require four seconds per spin no matter what.

Merlin, like all the games in this series, has little oddities that you may not initially notice or consider. First, as mentioned above, the spins each require four seconds; thus, the time remaining in seconds is always a multiple of four: 100 (1:40), 96 (1:36), 92 (1:32), 88 (1:28), 84 (1:24), 80 (1:20), 76 (1:16), 72 (1:12), 68 (1:08), 64 (1:04), 60 (1:00), 56, 52, 48, 44, 40, 36, 32, 28, 24, 20, 16, 12, 8, or 4 seconds. There are no in-between times. Secondly and similarly, since Merlin starts at zero and always moves in multiples of three feet, he is always located at a position that is a multiple of three: 0, 3, 6, 9, 12, 15, 18, 21, 24, 27, 30, 33, 36, 39, 42, 45, 48, 51, 54, 57, 60, 63, 66, 69, 72, 75, 78, 81, 84, 87, 90, 93, 96, 99, 102, 105, 108, or ??? feet (I've never seen a value above 108 feet). Again, there are no in-between levels. A player will never see Merlin at 59 feet.

Another feature of this set of slot machines is that the reset button cannot be used until the timer is less than 1:28. In other words, a player cannot reset the game until 1:24 or less time remains. At least four spins must always occur before the machine can be reset.

The Merlin slot machine does have two significant pieces of information on its display. One is the distance in feet that Merlin has already moved and the other is the amount of time of the initial hundred seconds remaining for Merlin to complete his movement. These two pieces of information can be used to determine if a particular machine is, on average, valuable to play.

First, in order for a Merlin slot machine to be, on average, valuable to play, there must be 52 feet or less remaining to be climbed to reach the bonus area, seventy feet and higher. The slot machine does not tell you that information in a direct sense. The machine displays how many feet Merlin has already moved. Consequently, the number of feet already climbed must be at least eighteen. I usually use twenty feet as the cutoff. Actually, 18, 21, or 24 feet are all very weak plays because there is still much of the distance to be traversed.

More importantly, for a Merlin slot machine to be, on average, of value to play, the amount of time remaining to be played should, when you begin slot play, be at least double the number of feet remaining to be moved to reach the bonus area. Thus, if there are 34 feet remaining to be climbed (the roughly halfway position to the first bonus level), you should have 68 seconds, i.e. one minute and eight seconds, remaining on the timer.

The factor of two used above actually seems a little too large. By my estimates, one can multiply the number of feet remaining to be traversed by 1.9 to obtain a better estimate of the minimum number of seconds needed. So for the halfway position mentioned above, you should have at least 64.6 (use 64) seconds remaining or, as the timer on the machine would say, one minute and four seconds.

Play on a Merlin machine that meets the above requirements should be at the maximum number of credits permitted per spin. It is imperative to move Merlin as much as possible with each ADVANCE symbol. There are a few anomalies where it is needless to wager the maximum of three credits per spin. For example, if you have moved Merlin 69 feet and there are only four or eight seconds remaining, then you should wager only one credit on the last spin and possibly next to last spin. However, these anomalies occur seldom enough that you can ignore them at comparatively little cost.

Play on a Merlin slot machine should be terminated when the distance counter resets to zero or if it becomes obvious that Merlin cannot within the remaining time accomplish the requirement of moving the seventy feet.

The Merlin slot machine is difficult to find in a condition which is profitable to play because most slot players only leave when it is obvious that Merlin will not complete the seventy foot minimum before the allotted time elapses.

# Merlin (Enlarged Bonus)

*Synopsis: Play maximum credits per spin when the number of feet remaining to travel is less than half the number of seconds remaining. Terminate play when the distance counter resets to zero.*

Merlin has been remade. This version is like Empire (Enlarged Bonus) and, with minor word changes, the information below is exactly like the material in Empire (Enlarged Bonus). However, it was felt that each game should have its own description.

This version of Merlin is basically like the previous version except that the bonuses and time allotments have been changed. Looking at the machine, the most noticeable difference is that the bonuses were significantly increased from the previous levels of 10, 15, and 25 to new and higher levels of 20, 40, and 250.

Now the casinos weren't suddenly going to start giving away money with these higher bonuses; to compensate, a new time allotment was introduced in order to make these slot machines function profitably for the casinos. The amount of time available to reach the bonus levels was changed. The time allotted was significantly reduced from two minutes to one minute and 24 seconds or, as the machine displays this, 1:24. No matter how it's written, you have only 84 seconds in which to obtain a bonus.

Let me assure you that having only 84 seconds instead of 120 seconds has a huge impact on obtaining a bonus. For all practical purposes, this machine is worthless to look for in order to get a valuable play.

First and foremost, I found that this version of Merlin was rarely left in a valuable state. This was, in part, because individuals didn't leave machines at which they perceived that they were doing well, but, I believe, moreso because the machines did not get into a valuable condition nearly as often.

Another occurrence, but of less importance, was that there was much more variability in the results of play on these machines. This type of Merlin had much larger wins but additionally had many more losing sessions. This, I believe, contributed to its unpopularity and eventual removal from several casinos.

The bright side of this version of Merlin is that the rules which determine if this machine will be valuable to play are exactly the same as previously. In other words, in order to, on average, profitably play this version of Merlin, you should locate a machine on which the number of feet remaining to be climbed to the first bonus is less than half the number of seconds remaining for climbing. This will put you into a relatively strong position to receive a bonus. Then you must play maximum credits per spin in order to quickly move Merlin to the bonus level. Play should be terminated immediately when the counter resets to the initial setting of zero feet traveled.

This strategy is effective to profitably play this version of Merlin. However, you will have difficulty finding machines satisfying these conditions. In fact, you'll have so much trouble that you will probably stop looking for good plays on this particular type of Merlin.

# Merlin (Random Bonus)

*Synopsis: Play maximum credits per spin when the number of units remaining to travel is less than half the number of seconds remaining. Terminate play when the distance counter resets to zero.*

Merlin has been remade again. This version is like Empire King in which the bonus award is a random amount of from ten to 1000 credits. With minor word changes, the information below is exactly like the material in Empire King. However, it was felt that each game should have its own description.

One minor difference in this version of the game is that it is unclear what are the dimensions of Merlin's travels. Is Merlin moving feet, yards, miles, etc.? To handle this dilemma, we will simply use the term units.

All Merlin games involve Merlin traveling to a castle. This version of the game involves reaching only one bonus level, which is called the Bonus Area. Any number of traveled units of 90 or over is considered to have placed Merlin in the Bonus Area. Merlin's reaching the Bonus Area will automatically begin the bonus round without requiring you to exhaust the remainder of the two minutes of time as is supplied on other machines in the series to reach higher bonus levels.

In this version of Merlin, there are two ways for Merlin to reach the Bonus Area and receive the bonus. One is for you to be lucky enough to have the Magical Instant Winner symbol land on the payline when a maximum bet of three credits has been made. The appearance of this symbol will immediately transport Merlin to the Bonus Area. The bonus is then awarded.

The second and commonest way for Merlin to reach the 90 unit level or higher is by traversing the 90 unit distance in smaller increments. This is done by being fortunate enough to have an Advance symbol land on the payline. When this occurs, Merlin will move upward by a number of units equal to three times the number of coins wagered on that particular spin for each Advance symbol. Merlin will thus move at most 27 units on a spin if the incredible outcome should be three Advance symbols on the payline while three coins were wagered.

The bonus given on this version of Merlin is a random amount which will range from ten to 1000 credits. Specifically, the bonus in credits will be one of the numbers 10, 15, 20, 25, 35, 40, 50, 75, 100, 250, 500, or 1000. Commonly, the bonus received is 35 credits; and, naturally enough, the average of all bonuses received is around 35 credits. Bonuses beyond 100 are definitely rarities.

In order to, on average, profitably play Merlin, you should locate a machine on which the number of units remaining to be traversed is less than half the number of seconds remaining for travel. This will put you into a relatively strong position to receive the bonus. Then you must play maximum credits per spin in order to quickly move Merlin to the Bonus Area. Play should be terminated immediately when the counters reset to the initial setting of two minutes and zero units traveled, which will occur if you receive the bonus or fail to obtain it.

It is not common to find this version of Merlin left in a valuable state. Novice players often seem to 'get it right' about when to give up on these machines.

# Money Factory

*Synopsis: Avoid play except at one credit per spin when sizable bundles of sixty (or more) or eighty (or more) are at or within one step of the final drop, or when a large bundle of several hundred is on the conveyor belt. Terminate play when the desired bundle is obtained.*

Money Factory is a banking game that produces bundles of "money" at assorted intervals and places them on a conveyor belt. Each bundle usually has a number on the outside which indicates the value of the bundle in credits. Occasionally, the bundle has a question mark on the outside and you are left in doubt about its value. The first rule regarding Money Factory is never to play to obtain a bundle with a question mark on its outside. Invariably, you will be disappointed.

In Money Factory, it is unclear exactly what causes the movement of the conveyor belt upon which the bundles are located. The movement of the conveyer belt, which is in discrete steps, appears to be random. Of course, when a bundle drops off the conveyor belt onto the transporter, you receive the number on the side as credits.

Money Factory is one of the games that I have not found to be a good experience. My negative experience is not alone and is confirmed by discussions I've had with others who commonly play various slot machines.

What little solid information I have is as follows. Money Factory is most profitably played with one coin per spin. The game should only be played when there is a bundle with sixty (or more) or eighty (or more) at or within one unit, respectively, of the final drop on the conveyor belt. Bundles of this size and location are usually not left by novice customers.

A more common find is one involving a bundle of several hundred credits which is a large number of steps from the end of the conveyor belt. Professional players do play to get these bundles. Their results are generally favorable; but because these machines have some considerable variability with that amount of play, you can suffer a sizable financial setback.

In all cases, play should be terminated on Money Factory when the desired bundle is obtained.

The above information may be somewhat biased because clearly these machines do have various settings. However, our experience suggests that you play these machines with considerable caution.

# Money Maze

*Synopsis: Although many strategies are available, generally play to move the gargoyle to a nearby (within three spaces) highlighted pay spot. Play the number of credits/spin equal to the number of spaces the gargoyle is from the highlighted pay spot. Terminate play when too tired from exhaustion to continue, the number of players decreases significantly, or told to leave the casino.*

I used to believe that the biggest money makers in slot machines were one dollar Piggy Bankin', Safe Cracker, and Shopping Spree slot machines. I was wrong. As I look back, those machines pale by comparison to Money Maze. After I finally learned to correctly play Money Maze, it was money, money, money and gobs more money. When my wife and I played, we could make 500 dollars a day each. And when you factor in that these are quarter machines with a max bet of 75 cents, you begin to realize that this was plainly extreme. If played correctly, this was virtually a no lose situation, like heads I win, tails you lose.

To my knowledge, Money Maze is only at Bellagio. It was, according to the scuttlebutt, made exclusively for that casino. This is really unimportant because if the game appears to be very popular, the ideas will be reproduced in a varied form that is similar but not too similar to be a copyright infringement.

So you can consider the information presented here to be both a specific lesson on how to play Money Maze and general directions on how to approach any similar game that may reach the casino market place.

After a few weeks, Money Maze was altered at Bellagio and the ability to win such large sums per diem ended. The proper procedure to play the game was affected by the changes. These variations will also be discussed below.

**Figure 1: Diagram of Maze**

# The Game

Money Maze involves a set of fifty machines linked into a single system. The individual machines are all three reel slot machines and much of the slot play is quite standard. Not all the slot machines in the system are exactly the same with regard to their pay schedules, but these variations pale in significance to the general play of the system of Money Maze. Also, I believe, and this is only an unsupported assumption, that the machines individually all have the same hold for the casino.

Figure 1 is a diagram of the maze that appears on each machine in Money Maze. This maze as it appears on the visual of the individual slot machines is attractively colored and also contains a small movable figure called a gargoyle. The machine does not use this term to describe the little figure on the screen which, in fact, is akin to a horny little devil's head. Some people have avoided playing the machines because they are put off by the appearance of the figure. So the slot personnel call the little figure a gargoyle, a grotesque ornamental figure [American Heritage Dictionary], rather than a devil as though that changed something.

Now Figure 1 may be a swell diagram to show what the screen on each machine looks like but is awkward to use in describing the play of the game. To remedy this, Figure 2 (page 104) was drawn up to clarify and describe the processes in properly playing Money Maze.

The gargoyle on each machine operates separately from those on other machines in the system and is initially at the position labeled S, the starting position. The gargoyle moves through the maze in response to the appearance of a gargoyle symbol appearing on the payline of the slot machine. The gargoyle on the visual will make a number of moves equal to the product of the number of gargoyle symbols on the payline and the number of credits wagered. Since there are three reels and the maximum wager is three credits, the maximum number of gargoyle moves on any reel spin is nine. Incidentally, the payline generally loses when a gargoyle appears on the payline. The pay schedule does not include gargoyle symbols.

**Figure 2: Maze with Labeled Positions**

Some novice players are often surprised when a gargoyle appears on a particular payline and generates no credits. It must be explained to the new players that the gargoyles are not wild symbols, a common initial misconception.

When a gargoyle symbol lands on the payline of the slot machine, you are supposed to press the spin button which will spin in a somewhat random manner the compass arrow located in the center of the visual and determine the direction in which the gargoyle figure moves. If you do not press the spin button within a short period, the machine is programmed to spin the compass arrow on its own and move the small figure.

During the play of the machine, the gargoyle moves along the pathways and only comes to rest on the numbered squares and the one labeled S, the starting position. The squares with circled letters have a number nearby which is a minimum of ten but often grows larger.

Landing on a square with a circled letter triggers the payment to the player of the number of credits of the nearby number. The gargoyle is then returned to the initial position, S, to begin a new trip through the maze.

During the play of Money Maze the individual squares with circled letters occasionally become slightly enlarged physically and highlighted. When this occurs, the numerical value associated with that circled letter square is increased significantly and remains enlarged until a gargoyle on one of the system's slot machines lands on that circled letter square. The circled letter square then returns to its usual size and is unhighlighted. At the same time, the associated number returns to the initial size of ten. Clearly, it is more profitable to the player of the machine for the gargoyle to land on a circled letter square when highlighted.

The highlighting of the circled letter squares is definitely dependent on coin-in and it is easily observed that the highlighting occurs far more often when more of the set of machines are in heavy use. It was also observed that when Money Maze was changed and the values of highlighted squares were reduced, the rate at which the highlighting of circled letter squares occurred was increased substantially.

Knowledgeable players often patiently wait for a circled letter square to become highlighted before attempting to move the machine's gargoyle. This is starting to get into the strategy of Money Maze which is primarily in following sections.

## Initial Strategy

The most novice strategy that will win money at Money Maze is to search through all the available machines of the fifty and play machines where the gargoyle is one move from any pay spot. Positions 2, 4, 11, 14, 15, 19, and 24 are the locations from which to make these plays. However, positions 2 and 4 are definitely the weakest plays. The play is at the rate of one credit per spin which will move the gargoyle one space when the symbol is on the payline. Even this very weak strategy will get the money. This strategy is occasionally used by knowledgeable players but only when the Money Maze system is inactive with no players or prospects of any.

## Elementary Strategy

A better strategy than the initial approach explained above is to combine the above procedure with playing a machine where the gargoyle is two positions away from a highlighted pay spot. Thus, you would also be playing from positions 1, 3, 10, 13, 14, 15, 17, 18, 22, and 23. This strategy incorporates the increased value of the pay spots when highlighted. Once again, positions 1 and 3 are the weakest. The play is still at the rate of one credit per spin which will move the gargoyle one space when the symbol is on the payline. If the pay spot becomes unhighlighted while you are two units away, terminate play.

This strategy will work poorly. When I say poorly, I do not mean to convey that the procedure will lose money or produce sizable swings in revenue, but rather that one can generally play far more profitably using more advanced and aggressive strategies.

## Advanced Strategy

The Advanced Strategy will generally win far better than either of the previous two strategies. It relies on playing only for highlighted pay spots. All play for unhighlighted spots is discarded as being of relatively minor financial importance in comparison. The gargoyles on machines are generally left in place to possibly be used later. In the Advanced Strategy, play is from positions 1, 2, 3, 4, 10, 11, 13, 14, 15, 17, 18, 19, 22, 23, and 24 and the amount wagered is dependent on the distance of the gargoyle from the highlighted pay spot. Sometimes with this strategy, a knowledgeable player will still play to remove all the gargoyles on positions 2, 4, 11, 14, 15, 19, and 24 even when the positions are unhighlighted. However, this is now done not so much because it is profitable but to dissuade novice players who may begin learning to play properly and become seriously competitive.

## Aggressive Strategy

Somewhat better than the Advanced Strategy is what we term the Aggressive Strategy. With this strategy, you will again play only for highlighted pay spots but now will play if the gargoyle is three or fewer spaces from the desired pay spot. Thus, you will be playing from any of the positions of the Advanced Strategy plus positions 8, 9, 16, 20, and 21. All told, that is positions 1, 2, 3, 4, 8, 9, 10, 11, 13, 14, 15, 16, 17, 18, 19, 20, 21, 22, 23, and 24. If fact, the only positions you do not play from are positions 5, 6, 7, 12, and S. The amount played is dependent on how far the gargoyle is from the highlighted pay spot: one, two, or three credits. This strategy is extremely aggressive but will definitely be a losing strategy if only used to obtain unhighlighted pay spots. This Aggressive Strategy can, as before, be coupled with play to remove all the gargoyles on positions 2, 4, 11, 14, 15, 19, and 24 even when the positions are unhighlighted. This is, as before, done not so much for profit but to dissuade novice players who may begin learning to play properly and become seriously competitive. Perhaps the most amazing thing about Money Maze is that the more aggressively you play, the more profitable the game can be.

## Passive Strategy

There is one final technique or strategy that is sometimes used to profitably play Money Maze. That is what we call the Passive Strategy; it will only win at about half the rate of the Advanced Strategy or the Aggressive Strategy. This is somewhat uncertain because the Passive Strategy can be used while playing and holding one to three slot machines.

Basically, the Passive Strategy works by selecting one to three slot machines in Money Maze. Then you play on the machine where the highlighted pay spot is near the gargoyle. In other words, instead of changing machines to find a gargoyle near the highlighted pay spot, you patiently wait for the spot near any gargoyle on the set of machines you are holding to become highlighted. The feature of repeatedly changing machines is eliminated.

Let us give a small example. Assume that one of the machines that you are holding has its gargoyle at the S position. You will move the gargoyle to position 1. Continuing, you will then move the gargoyle to either position 2 or 4. Then you will patiently wait until the pay spot that the gargoyle is near becomes highlighted. When the pay spot becomes highlighted, which eventually it will, you will then play one credit per spin until the gargoyle either lands on the pay spot (the process will then repeat itself from position S), the pay spot becomes unhighlighted (you will return to waiting), or the gargoyle passes by the pay spot by going to either position 5 or 6.

Let us assume that the gargoyle misses the pay spot and is at position 5. Then you will move the gargoyle to the next pay spot, usually moving one space at a time. Slowly you move the gargoyle to be adjacent to this unhighlighted pay spot and patiently wait for the pay spot to highlight. On highlighting, you endeavor to move the gargoyle to the pay spot and receive the enlarged bonus.

Whenever the gargoyle does land on a pay spot, the gargoyle is returned to position S and the entire process repeats itself.

As mentioned before, this Passive Strategy does not require you to repeatedly change machines. Many may find this a desirable feature even though the win rate is significantly reduced. However, this technique will not prevent you from being expelled from the casino. I know several individuals who were dismissed from Bellagio for successfully using this strategy.

# Strategy for Downgraded Variation

When Money Maze first appeared, the system was such that the unhighlighted pay spots were valued at ten credits each. When a pay spot became highlighted, its value was increased to fifty credits. This ten dollar variation (since these are quarter machines) was a very significant difference in the pay for landing on a pay spot. All the above strategies worked in playing the set of machines under those conditions. One day the system suddenly changed and the highlighted pay spots were only worth forty credits. The impact of this change was to decrease winnings by roughly 20%. This alteration did not, however, affect the use of the above playing strategies. All the above strategies still worked, just not as profitably.

After three days, the Money Maze system was altered again. This time the system was altered so that the highlighted pay spot was reduced to twenty credits, down from forty. The value of an unhighlighted pay spot remained ten all through the period of alteration.

With this final change, it was noticed that the pay spots, while highlighting to this lesser value, did highlight more often. However, in no way did highlighting more often financially compensate for the decrease in the highlighted value to keep a knowledgeable person's average earnings from the set of machines at the same level.

At that time, some number of the skilled players terminated their play because they felt they could find a more profitable use of their time elsewhere. It was still possible to profitably play Money Maze but the profit was radically reduced. My wife and I did not depart from Money Maze, however, because we wanted to determine for our readership how best to play under the new conditions.

With the new conditions that were imposed, namely highlighted pay spots worth twenty credits, we determined that the Initial and Elementary Strategies could both still be used profitably. The use of the Aggressive Strategy was totally ridiculous and definitely unprofitable. The Passive Strategy could also still be used profitably. What seemed to work most profitably under the new conditions was a variation of the Advanced Strategy.

In this variation, play for highlighted pay spots only occurred from positions 2, 4, 10, 11, 13, 14, 15, 17, 18, 19, 22, 23, and 24. Attempts for the pay spots labeled F and G were clearly minimized. This variation of the Advanced Strategy was profitable, although significantly reduced compared to previous standards.

## Coding

Coding is a feature of playing Money Maze well. And yet I think my wife and I were the only individuals doing coding at this set of machines. If you have a strong memory for remembering details that are constantly changing, then you won't need coding. But if not, then coding is almost indispensable.

When playing Money Maze with either the Advanced or Aggressive Strategy, it is important to be able to recall which of the fifty machines had the gargoyle in a desirable position in order to play for the currently highlighted pay spot.

Remembering this type of item in a constantly changing setting is a Herculean task, and the Herculean part is not in your arms and legs but in your head.

The easiest method of trying to remember what was where can be accomplished by coding. This coding can involve setting some unobtrusive object somewhere on the machine to indicate just where the gargoyle is on that machine. This coding will make return to the proper machine relatively quick and easy.

When my wife and I played at Money Maze, we used the ashtrays (change buckets, matchbooks, etc. are all acceptable) to code where the gargoyles were on all the machines which had a gargoyle in any reasonably good location. Then when a particular pay spot highlighted, it was simply a matter of looking at the ashtrays to decide which machine was the correct one to play. Of course, since the ashtrays were often being moved by customers and cleaning personnel, it was a continual effort to keep the system coded correctly while trying to profit through play at the machines. Nonetheless, coding proved to be extremely helpful.

# Downgrading Money Maze

Eventually, the Money Maze system at Bellagio was downgraded. The highlighting of the pay spots which originally altered the values of the pay spots from ten credits to fifty credits was changed so that the spots changed from ten to forty credits. Then three days later, the system was altered again so that the pay spot during highlighting changed from ten to twenty credits.

Money Maze could, after this final alteration, be played for roughly a hundred dollars per day by a knowledgeable person. I should stress here that this figure incorporates the fact that most knowledgeable players ceased playing and departed. The very few who remained, such as my wife and me who were still gathering data, played against very reduced competition. This created a playing situation where play in the system was virtually uncompetitive. So the figure above may be distorted to some extent.

Finally, in some sort of massive exclusion scheme, Bellagio began a routine of excluding anyone whom the floor persons sensed knew how to profitably play slot machines. So my wife and I were politely told to stay away. This is discussed elsewhere and the expulsions were not limited to Money Maze in particular.

However, prior to our dismissal we collected the data used in constructing Figure 3 (page 112), which is a limited collection of what we call the vector probabilities at various positions. We have used the term vector probabilities because the data possesses both magnitude and direction. Although it was not mentioned above, movements along the pathways of the maze by the gargoyle are not all equally likely. There is a very definite bias in the movements at various positions, e.g. a gargoyle at position 1 will with probability 37.6% move west to position 2, with probability 62.4% move east to position 3, and never (probability zero) return south to the starting position, S.

The numbers with their placement on the diagram indicate the direction and probability in percent of movement in that direction by the gargoyle figure if a gargoyle appears on the payline of the slot machine. Some positions have no data because we either never or very rarely played at that position or

**Figure 3: Vector Probabilities at Assorted Positions**

were told to leave before completing the collection of a sufficient quantity of data.

The data has been included for those of you who wish to examine the system in additional detail prior to a visit to Bellagio. Perhaps you will wish to consider various alternatives to the above playing strategies.

After the alteration of Money Maze through the reduction of the values of the highlighted spots, several months went by before the next significant change. The number of machines in the system was markedly reduced from fifty to 24. This surely made the system of far less value to play, especially when calculated on an hourly basis, probably by a factor of one half.

Then again some weeks later, the system was varied by reducing the number of machines to only twelve. Definitely, at this level, the only strategies which will work are the Initial and Elementary Strategies. Even then the techniques will not generate large amounts of revenue as previously.

# Monopoly: Reel Estate Version

*Synopsis: Never play.*

Monopoly slot machines come in several versions. A banking feature is possessed by one version, Reel Estate. The item that is banked is the highlighting of individual properties. Properties are highlighted by the player landing on the property through an electronic process somewhat similar to the board game. The player receives a bonus when all the properties of a particular color are highlighted. After the bonus is awarded, the set of properties is returned to the unhighlighted state and the process can repeat itself.

A potential player, on approaching such a machine, can easily see how many properties in each of the various sets are highlighted through previous play. If there are sufficient numbers of sets uncompleted by only one property, then the individual may choose to play to attempt to complete some of the sets and receive the associated bonus(es). (Part of the bonus for completing a set is a multiplication factor times the number of credits wagered, which appears to be a ploy to generate multi-coin wagering.) On completing each set of same colored properties, the player will receive one free spin in the second screen, irrelevant of the size of the wager.

Perhaps if I simply quote the information on the machine, you will appreciate more fully the item you are receiving. The machine states, "ACQUIRING ALL PROPERTIES IN ANY COLOR GROUP WILL CLEAR ALL PROPERTIES IN THAT COLOR GROUP AND AWARD A FREE SPIN IN THE SECOND SCREEN." (Capitalization is theirs.)

One free spin may seem to be an abysmally small award. However, that is not necessarily correct in this situation. That free spin in the second screen can generate some substantial funds. However, I know of absolutely no one who plays the Reel Estate version of Monopoly to get this banked item. In fact, most individuals, without a serious amount of examination of the game, don't even realize that it has a banking feature.

I can hardly express my indignation with the manufacturer for making this machine fit the category of a banking game.

The amount of play necessary to get to the second screen, coupled with the inherent difficulties in obtaining the single property to complete any particular set, seem to make this monetarily a questionable play at best. Plainly avoid playing this or any version of the Monopoly slot machines.

# Mystery Treasure

*Synopsis: When at least two sections of the map have been completed, play one credit per spin, terminating play on completion of the map.*

Mystery Treasure is on MULTI-PAY PLUS machines. It is a remake of Pirates Treasure. To call this game a remake of Pirates Treasure is to dignify the entire situation. Mystery Treasure is exactly the same game as Pirates Treasure with simply a name change. I have found nothing different between these two games in my examination of machines in the Las Vegas area.

Mystery Treasure, like Pirates Treasure, is somewhat uncommon in casinos in the Las Vegas area. What is banked in these games are certain reel alinements, namely three maps on a winning payline. These reel alinements are semi-difficult to obtain, since the alinement pays ten credits per credit wagered besides drawing the player nearer to the bonus.

When five proper alinements have been accomplished, a section of a map is obtained. More accurately, the next section of the map, which is already visible, is lit up or illuminated more intensely instead of being drab. Then when three sections of the map have been obtained, you receive a bonus which is automatically entered onto the credit meter.

Mystery Treasure, like Pirates Treasure, is, on average, profitable to play at one credit per spin when one section of the map is completed and over half of the alinements necessary for the second section of the map have been accomplished. Another way of saying this last part is that over half of the fifteen alinements necessary to complete the entire map must have been obtained. Play, of course, should be terminated when all three sections of the map have been obtained

Most knowledgeable players do not play Mystery Treasure when the slot machine has less than two sections of the map completed. They do not consider a machine with so few alinements accomplished to be worth their time and effort. There are always plenty of other types of machines to examine.

# Neptune's Treasure

*Synopsis: Play at one credit per spin on machines which have a figure one unit from a treasure chest, or two figures each two units from their respective treasure chests, or three figures which are each three units or less from their respective treasure chests. Terminate play when the machine does not meet any of the above conditions.*

Neptune's Treasure seems very much like an upside down Double Diamond Mine; but since the treasure chests are worth twenty credits, this game actually seems even more like an upside down Triple Diamond Mine. And that analysis is based on no data and simply reading the instructions.

These games come out so rapidly that my wife and I have trouble finding sizable numbers of machines left with the games in an advantageous mode. Hence, we are still in the process of collecting enough data to give reasonable estimates regarding the value of the machines. We can produce a winning playing strategy but cannot gather the quantities of data one should have to give solid numerical estimates.

On each reel of a Neptune's Treasure machine is a small sea figure unique to that reel which, when landing on the payline, moves a similar figure on the visual the number of units wagered on that spin. The sea figure is moved deeper into the depths toward an awaiting treasure chest.

When the sea creature arrives at the treasure chest, you will receive a bonus of twenty credits and the figure will return to the topmost position.

The one particularly annoying feature of these machines is that for the novice, it is very difficult to determine just how many units each figure is from the chest. The background does not readily lend itself to acting as a guide. So you are forewarned that this problem will exist initially and can only be overcome with a modicum of practice, preferably on quarter machines as opposed to dollar ones.

Note that this problem also exists in other games such as Balloon Bars Balloon Race. The reason for trying to overcome the dilemma in this case is that Neptune's Treasure machines are available to the public on a far larger scale.

A profitable way to play Neptune's Treasure is to locate a machine which has a figure one unit from a treasure chest, or two figures each two units from their respective treasure chests, or three figures which are each three units or less from their respective treasure chests. Having located an appropriate machine, play should be at one credit per spin.

Play should be terminated when the Neptune's Treasure slot machine does not meet any of the above conditions.

The above rule is primarily easy to remember. It does lack precision and is on the conservative side. Basically, you should, on average, win money with its use.

# Pay-Roll

*Synopsis: Play maximum credits per spin when there are two coins in any tube labeled 25, 100, or 1000. Terminate play when any tube of three coins is obtained.*

Pay-Roll seems to be simply a variation of Jewel in the Crown. The game banks coins instead of jewels. The coins are collected by play on the reels and are deposited in appropriate tubes labeled with the numbers: 5, 10, 25, 100, and 1000.

When in the course of ordinary slot play at max bet on Pay-Roll, you accumulate three coins in the same tube, you will receive on the credit meter the number of credits associated with that tube.

Coins are obtained by slot play with the maximum number of coins bet. The machines I have seen have only one payline and the maximum wager is two credits per spin. This is unlike Jewel in the Crown, which comes in game varieties with maximum bets of two and three credits. However, in my wandering through Las Vegas casinos, I have only seen Pay-Roll with a maximum wager of two. This may vary in other parts of the country.

For a Pay-Roll slot machine to be financially advantageous to play, the number of coins in any of the 25, 100, or 1000 rows should be two. If you locate such a machine, hopefully the 5 or 10 tube will not also contain two coins, because you will often suffer a loss by getting one of these tubes instead of completing the higher valued tube.

However, the rule is still the same; that is: for a Pay-Roll slot machine to be advantageous to play, the number of coins in either the 25, 100, or 1000 tube should be two.

Play should be terminated when three coins are obtained in a tube and the bonus awarded.

# Piggy Bankin'

*Synopsis: On $1, $2, and $5 machines with 18 or more credits in the piggy bank and on nickel and quarter machines with 21 or more credits in the piggy bank, play one credit per spin. Terminate play when a "Break the Bank" symbol appears on the payline.*

Piggy Bankin' slot machines have tended to be plain headaches for many casinos. The machines generate substantial funds but create problems of supervision because numbers of undesirable individuals haunt the machines for their good profit potential for the knowledgeable individual. This is especially true for the dollar Piggy Bankin' machines.

The dollar denomination of Piggy Bankin' has extreme profit potential because the item which is banked is actually dollar credits. These credits are readily banked, but removing the banked credits is sometimes rather time-consuming and boring. The dollar denomination of these machines has such profit potential that the machines are extremely corrupting — not just to individuals who play them but also to those working in the casinos.

To illustrate how corrupting they can be, let me go into the activities that occurred at the Tropicana Casino in Las Vegas. Knowledgeable players would sit around the casino for up to fourteen hours a day. I myself at one time used to visit the Tropicana six times a day: twice in the morning, twice in the afternoon, and twice in the evening. However, I definitely did not stay around the casino for such extended periods of time. My casino play was more of an "in and out" pattern.

Following the activities at the Tropicana for the newspaper with which I'm associated took an interesting turn when I saw that experienced players plainly began to encourage novice players to leave valuable machines. Although there are numerous ways to encourage such a departure, and the conditions often have to be right, corrupt players, instead of simply waiting for valuable machines to be vacated, began to work novices off the machines. In other words, experienced players began in a sense to cheat novice players out of their machines. This activity was reported by me to Tropicana security, who plainly expressed themselves as unconcerned.

Now, why would a security department be unconcerned about casino customers being fleeced of their valuable Piggy Bankin' slot machines? I was eventually told the answer by another individual (I feel a certain disgust with myself for not doping it out on my own). Subsequent events substantiated the information which indicated that the actions of the corrupt players were being tolerated for a usual reason, money. According to several sources, including some of these experienced players themselves, the necessary action to avoid being removed from

118

the Tropicana was to tip the security personnel. On further checking, it did appear that non-tipping individuals were asked (more like told) to stay away, while tippers were tolerated.

I personally was not about to tip anybody for the privilege of being in a casino, and especially security people, who are not in any way directly a part of the gaming process. But I did initiate a plan to annoy the individuals who thought they should be tipped. I realized that one of the things that really annoys someone who thinks he deserves a tip is to tip everyone else. And that is exactly what I did. From then on in the Tropicana, every time I hit a substantial jackpot, I passed around gratuities to everyone except security: the change girls, the hopper fillers, the floor person, even the workers at the various change booths. Everyone got a noticeable tip except, of course, security. I should elaborate on what I mean by noticeable. The gratuities that I dispensed were not only noticeable, they were distinctive and memorable. I gave ten dollar Red Lobster gift certificates. Part of the reason for giving this type of gratuity instead of cash is that some casinos require their personnel to share or pool tips with their coworkers. However, this type of food gratuity was not subject to such casino regulations.

My exclusion of security generated a definite response. After that, I was told to leave the Tropicana on the most ludicrous of pretenses: straightening the stools, finding money on the floor, writing notes on a small pad I carry in my shirt pocket, etc. These were like warning shots because my dismissals were for only a single day, or rather, the rest of the day. Eventually, with my repeated and continual non-tipping of security, I was permanently dismissed from the Tropicana.

I then decided to phone one of the supervisors in the security department and relate the information in my possession. He definitely didn't want to hear anything derogatory about the people in his department and was quick enough to brush me aside by suggesting I phone him back in about six months if I was interested in revisiting the Tropicana.

Unfortunately, with such an indifferent attitude, he eventually had the displeasure of reading about the actions of his departmental subordinates in the local newspaper, *Valley Explorer,* which contained additional details of this story.

The two major points of all the above are that these machines can be very valuable to play and that the machines can have a definite corrupting influence on people.

From the information that I have been able to glean from various sources, it appears that on Piggy Bankin' machines there are four settings used to determine the casino hold. Casinos generally use one of the three lower settings for the dollar and higher denomination machines, and usually use the highest setting for nickel and quarter Piggy Bankin' machines. With repeated play, you will discern the difference.

All Piggy Bankin' slot machines display a piggy bank on their visual. This piggy bank is seeded with an initial ten coins. Whenever you aline three blanks, the number of credits wagered is not lost but instead is transferred to the piggy bank. In this manner, additional coins are added to the piggy bank. As the bank grows, so the value of the machine grows. Clearly, what is being banked is the actual credits that are transferred into the piggy bank.

The bank is broken when the "Break the Bank" symbol, which is only on the right reel, lands on the payline. You then receive all the funds in the bank as credits on the credit meter. The machine then refills the bank with an initial ten credits.

The most advantageous procedure for profitably playing Piggy Bankin' machines is to wait until the piggy bank is sufficiently high and then play one credit per spin until the bank is broken. Then you should immediately terminate your play.

What is "sufficiently high" is different depending on the denomination of the machine that you are playing. For dollar and higher denomination machines, the piggy bank should contain at least 18 credits; nickel and quarter Piggy Bankin' machines should have a bank of at least 21. This is a reflection of the increased casino hold on nickel and quarter machines.

As an easy rule of thumb, a dollar machine with a bank of 25 is worth about eight credits (25 - 17 = 8) since on average the machine will generate an eight dollar profit. Similarly, a quarter machine with a bank of, for example, thirty is worth ten credits

(30 - 20 = 10) or $2.50. A nickel machine with a bank of 24 is worth on average four credits (24 - 20 = 4) or twenty cents. These formulas are not precise but are reasonable for general usage.

Another figure related to the Piggy Bankin' slot machines is that on average it will take about eighty spins to break the bank. The interesting thing about this tidbit of information is that after every spin, the average remains the same. In other words, after each spin you are basically back to the same situation and it will still on average take about eighty spins to break the bank.

# Pirate's Treasure

*Synopsis: When at least two sections of map have been completed, play one credit per spin, terminating play on completion of the map.*

Pirate's Treasure is uncommon in the Las Vegas area. What is banked in this game are certain reel alinements. These reel alinements are semi-difficult to obtain. When five proper alinements have been accomplished, a section of a map is obtained. More accurately, the next section of the map, which is already visible, is lit up or illuminated more intensely instead of being drab. Then when three sections of the map have been obtained, you receive a bonus which is automatically entered onto the credit meter.

I have always had a positive experience with this little game and always enjoy playing it through to completion, although it can be somewhat time-consuming. Pirate's Treasure is, on average, profitable to play at one credit per spin when one section of the map is completed and over half of the alinements necessary for the second section of the map have been accomplished. Another way of saying this last part is that over half of the 15 alinements necessary to complete the entire map must have been obtained. Play, of course, should be terminated when all three sections of the map have been obtained

Most knowledgeable players do not play Pirate's Treasure when the slot machine has fewer than two sections of the puzzle completed. They do not consider a machine with so few accomplished to be worth their time and effort. There are always plenty of other types of machines to go and check.

# Playoff: Deuces Wild

*Synopsis: Never play.*

Many of the Odyssey machines have a banking game called Deuces Wild Playoff. This game starts with a pot of 75 credits which increases by five credits after every 23 hands. On some of these games, the pot increases by five credits with every thirty hands. This is a setting that each casino can specify and affects the hold.

Now let me first assure you that not all Deuces Wild games are created equal. There is a version Full Pay Deuces Wild which has a pay schedule of 800, 200, 25, 15, 9, 5, 3, 2, 2, 1 per coin with max coins wagered. Of course, this is simply called Deuces Wild by the casinos but called Full Pay Deuces Wild by individuals who know how to play video poker profitably. Full Pay Deuces Wild is a video poker game with which many of the readers are familiar. It has a particular holding or playing strategy and can be profitably played in its own right with the holding strategy that is presented in many fine books, such as *Deuces Wild Video Poker* by Bob Dancer.

However, because the pay schedule for the Deuces Wild on the Odyssey is quite different from that of Full Pay Deuces Wild, the holding strategy for Full Pay Deuces Wild should not be used for playing on the Odyssey machines. This means that a new holding strategy would have to be developed for, and learned by, the reader to play this Deuces Wild with the very poor pay schedule 800, 250 (or 225), 20, 10, 8, 4, 3, 2, 1, 1 on the Odyssey machines. Note: this game has slightly varying pay schedules.

This slot machine game is simply not worth that type of effort by either you or me. Tucking special holding strategies into your gray matter can get to be more than a little bit of a tedium, but especially so when the strategy has only one use, i.e. this Odyssey game. But more annoying is that without some serious effort, such strategies can easily become confused with the proper and more commonly used Full Pay Deuces Wild holding strategy. Based on our experience, my recommendation with this game is to avoid play, primarily because it is generally not worth the time or effort involved.

# Playoff: Jacks or Better

*Synopsis: Play five credits per hand when the bonus pot contains at least 145 credits and discontinue play when bonus pot is re-established at 75 credits.*

Many of the Odyssey machines have a banking game called Jacks or Better Playoff. This game starts with a pot of 75 credits which increases five credits after every 16 hands. This game is significantly different from the game Deuces Wild Playoff which I recommended that you not play.

The pay schedule on Jacks or Better Playoff is 800, 50, 25, (9, 6) or (8, 5), 4, 3, 1, 1 per coin with max coins wagered. This is a weak pay schedule and does not warrant play in general. Technically, to be properly played, this game requires a holding strategy all its own. However, this Jacks or Better Playoff can be profitably played when the pot is substantial by using the strategy for 9-6 Jacks or Better, which has a pay schedule of 800, 50, 25, 9, 6, 4, 3, 2, 1 per coin with max coins wagered.

Technically, this game to be properly played requires a holding strategy all its own. As a consequence of some requests, I have in this edition included a strategy for the Jacks or Better (9,6) Playoff. It is given separately and can also be used with little ill effect with the Jacks or Better (8,5) Playoff. For those of you unfamiliar with reading this type of strategy chart, let me briefly explain. First, T, J, Q, K, A stand for ten, jack, queen, king, and ace, respectively. Also, the small s, e.g. KTs, means that the cards involved, king and ten, must be of the same suit. Then, the strategy chart works like a flow sheet in that you read down until you find a description of the hand that you currently possess. Then hold and draw appropriately. This strategy can be improved by including what are termed penalty cards; but that is too complicated for a book that is not about video poker.

Our experience with Jacks or Better Playoff is such that I recommend playing the game when the bonus pot is at or above 145 credits, using the given strategy and terminating play when the bonus pot is reestablished at 75 credits. With an initial amount of 145 credits in the bonus pot, the machine should, on average, generate about 16 to twenty credits. Each increase of five credits in the "initial" bonus pot will add about five credits to the average profit generated by playing the machine until the pot is won. Of course, each decrease of five credits in the "initial" bonus pot will deduct about five credits from the average profit generated by playing the machine until the pot is won. As I personally lost interest in this game, I ceased to play unless I encountered a bonus pot of at least 170. Eventually, I have reached the position where I plainly do not play unless the bonus pot contains at least 200 credits.

The factors which influenced me in these matters are given below. These factors will, with enough play, probably begin to affect your attitude about this game.

Initially, I came to dislike having to hold another strategy in my head, even if it was held only during the play of this one type of game. Also the strategy is for such a generally weak video poker game that I did not want any of its facets becoming confused with other strategies that I use regularly. Unless you are exceptionally thrilled with this particular game, you should avoid the possible confusion associated with learning another holding strategy.

On average, it requires 133 hands before a playoff occurs. This feature is built in and will not change, no matter how well or poorly you play. You may get three playoffs in the next six hands; but don't worry, you will, with continued play, eventually have intervals without playoffs that bring the average back to 133.

## Playoff: Jacks or Better (9,6) Strategy

any full house or better
4 royal
flush, straight, three of a kind, or two high pairs
4 any straight flush
KQJs, QJTs
high pair: JJ, QQ, KK, AA
3 royal
4 flush
4 open straight with 1 or more high cards
QJ9s, JT9s
4 open straight with no high cards
low pair: 22, 33, 44, 55, 66, 77, 88, 99, TT
QJ8s
3 straight flush with no gaps
KQ9s, KJ9s
AKQJ
QT9s, JT8s, J98s
two same suited high cards
4 inside straight with three high cards
3 straight flush with two gaps and one high card
3 straight flush with one gap and no high cards
234s
KQJ
4 inside straight with two high cards
QJ
JTs
KQ, KJ
QTs
AK, AQ, AJ
KTs
jack
3 flush with one high card
queen
king
3 straight flush with two gaps and no high cards
ATs
ace
4 inside straight with no high cards
3 flush with no high cards
draw five cards

Based on our experience, you will, on average, lose more than half of the playoffs. This is, in part, because the machine plays five card showdown practically perfectly, conditioned on the fact that the machine never seems to hold fewer than two cards. Also, note that there is a slight advantage for the slot machine in playing after you discard. The upshot of this is that it will, on average, require slightly more than two playoffs to win the bonus. This, in turn, means you should expect to be seated at the machine for roughly 266 hands.

Boredom and irritation can become real problems if you lose several playoffs in a row. The threat of tedium in an environment that should be fun-filled has caused me to avoid all but very strong plays on Jacks or Better Playoffs.

# Pushers

*Synopsis: Slowly play one coin at a time when the density of coins on the shelves is substantial with coins layered and especially overhanging the front edge. Terminate play after winning eight or more coins from the shelves or losing eight coins.*

If you play in casinos long enough, you will encounter pushers. Pushers come in several varieties: those that peddle pills and those that shove coins. The ones that push pills are there to make a drug sale; they tend to be eliminated by the casinos whenever noticed because casinos want you to get your highs at the gaming tables and machines. Casinos don't have to go through the niceties of proving that an individual is selling drugs. If the casino suspects any such activity, out the door the person goes. So drug dealing is primarily a street activity.

The pushers that are dealt with in this chapter are the machines that physically shove coins that the player puts into the coin drop slot. There are a few different styles but all that are current in the Las Vegas area seem to be called Flip-It. Whirl-Win is another name in the pusher business. If you find any in your area of the country that are a different brand, do not despair. The information supplied here can be used with very little alteration.

The attraction of pushers as a gaming device is that you can see all the action. There are no internal hidden settings or random number generators determining your destiny. The play area is surrounded by glass, letting you see all the gaming action.

In current models of pushers, coins (quarter and dollar denominations are available) are dropped by the player into one of four slots located across the front of the machine. The coins enter the machine in front of the playing area or shelves. Except for selecting in which slot to drop a coin, there is really no 'aiming' involved.

Each coin either falls through the machine, being returned to the customer via a lower tray, or strikes the impeller, hurling the coin high over the shelf area. The flying coins generally miss the baskets (special pays) along the machine's back wall. If you do receive a special pay, the winnings are not dispensed from coinage on the shelf, so the pusher aspect of the game continues unaffected.

On settling on the shelves, the coins, depending on their location, may encounter the pushers. The pushers run full time repeatedly shoving, lifting, and withdrawing. Of course, the shoving occurs only if there are coins on the shelves in the pushers' pathways.

Coins are shoved off the front shelf into openings, the largest of which leads most falling coins to the lower tray for the customer's usage. Generally, there are two smaller openings on either side of the spill area which guide a smaller part of the falling shelf material to an internal container for the casino.

The coins on the shelves are the banked item.

Variations of this game are commonly found in carnivals. And if I were at a carnival, I would be strongly averse to playing. Such enterprises can rig these games against the players even more substantially than the games may innately be. Some coins introduced into the machines by the proprietor may be slightly sticky, especially on the down side. Such coins are much more difficult to move across a playing area than smooth dry coins.

But casinos are not into this type of sneaky tomfoolery. You've got to admire businesses that handle carnival games in a professional manner. Or do you?

A major item in considering the playing of a particular pusher is the ratio of two distances. The first distance is the depth of the play area or pusher area. The other is the banking or coin area depth. If the ratio of the first to the second is significantly less than one, the machine should generally not be played. By examining the accompanying diagram, you may realize that if, in regard to depth, the coin area is large compared to the pusher area, then coins striking the impeller too frequently land in the coin area and fail to be of any service in removing coinage from the shelves.

In the casinos, some types of these machines have a raised front edge and some models have a raised front edge which appears to be adjustable. This feature could be used to affect the play on a particular game.

## Pusher Diagram
## Play and Banking Areas

| Play (Pusher) Area | $\updownarrow$ distance 1 |
|---|---|
| Banking (Coin) Area | $\updownarrow$ distance 2 |

The ratio of distance 1 to distance 2 is important.
Inserted coins landing in the coin area are ineffective.

The strategy (or strategies) for profitable play are rather lengthy. First, as in all banking games, machine selection is paramount. A 'good' machine must have a significant coin density. There cannot be gaps in the coinage on the shelves. Play on such a low density machine will often result in your filling that gap.

Having some layers of coins is a good feature and a part of the overall density consideration. However, stacks of coins, especially near the edge, are a sucker's play. You might wonder how such a stack came to be. In a casino, an ignorant floor person probably set the stack in the machine during a fill of a pusher. Fills do occur because sometimes a customer shakes the machine so severely that the shelves are basically emptied of coinage. Often in an arcade, the proprietor sets the stack there. Would this proprietor glue the stack down? No! That would be totally unnecessary. The stack is generally too heavy to move appreciably. The stack does move over a long period of time, but it will not be reaching the edge before the proprietor has a sizable opportunity to relocate it further back from the edge. Coins introduced into a machine with a stack tend to flow by and around the stack. Never consider a stack to be a positive feature when examining a pusher. In fact, the stack may reflect on the establishment.

A positive feature to look for on a pusher is overhangs. Coins partially dangling over the front edge are a source of enticement and are the best way to make a small amount on a pusher. Overhangs are a very desirable feature.

Another item that you should check before playing one of these types of machines is if the pushers are actually touching the coins farthest from the shelf's edge. It would be unusual if this were not the case, and a definite reason not to play the machine.

Having located an appropriate machine, the play of a pusher seems to be quite simple. Actually, you do have quite a few options in the play of a pusher. Since there are commonly four slots into which you may introduce coinage, you can drop a coin into an appropriate slot to attempt to land the coin in the area directly ahead of the slot. Introducing your coins into the machine in that manner will only aid a little in placing the coins as you desire.

More commonly, the two central slots are used because the customer's pay area is usually in the central portion of the machine. Again, even introducing your coins into the central slots will only aid in locating them in the central portion of the machine.

Coins should be introduced into the machine one at a time, awaiting the results of the previous coin insertion. It is immensely exciting to insert two, three, or four coins simultaneously or in rapid succession; but this is not nearly as effective as single coin play. Among other things, by observing each individual coin play, you gain some skill and insight for the vagaries of that particular pusher.

The amount of play on a pusher is a critical item. Assuming you have found a machine which you consider to be favorable for play, my recommendation is that you limit your play to no more than eight coins. This assumes that the coins get into play, e.g. don't just fall through into the lower tray. If you have played eight coins to no avail, then my opinion is that you very possibly have not evaluated the machine correctly. In the hunt for a 'good' play, you have probably settled for something marginal at best and, if you are inexperienced, have probably begun play on a somewhat poor machine. You should generally terminate your play.

You must bear in mind that these machines will not produce sizable wins. And most certainly, they will not produce sizable wins twice in a row for you. There must be intervening players reloading the shelves for your next play.

Pushers can generally only be played for many small wins at scattered machines. One of the major problems for many winning players is knowing when to quit. After a win of eight coins or more, you should usually terminate play on a pusher.

To give you some feeling for the scale of the winnings, let me give these guidelines. A win of forty coins from the shelves is extreme. Wins of twenty coins from shelves are large. A win of eight coins from shelves is reasonable.

Let me remind you that the figures in the above two paragraphs do not include basket wins. Those wins are simply rarities and not a part of the banking play discussed here.

There are a few questionable strategies used in this game. First, you can shake the machine. If shaken to any significant extent, the pusher will go on tilt and not permit coins to fall into the lower tray. About the only thing possible in this regard is to strike the heavy machine, which I believe you will find ineffective.

A definitely bad strategy is to introduce slugs or worthless tokens into the slot machine. The introduction of such material, which will be sitting in plain sight on the shelves, will result in your prosecution. Of course, if you carry a white cane and wear sunglasses, you might try to convince the arresting officers that you didn't know you had worthless tokens and the change girl must have pulled a fast one on you when selling you change and since your eye surgery, . . . and so on. But I don't think they'll believe your story.

Another questionable strategy to play pushers is to use coins of a lesser denomination. Inserting such coins will at least give you the excuse that you believed the machine was multi-denominational. There are multi-denominational slot machines, but I have never heard of them with regard to pushers. If you have quickly inserted many different types of lower denomination coins already, you might point out that the reason you're using pennies is because after you saw all the different coins in the machine, you considered that pennies were possibly the most cost effective way to play the machine. If the casino doesn't, at the least, kick you out after that lame story, I would be amazed.

However, pushers, like all slot machines, have methods of rejecting incorrect coinage and the variant coins should simply fall through into the tray.

As a related note, I should comment that once I actually did play a pusher, attempting to win coins of greater value than those I was introducing into the machine. The situation occurred at Silver City and the machine was of a quarter denomination. A previous customer had played silver quarters in the pusher and a considerable number of them were in plain view. At that time, silver quarters were worth roughly a dollar each, so it was definitely advantageous to play clad quarters to obtain silver quarters. This, of course, was a very unusual and profitable play. But it does indicate that you should always try to be alert.

# Racing 7's (5, 10, 20 Version)

*Synopsis: When the number of marks remaining for any seven is two or fewer, play one credit per spin until the finish line is reached by one of the sevens.*

Racing 7's (5, 10, 20 Version), like Racing 7's (10, 25, 200 Version) discussed next, pictures three straight tracks of equal length with small markings and a set of three sevens, one on each track. The three sevens are colored red, white, and blue and have associated values of 20, 10, and 5 credits respectively.

The game of Racing 7's (5, 10, 20 Version) is initiated with each symbol at the starting position of the track. Play proceeds as with any slot machine except that whenever a seven (or sevens) land(s) on a payline, the seven of that color is advanced on the race track a number of units for each seven corresponding to the number of credits wagered. It is not necessary that the seven on the payline be a part of a winning combination or that the payline be a winner. The seven only has to land on the payline.

The red, white, and blue sevens advance across the track, and when one of them reaches the finish line, a checkered flag is waved. You then receive the number of credits associated with the winning color. In case of a tie (unheard of in my experience), you will have the values of both colors transferred to the credit meter.

Unlike the other version of Racing 7's, all the colors of sevens in this game are known to win. However, based on our experience, you must find a seven (any color) two units or less from the finish line for the machine to be advantageous to play. Then, playing at one credit per spin and terminating play when the finish line is reached by one of the sevens, you will, on average, be a winner.

Finding a machine that satisfies the condition of being so incredibly close to the finish line is extreme, and virtually no novice player leaves the machine in that state. Certainly, I have won on machines which had sevens at slightly greater distances from the finish line; nonetheless, the figures work out that a seven should be that close to the finish for the machine, on average, to favor the player. I considered making the advice for this machine "Never play," or "Avoid play." Instead, you decide what you want to do.

# Racing 7's (10, 25, 200 Version)

*Synopsis: When the number of marks remaining for the blue seven is four or fewer, play one credit per spin until the finish line is reached by one of the sevens.*

Racing 7's (10, 25, 200 Version) pictures three straight tracks of equal length with small markings, and a set of three sevens, one on each track. The three sevens are colored red, white, and blue and have associated values of 200, 25, and 10 credits respectively.

The game of Racing 7's is initiated with each symbol at the starting position of the track. Play proceeds as with any slot machine, except that whenever a seven (or sevens) land(s) on a payline, the seven of that color is advanced on the race track a number of units for each seven corresponding to the number of credits wagered. It is not necessary that the seven on the payline be a part of a winning combination or that the payline be a winner. The seven only has to land on the payline.

The red, white, and blue sevens advance across the track, and when one of them reaches the finish line, a checkered flag is waved. You then receive the number of credits associated with the winning color. In case of a tie (what a rarity!), you will have the values of both colors transferred to the credit meter.

In my experience with this machine, I have never known of anyone being paid the bonus for the red seven (valued at 200), winning the race. Additionally, I have never had the white seven, valued at 25, win the race, although I recall some few close races between the white and blue seven. In every race we have experienced, the blue seven has been the winner and we have received the ten-credit bonus.

When the blue seven is four or fewer units or markings from the finish line, the machine is advantageous to play. The average cost of moving the blue seven one marking is somewhat over two credits. Since the blue seven is worth ten credits, the blue seven should be four or fewer markings from the finish line for the Racing 7's (10, 25, 200 Version) machine to be advantageous to play.

Machines are rarely left with the blue seven that close to the finish line. If a machine is left in that position, it should be played one credit at a time until the finish line is reached by one of the sevens. Then play should be terminated.

# Red Ball

*Synopsis: With twenty under either 3x3, or fifteen under both 3x3s, play one credit per line per spin until the machine does not satisfy either of the above conditions.*

Red Ball is played on a video screen and is a nickel machine. There are three paylines and the proper play is to play one credit per line until the banked items are obtained.

Each of the three paylines has a number associated with it, ranging from one to four, designated by 1X, 2X, 3X, and 4X, and located in front of the payline. These change during the course of play and affect the pays by multiplying the pay on the individual payline. This, however, is not an item to consider seriously when deciding whether to play a particular Red Ball slot machine.

Adjacent to the three reels on the video screen are two 3x3 squares which resemble tic-tac-toe boards. One of these applies to the red balls while the other is for the black balls. Under each of these tic-tac-toe boards is a number indicating how many credits you will receive for completing the board.

Each 3x3 board is completed by red and black balls landing in the corresponding positions of the nine spots of the three reels. A ball landing in a position on the reels that is empty on the corresponding board of that color will trigger filling that position on the board. If, however, that position on the tic-tac-toe board is already filled, then the amount wagered on that line is added to the amount beneath the particular board.

It is the amounts under these two boards that determine whether a particular Red Ball slot machine is advantageous to play. When either of the numbers under the boards is twenty or more, the Red Ball slot machine is advantageous. If both numbers under the tic-tac-toe boards are fifteen or more, again, the machine is advantageous to play. The machine should be played at a rate of one credit per line per spin until the machine reaches a status such that it does not qualify as advantageous to play.

# Red Hot 7's

*Synopsis: Play one credit per line per spin when three or more sevens have been completed and terminate play when the five free spins of the bonus round have been used.*

Red Hot 7's is found on multi-game machines called Winning Touch. Commonly, these are penny and nickel machines. What is banked in this game are fillings. Well, sort of! There are five sevens already on display in a line near the top of the screen. These are filled with red "paint" as the game progresses. The following chart is a schematic of the filling process. The sevens are filled when sevens are on a winning payline. Each seven on the winning payline contributes to the filling of the five sections of the large seven near the top of the screen.

Red Hot 7's can, on average, be profitably played when three or more of the five sevens have been completed and are filled in as shown by the sixth symbol in the f chart.

The average profitability in credits of Red Hot 7's is given in the table on page 136. When you also consider that these are penny and nickel slot machines, you can appreciate that you will have to locate and play large numbers of these machines in order to have a reasonable per-hour profit.

## Red Hot 7's: Schematic of the Process of Filling of Sevens

| Empty | One | Two | Three | Four | Filled |
| Seven | Section | Sections | Sections | Sections | Seven |
| | Filled | Filled | Filled | Filled | |

# Red Hot 7's
## Average Profit During Advantageous Periods

| Starting Position (7's & Fills) | Average Profit in Credits |
|---|---|
| 3 & 0 | 7.3 |
| 3 & 1 | 18.7 |
| 3 & 2 | 30.1 |
| 3 & 3 | 41.5 |
| 3 & 4 | 52.9 |
| 4 & 0 | 64.3 |
| 4 & 1 | 75.7 |
| 4 & 2 | 87.1 |
| 4 & 3 | 98.5 |
| 4 & 4 | 109.9 |

# Red Hot 7's (Symbol Score Version)

*Synopsis: Play one credit per line per spin, a total of five credits, when there are three or more 7's or 600 or more points and terminate play when the five spins of the bonus round have been obtained.*

Red Hot 7's, commonly found on Winning Touch penny and nickel machines, comes in another variety. No, I don't mean quarter and dollar varieties.

Previously, Red Hot 7's was such that you could play advantageously when there were three or more filled sevens on the display. Then you played at one credit per line on each of the five paylines until the five sevens at the top of the screen were filled with "paint." This paint was added by having a seven on a winning payline and there had to be five such occurrences to completely fill an empty seven at the top of the screen with paint. With the game in this format, you could profitably play one credit per line on only one payline for a minor increase in profitability of the machine. However, playing a single line for a single credit was not recommend because an inordinate amount of time would be required to obtain the bonus.

Now the new version of Red Hot 7's comes in a variety which we have labeled Red Hot 7's (Symbol Score Version). We have gone to this descriptive device because the handling of the banked item has changed radically. Note: the pay schedule has remained unchanged. What is being discussed here is strictly a variation introduced into the game as it applies to the banked item, the filling of the sevens.

When playing this newer version of Red Hot 7's, instead of filling the sevens directly, you accumulate points. To obtain points, a seven must appear on a winning payline. Then the number of points received for each seven on the winning payline will depend on the total number of credits wagered. If the number of credits wagered is between one and four inclusive, you will receive thirty points for each such seven. If the number of credits wagered is between five and nine inclusive, you will receive fifty points for each such seven. And finally, if the number of credits wagered is ten, you will receive sixty points for each such seven. This is all given in the accompanying chart.

You need to accumulate two hundred points to obtain a seven. When five sevens, i.e. one thousand points, are obtained, you receive the awards generated by the bonus round.

The current number of accumulated points is displayed on the video screen in two distinct formats. In one format, the system displays a number of accumulated sevens (valued at two hundred points each) and a symbol score, which is the number of points accumulated toward the next seven. (Example: 7  7 SYMBOL SCORE = 190). In the other format, the system simply informs you of the total number of accumulated bonus points (Example: TOTAL BONUS ... 590).

This version of Red Hot 7's can still, on average, be profitably played when three or more of the five sevens have been completed, i.e. six hundred or more points have been accumulated. However, now the game should definitely be played at five credits per spin and with no additional profitability for playing a single credit on only one line.

Initially, you might suspect that needing only four sevens (instead of five) on paylines to get a bonus seven would make the machine more valuable. The limited data I have does not bear that out at this point. Seemingly, needing only four is better than the previous version where you needed five; but the conclusion seems to be that the sevens on paylines are more difficult to obtain.

Wait a minute! Are we starting to talk about profit on penny and nickel machines? Get real! Try to appreciate the large number of machines that you will have to locate and play in order to have a reasonable per hour profit.

### Red Hot 7's (Symbol Score Version)
### Bonus Point Awards

| Number of Credits Wagered | Bonus Points per Seven |
|---|---|
| 1-4 | 30 |
| 5-9 | 50 |
| 10 | 60 |

# Riddle of the Sphinx

*Synopsis: If the top of any column has three matching Golden Egyptian Symbols, play the number of credits associated with that column. If there are two or more such columns, play the number of credits associated with the larger column. Terminate play when there are no columns whose tops have three matching Golden Egyptian Symbols.*

Riddle of the Sphinx is rather majestic musically as the game begins to appear on the screen of the Oddysey machine. With doors swinging wide to reveal the game's current status, you can learn in a moment if the machine is favorably inclined. On Riddle of the Sphinx you can play one to six coins per spin; however, the banking feature of this game does not operate unless at least four coins per spin are played. The items that are banked are called Golden Egyptian Symbols, of which there are three distinct types. These banked items can produce a bonus of 50, 75, or 125 credits under certain conditions.

If you wager only one, two, or three coins per spin, the game functions as an ordinary slot machine in video form. However, when four, five, or six credits per spin are wagered, Golden Egyptian Symbols that appear on the payline can be banked. If four credits per spin are played, Golden Egyptian Symbols appearing in the left position of the payline will be banked into the top of the four-coin column (column on the extreme left). If five credits per spin are played, Golden Egyptian Symbols appearing in the left and center positions of the payline will be banked into the top of the corresponding position of the four-coin and five-coin columns (left and center columns). If six credits per spin are played, all Golden Egyptian Symbols that appear on the payline will be banked into the top of the corresponding columns on the sarcophagus.

When there are four matching symbols in any column, you are awarded the number of credits associated with that column, i.e., 50, 75, or 125 credits. However, the game has another twist to it in that if the four matching symbols are queens' heads, you are awarded twice the column value and if the four symbols are all pharaohs' heads, you are awarded five times the column value.

Riddle of the Sphinx can be profitable to play under certain rarely occurring conditions. If there are three matching Golden Egyptian Symbols at the top of any column, play the number of credits associated with that column. However, if there are two or more such columns, play the number of credits associated with the larger or largest of these columns. Play should be terminated when there are no columns having three matching Golden Egyptian Symbols at the top.

A word of caution is in order here. Having three queens' heads or three pharaohs' heads at the top of any column does not generally make the situation substantially more beneficial financially because these symbols are correspondingly harder to obtain. The column is unfortunately often added to with a nonmatching symbol. For example, having three pharaohs' heads at the top of the third column is an advantageous play; but be assured that if this is the only column with three matching symbols, you will experience sizable amounts of volatility in your bankroll in your pursuit of such bonuses.

Riddle of the Sphinx will occasionally add some variety to your slot play, but generally it is difficult to find this game in a condition which is, on average, profitable to play. Most novice players, expending six coins per spin, realize that three matching heads at the top of a column is a prize worth pursuing.

# Ring 'Em Up

*Synopsis: Never play.*

Ring 'Em Up is another banking game where a bonus is paid for a rather rare slot event. The bonus can be as high as 40,000 credits or nearly so because the bonus is paid out automatically if it reaches the forty thousand credit value. The bonuses that I have seen are so much lower and grow so slowly that I doubt that a bonus ever reaches such a high level.

On Ring 'Em Up, a bonus amount of credits is clearly displayed and is the item that is banked. The player receives this bonus when eight coins are wagered and nine fruits appear in the 3x3 pattern on the screen.

The danger in playing Ring 'Em Up when the bonus seems high is that the internal machine settings are unknown and, except for the casinos and the slot manufacturer, no one has any information about the play of this machine. Playing a slot machine for a very rare event is not a wise move. The machine may be set to exact a literal fortune before releasing its bonus fund. In fact, a high bonus in itself can be superficially thought of as an indication of a tight setting on the machine. Otherwise, why is the bonus so high?

With such uncertainties in the situation, it is unwise to play the unknown number of spins needed to have a reasonable chance to obtain the bonus. The very real danger of taking a significant loss while chasing such a bonus causes most professional players to back away from playing this machine.

Besides these financial considerations, the amount of time necessary to obtain the bonus can easily make Ring 'Em Up a poor play. The amount of time necessary to obtain the bonus can often be a couple of hours as a minimum and that involves using the spin and stop spin buttons in immediate succession.

With these serious drawbacks, Ring 'Em Up should be avoided. And after all, there are plenty of other advantageous slot machines available at which to spend your time.

# Road Rally

*Synopsis: Play maximum credits per spin when at least 21 miles are completed by your racer and the amount of time in seconds remaining is at least double the number of miles remaining to be traversed to reach the bonus area. Terminate play when the mileage indicator returns to zero or it becomes obvious that your racer will not reach the bonus area before the allotted time elapses.*

Road Rally is a game that has fallen on hard times. The game was quite similar to Empire, Isle of Pearls, and Spacequest, in that you could advantageously play the slot machine when a figure (a race car in Road Rally) was half or more of the distance to the bonus area while a third or less of the allotted time had elapsed. Machines in this condition could be found occasionally.

However, Road Rally had a feature that seemed to discourage player participation. The physical setup of Road Rally usually involved several slot machines placed in front of a race track. Each of the several machines operated independently of the others and only used the track to show each racer's position. Unfortunately, this layout gave the appearance that the players were competing for some prize in a race against each other. Individuals were reluctant to sit down when another car was clearly ahead. With diminished play, the machines have gradually disappeared from the gaming scene.

With their disappearance came a replacement, an upgraded version, called Bonus Road Rally which is described below. But in case you should locate an older machine, we have the following instructions for advantageous play.

A Road Rally slot machine is advantageous to play when the amount of time in seconds remaining is at least double the number of miles remaining to be traversed by the racer to reach the bonus area. This criterion determines that at least 21 miles must definitely have been completed to play the machine advantageously. On locating such a Road Rally slot machine, which will really be a great challenge since these machines seem to be gone, the proper play is maximum credits per spin.

There are a few anomalies to the above discussion, such as the situation in which you find a racer with 69 miles completed and the timer having only a few seconds remaining to be used. In this case, you are advised to play one credit per spin. But these anomalies are clear in the play of the game and even if they are overlooked, you will not, on average, be hurt significantly.

Play on Road Rally should be terminated when the mileage indicator returns to zero or it becomes obvious that your racer will not reach the bonus area before the allotted time elapses.

# Road Rally (Bonus Version)

*Synopsis: Play maximum credits per spin when at least 21 miles are completed by the racer, and the distance remaining for the racer to reach the bonus area is less than or equal to three-quarters the distance remaining to be traversed by the pace car to reach the finish line. Terminate play when the mileage indicators return to zero, or it is obvious that the racer will not reach the bonus area before the pace car reaches the finish line.*

Bonus Road Rally is the result of remaking Road Rally. It is extremely similar to Chuck Wagons, which is itself a game quite similar to Empire, Isle of Pearls, and Spacequest. Unlike its predecessor, Road Rally, this newer version of the game has clearly individualized play and each of these new machines unquestionably operates independently.

In Bonus Road Rally, you are attempting to move your race car to the finish line and into the bonus area for a bonus of 10, 15, or 25 credits. To be a winner, you must move your racer into the bonus area before the pace car reaches the finish line. This competing pace car moves with every spin of the reels and functions as a timing device, while your racer only moves when an ADVANCE symbol is on the payline. The distance moved by the pace car is such that you are assured 25 slot plays or spins before the game is terminated by the pace car reaching the finish line.

To play Bonus Road Rally advantageously, you need to locate a machine on which the racer has completed at least 21 miles of the seventy miles to reach the bonus area. Actually, 21 (or 24 or 27) miles is a very weak play because there is still much of the distance to be completed to reach the bonus area at seventy miles.

The reason for pointing out this 21-mile criterion is that you can easily use it to determine at a glance that many machines are not favorable for play.

Additionally, for a Bonus Road Rally slot machine to be, on average, of value to play, the number of miles remaining to be traversed to reach the bonus area by the pace car should, at the beginning of your slot play, be at least 1.33 times the number of miles remaining to be traversed by the racer. Thus, if there are 34 miles remaining to be traversed (the position halfway to the bonus area) by the racer, the pace car should have at least 45 miles to go to the finish line.

Since 1.33 is extremely close to the fraction 4/3, you may wish instead to use this fraction for "in the head" calculations. So, for the halfway position mentioned above, using the factor 4/3, you would again want to have at least 45 miles remaining for the pace car to reach the checkered finish line.

An equivalent alternative to the above is that the distance remaining for the racer to reach the bonus area must be less than or equal to three-quarters of the distance remaining for the pace car to reach the finish line. If you find this statement more comprehensible (and many prefer fractions that are less than one to those larger than one), then use this equivalent statement appropriately.

Such machines can be found occasionally. Having located an appropriate Bonus Road Rally, you must move the racer as quickly as possible to the bonus area. Consequently, play should be at maximum coins per spin, which will move the racer three miles times the number of credits played on that spin for each ADVANCE symbol on the payline. There are a few minor exceptions to this play-at-maximum-coins rule, but they are usually clear in the particular situations and can be ignored without significant financial loss.

Play on Bonus Road Rally should be terminated when mileage indicators return to zero or it becomes obvious that the racer cannot reach the bonus area before the pace car reaches the finish line.

# Royal Hot 7's

*Synopsis: Play one credit per line per spin when three or more sevens have been completed. Terminate play when the five free spins of the bonus round have been obtained.*

Royal Hot 7's is similar to Red Hot 7's but with a slightly varied pay schedule, in part because there are wild symbols called crowns which affect the payouts. With these additional wild symbols, the game has to be a little different. But from our perspective of banking, virtually nothing of significance has been altered. Royal Hot 7's can, on average, be profitably played when three or more of the five sevens have been completed and are filled in as indicated by the sixth symbol in the following chart.

Royal Hot 7's is found on a machine called Winning Touch. However, this Winning Touch machine is a slightly different model from the Winning Touch machines on which Red Hot 7's is found. This is of little importance to us but is noticeable in that the Royal Hot 7's seems to be on quarter machines rather than nickel and penny slot machines.

**Royal Hot 7's: Schematic of the Process of Filling of Sevens**

| Empty Seven | One Section Filled | Two Sections Filled | Three Sections Filled | Four Sections Filled | Filled Seven |

# Rue de Riches

*Synopsis: Avoid play because of extreme variability. Never play unless there are at least two coins of each of three denominations or two coins of each of two denominations and one of the two denominations is fifty. Play at three credits per spin. Terminate play when the above criterion is not met.*

Rue de Riches is a game made especially for Paris. Actually, the game wasn't made for Paris; it was made by Paris. Rue de Riches was created by Charlie Lombardo, Senior Vice President of Slot Operations at Paris, who worked out the mathematics for this game and was personally involved in the designing of the visual presentation. My wife and I were fortunate enough to meet and interview Mr. Lombardo. Many of our readers may not realize that some casino executives are very talented and are involved in such facets of gaming.

Rue de Riches is on a three reel slot machine with an elevated visual much like the diagram presented with this chapter. Coins or tokens of a French appearance are symbols on the reels and are also a part of the pay schedule. These coins are in five denominations: 10, 15, 20, 25, and 50. Whenever a coin (or coins) appears on the single payline, you receive three times the amount wagered for each coin on the payline. In addition, if you have wagered three credits on that particular spin, you receive a coin (or coins) of the same denomination(s) in the display above the reels.

The visual display of the coins is filled from bottom to top. When you accumulate three coins of any particular denomination, the machine enters a bonus round. The three matching coins are flipped, electronically of course, and you receive a bonus based on the outcome of tossing the three coins.

The bonus you receive as credits on the machine is as follows. For each coin falling with the denomination showing, you receive the value of the coin in credits. If perchance the three coins should all land without the denomination of any coin showing, then you will receive a bonus of six times the denomination of the coins.

From my limited experience with this game, it does appear that the outcomes of the flipping of coins are as would occur with three real and tangible coins that are unbiased. Mr. Lombardo also confirmed that this was the case. Those percentages are given in the following table.

## Percentages Expected with Random Coin Tossing

| No Coins With Denomination Showing | One Coin With Denomination Showing | Two Coins With Denomination Showing | Three Coins With Denomination Showing |
|---|---|---|---|
| 12.5 | 37.5 | 37.5 | 12.5 |

Further calculations show that, on average, you will receive credits of 2.25 times the denomination as your bonus when obtaining the third coin.

To profitably play Rue de Riches, it is recommended that you locate a slot machine with at least three denominations each con-

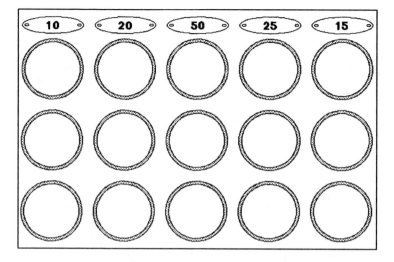

| 10 | 20 | 50 | 25 | 15 |

**Diagram of Rue de Riches**

taining two coins. Finding such a machine will be a sizable challenge. Patrons tend not to leave their machines in such a state.

Another way to profitably play Rue de Riches is to locate a machine with two denominations containing two coins and one of these two denominations is fifty. Finding such a machine is less of a challenge. Patrons more readily leave their machines in such a state. However, the results of your play will be more marginal.

Finding such machines, you should play three credits per spin until the above criteria are not satisfied by the machine.

Even this type of play will often not be profitable in the short run. What causes Rue de Riches to often be unprofitable to play is the pay structure. Most of these machines have a pay schedule which seems reasonable enough; but with the reels containing numerous wild symbols which, besides being wild, offer double, quintuple (5X), and even dectuple (10X) pays, the machine is biased toward a few large wins rather than many smaller wins.

This type of pay structure creates a considerable amount of variability in the results. In other words, the average may remain the same while there are far larger swings in the individual results.

Let me illustrate this with a small silly numerical example. Let us assume you play some type of banking slot machine five times and your profit on each one is -5, 2, 4, 6, and 8 credits. The negative value of profit is commonly called a loss.

The average of these five outcomes is 3 credits.

Now let us assume you play some other type of banking slot machine five times and your profit on each one is -15, -10, -5, -2, and 47 credits. Again, the negative values are losses.

The average of these five outcomes is also 3 credits.

Both of these situations lead to an average of 3 credits per machine played. However, in the second case, most of the individual results are negative.

This is the type of situation one is dealing with in Rue de Riches and because of the volatile results, in my opinion, Rue de Riches is a very poor game to play. I have had generally unfavorable results.

I recommend that you avoid all but very strong plays at Rue de Riches; unless you plan to be playing this game an extremely large number of times. Otherwise, you'll start to feel you're on the road to the poorhouse. This is something you will definitely rue.

# Safe Buster

*Synopsis: If two Xs are present, play three credits per spin until a third X is obtained.*

Safe Buster seems to be popular in the rather few casinos that have installed these machines. Beyond its common three reel activity, the game involves the spinning of a safe combination dial. This dial, located overhead, automatically spins whenever you have wagered the maximum number of coins and lost on the reel payline. When the dial lands on the next number of the three-number combination, it is noted by an X being clearly placed across the obtained number.

The safe is automatically opened when the dial lands on the final number of the safe combination. The bonus for unlocking the safe is an amount which is generated by the multiplication of two numbers. The first number of this product is obtained by the

Safe Buster slot machine automatically spinning the reels until a winning combination appears on the payline. The value of this reel spin (based on max coins played) is one of the numbers used for the product. The second number used to obtain the product is a randomly generated integer between one and ten, both inclusive, and appears on the slot machine's visual. The term random should be qualified by stating that in a sizable amount of play, I have never seen this integer be smaller than four. An amount equal to the product of these two numbers is awarded as credits for unlocking the safe. The game then resets with three new numbers in the combination.

The item which is banked in Safe Buster is the obtained numbers in the safe combination which are clearly Xed out. The proper way to profitably play Safe Buster is to begin on a vacated machine which has two Xs. The machine should then be played at the maximum number of coins in order to obtain the dial spins to receive the bonus award. Play should be terminated when the final number of the combination is Xed out. In this game, there is an oddity. You want to win on each spin of the reels on a slot machine; yet in order to end this particular game, you must lose on a reel play in order to obtain a winning dial spin.

The average cost of obtaining an X is 20.6 credits. The average of the bonus is 38.6 credits. Clearly, it is, on average, unprofitable to begin play when only one X has been obtained.

# Safe Busters

*Synopsis: If two X's are present, play six credits per spin until a third X is obtained. Then terminate play.*

Safe Busters is a remake of Safe Buster. So if you feel the presentation here is too abbreviated, you may wish to check the chapter called Safe Buster. I have never understood what was accomplished by this remaking of the Safe Buster game. It may be that some companies simply need to design a new model every year.

The new game requires a maximum bet of six credits per spin in order to obtain the bonus. The first five coins are a wager on each of the five paylines: three across and two diagonal to the three reels. The sixth coin involves only the banking feature. Because of the need to play six coins, you may expect more variability in the final results on these machines.

The changes in this game from its predecessor are generally unnecessary to elaborate. The one change that is especially noteworthy is that it is now unnecessary to lose on the reels in order to get the safe dial to spin to obtain a combination number. The bonus round has also been modified in that, among other things, you must repeatedly press the spin button to obtain the bonus.

But these items are clear during the play of Safe Busters.

To profitably play Safe Busters, you should locate a machine on which two X's have been obtained by the previous player(s). Then playing six coins per spin, you should obtain a final X and receive the bonus spins. The game will then reset to its initial setting of no X's and you should terminate your play at that time.

As a final comment, I should mention that some of you, after examining Safe Busters, may be tempted to calculate the probability of obtaining the maximum bonus of 4000 credits. Be warned that the figure you calculate may be totally incorrect because the spinning of the safe dial does not appear to be random with a probability of 12.5% for each of the eight outcomes. The spinning of wheels electronically is not required by law to be random in that sense of the word.

# Safe Cracker

*Synopsis: On dollar machines with twenty or more coins in the safe and on quarter machines with 25 or more coins in the safe, play one credit per spin until the safe is opened.*

Safe Cracker is not commonly available. It is a complicated game and most casinos that have offered the game have later removed the machines.

Safe Cracker machines have a pretend safe which contains an initial sum of coins. These coins are the same value as the machine denomination; quarter machines have quarters in their safes, while dollar machines have dollars within their safes. Additional funds are added to the safe whenever a money bag of coins appears on the payline. The bags can contain anywhere from two to five hundred coins. In this manner, the funds in the safe can grow during the play of the machine.

The object of the game is to obtain the five-digit combination to the safe. This is done by spinning the reels in the standard manner. Whenever a dial appears on the payline, a digit in the combination is revealed. When all five digits in the combination are obtained, the safe is "cracked" and a bonus is paid.

The bonus is the number of coins in the safe multiplied by the assigned poker hand value of the five digits. Let me explain. The five digits in the combination constitute a poker hand, e.g. nothing, one pair, two pair, three of a kind, etc. The various types of poker hands (made with the five digits) each have an assigned value. There is a table of these values on the machine, which can easily be read. It is this value, always greater than or equal to one, which is multiplied by the number of coins in the safe to determine the bonus awarded for opening the safe.

The safe can also be opened by alining three bombs on the payline. This alinement blows the safe open and is generally detrimental because you are awarded only the coins in the safe without the benefit of the multiplying factor.

The exact rules describing when it is profitable, on average, to play Safe Cracker are quite complicated. However, two easy rules of thumb can be applied. If the Safe Cracker slot machine is a dollar machine, then it can, on average, be played when the safe contains twenty or more coins. If the Safe Cracker slot machine is of a quarter denomination, then it can, on average, be played when the safe contains 25 or more coins. In general, quarter slot machines have a higher hold than dollar slot machines. In the case of Safe Cracker, it appears that the casino hold on the quarter Safe Cracker machines is the result of more of them blowing open.

The best method of play is one credit per spin until the funds in the safe are obtained.

On unplayed Safe Cracker slot machines, the information about the contents of the safe is generally not displayed on the visual. If you play the machine for a single spin, the machine will put the critical information on the display. However, who seriously wants to spend even one coin to learn that a machine is not advantageous to play?

This important information can be obtained in another manner. There is an anomaly to the Safe Cracker slot machine that should be mentioned. Since before playing, you wish to learn the amount in the safe, which is generally not known, you should insert a piece of currency into the bill acceptor as though you were preparing to play. The machine will reveal just how much is in the safe. You can then either continue to play or press Cash Out, have your funds returned, and be much the wiser about the contents of the safe.

# Shopping Spree

*Synopsis: With 29 or more frequent shopper points accumulated, play two credits per spin until fifty frequent shopper points are obtained.*

Shopping Spree has become a rarity in the Las Vegas area. It comes in two denominations: quarter and dollar varieties.

The item that is banked on a Shopping Spree slot machine is frequent shopper points. The machine starts with zero points; when the number of points reaches fifty, you receive a bonus. The bonus consists of twenty credits plus ten spins of the reels at the maximum bet.

Shopping Spree is advantageous to play when the number of frequent shopper points exceeds 28. Technically, playing a machine with 28 points will on average be neutral to your pocketbook. However, you could be gaining points on your slot account.

The best method to play Shopping Spree is to play two credits per spin. This is because you should endeavor to play the slot machine as little as possible and the number of spins necessary to accumulate the desired points is reduced by playing the maximum wager, two coins, per spin. The only time you should deviate from this play is if there are 49 frequent shopper points, in which case play should be at one credit per spin until the bonus is received. Then, of course, you are generally financially ahead if you terminate your play after receiving the bonus.

# Slot Bingo

*Synopsis: Play at one credit per spin after fifty numbers have been obtained on either flashboard. Terminate play when an appropriate bingo occurs.*

Slot Bingo seems to be bingo the way you always wanted it. You will definitely get a bingo before everyone else and the prize will definitely be yours. Even the cards are free. The only expense is paying to have the numbers drawn, but that expense can be substantial.

Slot Bingo is new on the Las Vegas scene. This slot machine banks the numbers of a bingo game. In fact, it banks the numbers of two Bingo games that are being played simultaneously.

The two simultaneous games of bingo are distinguished by being labeled red and green. Numbers are "called" in a red game by having a RED NUMBER symbol appear on the payline. Similarly, a number is "called" in a green game by having a GREEN NUMBER symbol appear on the payline. Technically, the number of bingo numbers called for a particular color is the number of credits bet times the number of RED NUMBER or GREEN NUMBER symbols that appear on the payline. These called or drawn numbers are shown on flashboards and, if appropriate, marked on the bingo cards. Note that the appearance of the RED NUMBER and GREEN NUMBER symbols on the payline generally means the payline is not a wining combination.

When a standard straight line bingo (horizontal, vertical, or diagonal) occurs on either game, you are awarded a bonus. The bonus is dependent on how many bingo numbers have been called in that game when the bingo occurs. If this number is between four (the machine incorrectly indicates one, two, and three are acceptable) and 24, you are awarded one hundred credits. If this number is between 25 and 60, you are awarded twenty credits. And if this number is between 61 and 71 (the machine incorrectly indicates 72, 73, 74, and 75 are acceptable), you are again awarded one hundred credits.

However, by my estimates, a single card getting a bingo within the first 24 numbers occurs in less than 5% of the games. Similarly, not getting a straight line bingo within sixty numbers is even more difficult and occurs in less than one percent of the games. Feel assured that if you play Slot Bingo, you will almost certainly get the award of twenty credits.

One of the sure ways to have the advantage on Slot Bingo is to begin to play this game after sixty bingo numbers have already been called on either game. This, of course, will clearly put you in the position of obtaining the hundred-credit bonus. Unlike the bonus of one hundred credits which is offered for a bingo in under 25 numbers, this bonus will not slip away when you obtain additional numbers. Since the situation of having sixty numbers called without a bingo occurs less than 1% of the time, and then in addition the novice player would have to leave the machine, let me assure you that this type of machine has, to my knowledge, never been found.

Somewhat more common is to find a machine where fifty numbers have been called on one of the bingo games. This is a strong play and generally the number of spots filled on the bingo card of that game is irrelevant. Many spots will already be filled.

When less than fifty numbers have already been called, the situation becomes considerably more involved. The factors which determine if a Slot Bingo machine is advantageous to play are the number of bingo numbers already drawn, the number of spots filled on the card, and the positioning of the filled spots with particular emphasis on the number of four-spot potential bingos. This last item is of major importance in examining the game's potential average benefit to you. Also, you could include the status of the other bingo game in attempting to determine the possible advantage in playing the Slot Bingo machine. However, it is quite unusual to have two attractive cards on a Slot Bingo machine.

At this point, the play of a Slot Bingo machine starts to become a study of the game of bingo. That is beyond the scope of this book. The tragedy is that there is no book, to my knowledge, that seriously deals with the intricacies of bingo in general.

To illustrate the type of item that starts to become important in dealing with an examination of the various possible semi-completed bingo cards, consider the cards presented in the chart below. Card 1 has twenty spots filled, but only five uncalled numbers will result in a straight line bingo. Card 2 has only sixteen spots filled, but nine uncalled numbers will result in a bingo. In Slot Bingo, Card 2 is clearly preferable to Card 1.

Generally, when fewer than fifty numbers have been called in a Slot Bingo game, consider the number of four-spot potential bingos before playing the machine. This will aid you considerably, although I can give you no definite guidelines at this time.

If you do decide to play a particular Slot Bingo machine, play should be at one credit per spin until a bingo occurs on the appropriate card. You will, as a rule, find it particularly annoying to have numbers drawn for the card that you are not seriously pursuing, since these alinements will mean that your payline is generally not a winning combination. But that's Slot Bingo.

# Slot Bingo
## Examples of Partially Filled Cards
### Card #1             Card #2

# Spacequest

*Synopsis: Play three credits per spin when the amount of time in seconds remaining is at least double the number of lightyears remaining to reach the bonus area. Terminate play when the ascent is completed, or it becomes obvious that the spaceman will not reach the initial bonus level before time expires. [Note: Spacequest slot machine instructions use the term "lightyear" instead of the dictionary approved spellings "light-year" and the less common "light year."]*

I first observed a Spacequest slot machine located at the Las Vegas Hilton in conjunction with Star Trek: The Experience. Spacequest is simply the same game as Empire and Isle of Pearls. The pay schedules, etc., are identical. No! Not similar! Identical! Were it not for superficial changes such as variation of the outside design and minor wording alterations on these machines, not one thing would be different. Coke, Pepsi, and Royal Crown have more variation than these three slot machines. So if the information below sounds familiar, don't be surprised.

These three slot machines are currently about as close to arcade games as the the gaming industry has produced recently. The three machines are still games of chance with no skill factor. However, it is the small animated figures that have given the games an arcade quality and appearance. One can only wonder if the Disney studios are considering ways to put Mickey Mouse and Donald Duck into the gaming scene.

In the slot machine, the spaceman needs to ascend at least seventy lightyears in one minute and forty seconds (one hundred seconds) or 25 spins, whichever comes second, in order for you to be a winner. Play is such that each $U^P$ symbol on the payline yields three lightyears times the number of credits wagered: one, two, or three. The machine displays a counter that informs you what height or elevation the spaceman has attained and a timer that shows the amount of transport time remaining for the ascent to be completed.

The spaceman's ascent must reach an elevation of at least seventy lightyears for you to receive a bonus. But if the spaceman reaches additional specified elevations of ninety lightyears or 110 lightyears, you will obtain, instead of ten credits, a higher reward of 15 or 25 credits respectively at the completion of the spaceman's ascent.

I have never observed the spaceman to use the hundred seconds of transport time without using the minimum of 25 spins. So the 25 spins are generally not a factor in determining if a Spacequest machine is valuable to play. This slot machine has two significant pieces of information on its display. One is the elevation in lightyears that the spaceman has already ascended and the other is the amount of time of the initial hundred seconds remaining for the spaceman to complete the ascent. These two pieces of information can be used to determine if a particular machine is, on average, valuable to play.

First, in order for a Spacequest slot machine to be, on average, of value to play, the amount of transport time remaining should, at the beginning of your play, be at least double the number of lightyears remaining to reach the bonus area. Thus, if there are 34 lightyears remaining to be ascended (roughly the half-way position to the bonus area), you should have 68 seconds, i.e. one minute and eight seconds, of transport time remaining.

There are small anomalies to this rule, of course, because of the discrete nature of the timing device and the elevation measurement. Time, which is always continuous, is a discrete item on these machines and seems repeatedly to be a multiple of four seconds, while the elevation measurement is always an integer and a multiple of three and thus a discrete item.

Thus, there are small oddities, such as if the spaceman has completed 63 lightyears and seven remain to ascend, then if 12 seconds remain, the game is favorable. The rule about the ratio of time and distance remaining to ascend has some flexibility, especially near the end of the game. Clearly, the rule is not carved in stone but should generally serve you well.

A consequence of this rule is that for a Spacequest slot machine to be, on average, valuable to play, there must be 49 lightyears or less remaining to reach the first bonus level (seventy lightyears). The slot machine does not tell you that information directly. The machine displays how many lightyears the spaceman has already ascended. Consequently, the number of lightyears already traversed must be at least 21. Actually, 21,

24, and 27 lightyears are very weak plays because there is still much of the distance to be traveled.

Play on a Spacequest slot machine that meets the above requirements should be at the maximum number of credits permitted per spin. It is imperative to move the spaceman as much as possible with each U$^P$ symbol. There are a few anomalies where it is unnecessary to wager the maximum of three credits per spin. For example, if you have moved the spaceman 69 lightyears and there are only a few seconds remaining, then you should wager only one credit per spin. However, these anomalies occur seldom enough that you can ignore them at comparatively little cost. A Spacequest slot machine is difficult to find in a condition which is profitable to play because most slot players only leave when it is obvious that the spaceman will not complete his ascent within the transport time allotted.

# Super 7's

*Synopsis: With three or more square sevens, wager five credits per spin, terminating play when the bonus is obtained.*

Super 7's is one of the games on Game King machines. It can sometimes be found on bars with inlaid machines. The game comes in nickel, quarter and dollar denominations, all of which should be played the same way.

The item that is banked on Super 7's is, not surprisingly, sevens. Whenever any of the played paylines has a winning combination, the machine counts the number of sevens on that payline. Sometimes a single seven will be counted more than once because of the layout of the five paylines. This number of sevens is then accounted for on the video display. Whenever a total of five sevens has been obtained on winning paylines, a seven in a square is displayed on the screen. Then when five of these squares with sevens are obtained, the machine rewards you with a bonus of forty credits plus five spins at a wager of two credits per line for all five lines. In addition, these five spins will pay at double the usual amount for winning paylines.

If you were to begin from the lowest point, you would need to accumulate 25 sevens on winning paylines to earn the bonus of forty credits and five spins.

Super 7's is advantageous to play when at least three of the square sevens have been obtained. At that point, you can, on average, be a winner by wagering one credit per payline, i.e. five credits per spin, until the fifth seven in a square is obtained and the bonus is received. Then continued play is not to your advantage.

It should be noted that it is very slightly more profitable instead to play one credit per line and play only one line per spin. This will actually save you a small amount of expenditure because with standard five-line play, you will not win simultaneously on all five lines. However, you can conceivably win on each played payline on all spins with one credit bet on one line. The trade-off is that although you will save a very small amount financially while trying to obtain the bonus, it will take a much, much longer time to accomplish that goal. Certainly the pros don't fuss with these minimal savings.

The following table will give you a rough idea of what to expect as an average profit on a particular advantageous machine.

## Super 7's: Average Profit During Advantageous Periods

| Initial Status of Machine | Average Profit in Credits |
|---|---|
| NEXT SYMBOL IN 1 [7][7] | 6.5 |
| NEXT SYMBOL IN 5 [7][7][7] | 14.4 |
| NEXT SYMBOL IN 4 [7][7][7] | 22.4 |
| NEXT SYMBOL IN 3 [7][7][7] | 30.3 |
| NEXT SYMBOL IN 2 [7][7][7] | 38.2 |
| NEXT SYMBOL IN 1 [7][7][7] | 46.1 |
| NEXT SYMBOL IN 5 [7][7][7][7] | 54.1 |
| NEXT SYMBOL IN 4 [7][7][7][7] | 62.0 |
| NEXT SYMBOL IN 3 [7][7][7][7] | 69.9 |
| NEXT SYMBOL IN 2 [7][7][7][7] | 77.8 |
| NEXT SYMBOL IN 1 [7][7][7][7] | 85.8 |

# Super 8 Line

*Synopsis: Never play.*

Super 8 Line is a banking game where a bonus is paid for a rather rare slot event. The bonus can be as high as 25,000 credits; even on a nickel machine, that is sizable. Generally, the bonus is much lower and it does take some time for such an extremely high level to be reached.

The danger in playing Super 8 Line when the bonus is high is that the internal machine settings are not known except to the casino and manufacturers. Thus, the machine may be set to exact a literal fortune before releasing its bonus fund. In fact, such a high bonus in itself can be superficially thought of as an indication of a tight setting on the machine. Otherwise, why is the bonus so high?

Playing the maximum wager, a requirement to obtain the bonus, will cost forty credits per spin. The internal settings can be such that the average potential benefit, or technically the expected value of the next spin, may not be a positive quantity even at the 25,000 bonus level.

Even if a particular machine's settings are not actually such that the player is in a long-run disadvantageous position, the amount of time necessary to obtain the bonus can easily make this a rather poor slot play.

With such uncertainties in the situation, it is unwise to play the thousands or tens of thousands of spins required to have a reasonable chance to obtain the bonus.

# Super 8 Race

*Synopsis: Never play.*

Super 8 Race is another banking game where a bonus is paid for a rather rare slot event. In many respects, this game resembles Super 8 Line. A bonus number of credits is displayed and is the item that is banked. The player receives this bonus when maximum coins are wagered and nine fruits appear on the screen.

Like Super 8 Line, the problem in playing this Super 8 Race when the bonus is high is the unknown internal machine settings. The very real danger of taking a significant loss while chasing the bonus causes most professional players to back away from this machine. After all, there are plenty of other advantageous slot machines available.

# Super Double Diamond Mine

*Synopsis: Play at one credit per spin on machines which have nine diamonds in one shaft, or eight diamonds in each of two shafts, or seven or more diamonds in each of the three shafts. However, play maximum coins per spin when any diamond dust stack is within two units of the top of its shaft. Terminate play when the machine does not meet any of the above conditions.*

Super Double Diamond Mine seems basically quite similar to Double Diamond Mine with the stipulation that the diamonds are more difficult to obtain. Thus, in that sense, the game is more like Triple Diamond Mine. But since the diamonds that are collected are worth only one credit each rather than two, the similarity to Double Diamond Mine is still present.

Super Double Diamond Mine is distinctive in appearance because it has on its visual two sets of three shafts: one to hold distinct diamonds and a second to hold diamond dust.

Like both of these other games of which this is a hybrid, each of the three reels contains some diamond symbols. These symbols do nothing as far as the pay table is concerned and alining three diamonds on the payline will not in any direct way earn you additional credits.

Instead, a diamond or diamonds appearing on the payline will each trigger the slot machine to drop a number of diamonds equal to the number of credits wagered into the corresponding mine shaft(s) that contain diamonds and at the same time to drop a small quantity of diamond dust into the corresponding mine shaft(s) that contain diamond dust. When any mine shaft is filled with a total of ten diamonds, the shaft is emptied of diamonds and you receive ten credits. In a similar manner, when any mine shaft is filled with diamond dust, the shaft is emptied and you receive a certain number of credits. Just how many is still to be discussed.

Clearly, the items that are banked in Super Double Diamond Mine are the diamonds and diamond dust in the mine shafts.

In a general sense, the diamond dust is handled on the machine in a somewhat unclear manner. On the machines that I have observed, the machines are linked with respect to the diamond dust. That is: the diamond dust and the accumulated piles of such dust along with its accumulated awards, etc. are held in common on all machines. My experience is generally with sets of machines numbering roughly ten.

This linkage is common to the machines that I have observed but the machines would not necessarily have to be installed with this feature and could operate independently. The information presented below is conditioned on the existence of a linked system. However, the parts of the presentation not related to the linkage, namely the distinct diamonds in shafts, etc., are not affected.

The proper play of a Super Double Diamond Mine is to play one credit per spin on any machine which has nine diamonds in any one of its shafts. This, however, can be enlarged upon by adding that it is also profitable to play at the rate of one credit per spin any of these machines that have two shafts containing eight diamonds each. And expanding upon that, it should be noted that you can also profitably play any Super Double Diamond Mine that has three shafts each containing at least seven diamonds, and again this is at the rate of one credit per spin. These plays are not as profitable as they are on a Double Diamond Mine or Triple Diamond Mine, and, in fact, seem somewhat marginal by comparison.

Now the play involving the diamond dust is in a category by itself. The diamond dust is collected in three shafts that each have a value at the top of the shaft. The value starts at zero and increases as the shaft is filled with diamond dust. The linkage of the machines means that the pile of diamond dust on any machine can enlarge even while the machine is not being played. The three shafts collect diamond dust at different rates and have different values at the top of the shaft. The largest amounts that will occur at the tops of the shafts range from roughly twenty credits to over four hundred. I hesitate to give numbers about the top figures on these shafts because, I believe, these figures can be set by the casino and manufacturer and may differ significantly at various establishments.

Nonetheless, the first diamond dust shaft (moving left to right) tends to be worth several hundred (at least four hundred) credits, the second about forty credits, and the third shaft tends to be valued at about twenty credits on the systems I have seen. As noted before, the shafts do not fill with diamond dust at the same rate. The speed of filling is, of course, related to the final values occurring on each shaft, with the shafts with larger values filling more slowly.

The machine which completes the filling of the shaft with dust receives the final amount appearing at the top of the shaft. However, "filling a shaft" means different things with different shafts. With the second and third shafts, as numbered above, fill-ing the shaft means that the stack of diamond dust on the display will reach to the very pinnacle of the shaft before releasing those credits to the winning machine.

But the first shaft acts differently in regard to what it means to be filled. With the first shaft, the Super Double Diamond Mine system is designed such that an undisclosed number is chosen by the system as the amount of diamond dust to constitute a filled shaft. This is a random number in that it is an unknown integer between about four hundred and roughly eight hundred. I have never noticed the random number beyond this range. Now the machine which completes the filling of this shaft with dust by reaching the designated unknown number receives that final amount appearing at the top of the shaft.

The proper play of a Super Double Diamond Mine in order to obtain one of the values of credits associated with the second and third shafts of diamond dust is to only play when the shaft is within two credits of being filled. This means that on the system on which you are playing, you should have some previous experience. Lacking that, you would have to watch the display of diamond dust and evaluate the closeness of the pile to a complete filling. The shaft must be very full. Then begin playing maximum credits per spin. The most common mistake that I have seen players make in this regard is to wager only one credit per spin. It is necessary to be the one who places the final amount of diamond dust on the pile to receive the bonus award, so you must be the one dropping in the diamond dust. You want to be dropping in as much as possible. Playing maximum credits is imperative since you will probably have competition whenever endeavoring to obtain one of these two piles.

It is very common to have a set of Super Double Diamond Mines fill with players just as the filling of one of the diamond dust shafts nears completion. There is an intense period of extremely active play at all the machines. Then when the bonus is won, virtually the entire group cashes out and departs. Hmmm, could these players be knowledgeable about just how to best play these machines?

Now the play of the Super Double Diamond Mine machine in order to obtain the credits associated with the first shaft of diamond dust is in its own category. This shaft dispenses its contents when the unknown number is reached. Since the sets of machines with which I have had experience may not be quite the same as others, use the following advice with some caution.

Knowledgeable individuals begin to fill the set of machines when the number in the shaft is near four hundred. Most then begin to play maximum coins per spin until the first shaft is emptied. One of the individuals at the ten machines will win this using this technique. This appears to be a profitable approach to obtain the bonus associated with the first shaft.

Now if you feel uncomfortable playing rapidly at maximum coins to obtain the bonus in the first shaft, let me offer another winning strategy to use in this case. As the other players who are endeavoring to get the bonus in the first shaft rapidly play the set of machines, wait patiently until the diamond dust in the second and third shafts reaches the top of those shafts and only play to get those bonuses. Those two shafts will fill repeatedly while the other individuals struggle to obtain the top prize in the first shaft.

Trying to obtain only the bonuses associated with the second and third shafts will not generate the large swings in your funds that occur with chasing the top prize in the first shaft.

As a final comment, it is possible that you may be playing on a machine that has a diamond dust shaft that is very near the top and also a regular diamond shaft or shafts that qualify for play in their own right. In such cases, play maximum credits per spin until the diamond dust bonus is eliminated and then revert to regular play at one credit per spin if the standard shafts necessitate it.

Play should be terminated on a Super Double Diamond Mine when the slot machine does not satisfy the above conditions for any of the six shafts.

Good luck with this machine. You will probably find it an interesting experience if you ever play for the most valuable of the diamond dust shafts.

# Temperature's Rising

*Synopsis: When the number of degrees remaining is less than or equal to the bonus, play one credit per spin until the bonus is won.*

Temperature's Rising is easily spotted because each machine clearly shows a red thermometer with the temperature written below it. There are a large number of semi-variations of this machine. When I say semi-variations, I should clarify what I mean.

All the Temperature's Rising slot machines seem to be the type with three reels. The variations are in the thermometer and the bonus system. Different machines have different levels to which the temperature on the thermometer must rise in order to "break" the thermometer for the bonus award. Besides that, often the machines offer different bonuses. Usually the bonus, which is clearly printed near the thermometer, is larger on machines which require a higher temperature to break the thermometer.

Degrees on the thermometer are obtained by winning on the payline. The number of credits of each win is the number of degrees that the temperature is raised. When the thermometer is broken by reaching the proper temperature, the bonus is awarded on the credit meter and the thermometer is reset at or near zero.

From the small sampling of machines that we have tried, for a Temperature's Rising machine to be, on average, advantageous to play, the temperature should be a number of degrees from breaking the thermometer less than or equal to the number of credits which will be received as a bonus. Play should be at one credit per spin and terminated when the bonus is won and the thermometer is reset.

# Tour de Slot

*Synopsis: Play three credits per spin when any cyclist is one space from the end of a route which has fifty or more as the indicated bonus or two spaces from the end of a route which has one hundred or more as the bonus or three spaces from the end of a route which has a bonus of 150 credits. Terminate play when the requirements for play are not met.*

Tour de Slot is, except for cosmetic variations, identical to An American in Paris. Both these games are exclusive to Paris; even their sister properties, Bally's, etc. do not have these or similar versions of this game. With such limited distribution, it was debatable whether to include this game in the book. However, it was felt the game was of such a different variety that it would serve as an example concerning other games that might be developed and presented to the public. So the information is included.

The play on Tour de Slot is composed of two parts. There is the spinning of the three reels with results which are paid as ordinarily through reference to the pay tables. Then additionally, there can be some reel alinements which effect a banking feature on the visual.

The visual, located above the reels, pictures a white circular area from which six routes each wind to one of six attractions of France. To an extent, this game and An American in Paris compare to a six-legged octopus.

The routes, which are of varying lengths, are composed of distinct spaces similar to the divisions on a sidewalk. Six cyclists with identifying colored shirts each move from the central circular area to the end of their particular route. The movement of the cyclists follows the discrete pattern of the route and toward a number located near its end.

When a cyclists reaches the end of a route, you are awarded a bonus on the credit meter. The bonus is a number of credits equal to the number located near the end of the particular route. The cyclist is then returned to the white circular area to begin a new trip on the same route. The number near the end of that route and used to determine the last bonus is then altered.

The accompanying chart shows the relationship of the various destinations, route lengths, cyclist colors, and reel positions. On examination, you may be interested to note that each of the cyclists is limited to appearing on one reel. Thus, you can move any cyclist only one space per spin.

A profitable method to play Tour de Slot is to locate a machine on which any cyclist is one space from the end of a route which has fifty or more as the indicated bonus or two spaces from the end of a route which has one hundred or more as the bonus or three spaces from the end of a route which has a bonus of 150 credits.

After locating such a machine, you must play the maximum of three credits per spin until the appropriate cyclist is moved to the end of the route and the desired bonus is obtained.

Play is terminated if the machine no longer meets any requirement for play.

The advice given above is conservative. You can actually play machines with the cyclists at greater distances from the end of the routes. However, the play quickly begins to become marginal and, coupled with the fact that results on these games are quite variable, you will probably find more satisfaction in just playing machines with strong settings.

As a final suggestion, never be tempted by a bonus of less than fifty which has the cyclist only a single space from the route's end. On average, you will be financially disappointed. A cyclist only a single space from a small bonus is helpful during play for a larger bonus, but should not be played on its own merit.

## Tour de Slot Informational Chart

| DESTINATION | ROUTE LENGTH (in Spaces) | CYCLIST COLOR | REEL POSITION (Left to Right) |
|---|---|---|---|
| Building with Flag | 10 | Purple | 1 |
| Broad Mountain | 4 | Dark Blue | 1 |
| L'Arc de Triomphe | 5 | Red | 2 |
| Steep Mountain | 6 | Light Blue | 2 |
| Wine Bottle | 9 | White | 3 |
| Beach Umbrella | 7 | Yellow | 3 |

# Treasure Quest

*Synopsis: Play one credit per line per spin, on each of the five paylines, when three or more treasure chests have been completed. Terminate play when the five free spins of the bonus round have been used.*

Initial
Treasure Chest

Filled to
First Level

Filled to
Second Level

Filled to
Third Level

Filled to
Fourth Level

Open
Treasure Chest

Treasure Quest is found on Winning Touch slot machines. Particularly, it appears to be on the Winning Touch machines that do not have Royal Hot 7's. This almost undoubtedly is because Treasure Quest is virtually the same game as Royal Hot 7's, which is, in turn, extremely similar to Red Hot 7's.

Treasure Quest is best played at one credit per line per spin on each of its five paylines, when three or more of the treasure chests are open or completed as shown in the illustrations above. Play should be terminated when the five free spins of the bonus round have been obtained. During this bonus round, treasure chests on the paylines are wild symbols. This method of play will, on average, produce profitable results.

Like many similar banking games, you can play Treasure Quest at one credit per line on only a single payline. This will, on average, produce slightly more profitable results. However, the entire process of reaching the bonus round will take roughly five times as many spins and, in addition, generally produce a very irritable player.

# Triple Cash Winfall

*Synopsis: Play at one credit per spin on machines which have nine coins in one stack, eight coins in each of two stacks or seven or more coins in each of the three stacks. Terminate play when the machine does not meet any of the above conditions.*

Triple Cash Winfall is very similar to Double Diamond Mine, and even more like Triple Diamond Mine (discussed later) which seems to be rarer to find in casinos than Double Diamond Mine.

In Triple Cash Winfall, a dollar sign landing on the three-reel payline causes a coin to fall onto the corresponding stack of coins on a visual above the reels. When ten of these coins are accumulated in one stack, you are awarded two credits per coin and that particular stack vanishes. A new stack in that position is then formed as dollar signs continue to land on the payline. Clearly, the item banked is the stacked coins.

The play of Triple Cash Winfall is the same as either Double or Triple Diamond Mine. It is suggested that you play one credit per spin on any machine which has nine coins in any one of its stacks. It is also profitable to play at the rate of one credit per spin any of Triple Cash Winfall machines that have two stacks containing eight coins each, and you can also profitably play a machine that has three stacks each containing at least seven coins, at the rate of one credit per spin. Again, these rules are on the conservative side but quite easy to remember.

Play on Triple Cash Winfall should be terminated when the conditions indicating favorable play no longer exist. In other words, stop playing when the machine does not meet the above standards.

Triple Cash Winfall, like Triple Diamond Mine, has a relatively slow rate of accumulation of the banked items which are worth two credits each on completion of the collection of the set of ten. In this respect, the machine's performance is slightly different than that of Double Diamond Mine.

# Triple Diamond Baseball Diamond

*Synopsis: Play at one credit per spin when there is a total of at least 25 runs and indicated runs, and terminate play upon receiving a HOME RUN on the payline.*

Take me out to the casino, take me out to the crowd, buy me some . . . Triple Diamond Baseball Diamond is a play on one of the favorites, baseball, a game that virtually everybody knows. As slot players spin the reels, small figures move around the baseball diamond as singles, doubles, triples, and home runs are "hit" by the corresponding term (1 SINGLE, 2 DOUBLE, 3 TRIPLE, and HOME RUN) landing on the third reel of the payline. In Triple Diamond Baseball Diamond, the item that is banked is the credits that are wagered on a spin in which a baseball term lands on the payline. Thus, a wager is sometimes banked because the credits are transferred to a baseball player moving around the bases. Note that each runner on the visual has a baseball over his head, which contains the number of credits wagered on the particular spin during which he got on base.

As play progresses, the baseball symbols advance all base runners by the corresponding number of bases. When a particular runner passes home plate, the number on the baseball over his head is added to the accumulated total of runs scored. This total continues to grow until a home run is hit by the appropriate symbol appearing on the payline. When a HOME RUN is obtained on the third reel's payline, the bases are cleared and the entire accumulation of runs is added to your credits at a rate of one credit per run.

Since the home run bonus can be obtained by playing one credit per spin, you are advised to wager at a rate of one credit per spin when there are a total of 25 or more runs and indicated runs displayed on the visual. The term "indicated runs" is used here to stress that you, when checking a machine, should add together the number of runs already scored and the numbers in the baseballs over any runners on base to determine the total for the Triple Diamond Baseball Diamond machine. Play should be terminated when the bases are cleared by a HOME RUN.

One final comment about Triple Diamond Baseball Diamond: the only way to be out in this game is to be out of money.

# Triple Diamond Mine

*Synopsis: Play at one credit per spin on machines which have nine diamonds in one shaft, eight diamonds in each of two shafts or seven or more diamonds in each of the three shafts. Terminate play when the machine does not meet any of the above conditions.*

Triple Diamond Mine is virtually identical to Double Diamond Mine. As in Double Diamond Mine, the items that are banked in Triple Diamond Mine are the diamonds in the mine shafts. The first noticeable difference you will usually observe during play is that diamonds are more difficult to obtain. This is because they are worth two credits each on completion of the collection of ten diamonds in a shaft.

A profitable way, on average, to play Triple Diamond Mine is to play one credit per spin on any machine which has nine diamonds in any one of its shafts, two shafts each containing eight diamonds, or three shafts each containing at least seven diamonds. This rule is on the conservative side but quite easy to remember.

Play on a Triple Diamond Mine should be terminated when the conditions indicating favorable play no longer exist. In other words, stop playing when the machine does not meet any of the above conditions.

Triple Diamond Mine machines are not nearly as common in casinos as the Double Diamond Mine machines. The two machines look so much alike that except for the slightly different performance and a few words on the machines, you would be hard pressed to sort them.

# Vacation U.S.A.

*Synopsis: Guidelines: In all situations, play one credit on only one payline. When the last bet is one credit and seven or more of either route is completed, play until the bonus for that route is obtained. When the last bet is ten credits and five or more of either route is completed, play until bonus for that route is obtained. When the last bet is fifty credits and three or more of either route is completed, play until the bonus for that route is obtained.*

Vacation U.S.A. is a game that sits alone in the physical framework of an Odyssey machine. It was sitting that way in a five cent denomination at all the casinos that I visited. After many weeks, I noticed that it had been put on the standard Odyssey machines in a quarter denomination with other games. In this setting, one was forced to call the game into play by the usual method of touching the screen.

It may sound strange to say this, but Vacation U.S.A. is very different from many other slot games because of a feature that all, or at least many, of the other games probably possess. That feature is that the bonus round in a general sense and the average amount received in the bonus round in particular are a function of the coin-in. As an easy example of this phenomenon, consider the game Lady of Fortune. During the bonus round involving the placing of the player's hand against the screen, you will notice that there is a semi-circle of numbers surrounding the lady's hand on the screen. These numbers appear to be generally indicative of the size of the bonus that the player will receive. Also those numbers appear to be related to the amount inserted into the machine since the last bonus round or what is commonly called the coin-in since the last bonus round.

This feature of the bonus being a function of the coin-in may be mildly noticeable in various other games; but in Vacation U.S.A., it is strongly noticeable. In fact, the feature is so strong that the decision about whether a particular machine is advantageous to play will sometimes be based on indications of both the number of road signs previously collected and the amount wagered by the previous player. However, we are getting ahead of ourselves. Suffice it to quote the machine from under the "Help?" button, "Bonus round awards are based on the average coin-in since the previous round of that bonus."

First , we will discuss the general play of a Vacation U.S.A. In the center of the screen, the game displays a 4x4 rectangle. This rectangle has sixteen areas which spin during standard machine play. On each spin, the sixteen areas each produce a symbol which can be used to generate pays according to the pay schedule.

The pay schedule is primarily structured on paylines of length four and pays in either direction. On Vacation U.S.A., there are a total of ten paylines: four horizontal, four vertical, and two diagonal. On each payline, you may wager from zero to five credits per spin. However, the minimum wager is one line at one credit per spin.

In addition to the linear pays, there are also pays called scatter awards. These scatter awards are only earned if you wager at least one credit per spin on each of the ten paylines.

There is one other way to obtain credits from this machine and that involves the banking feature. What is banked in Vacation U.S.A. are interstate road signs.

Displayed on the lower left side of the screen of this machine is a U.S. map with two east-west cross-country interstate routes: Interstate Route 80 and the more southerly Interstate Route 40. Whenever an interstate symbol either 40 or 80 appears in the 4x4 rectangle on the screen, regardless of the number of credits wagered, the game will award you the symbol by marking it appropriately on the U.S. map. After obtaining a set of ten of either interstate symbols, you are moved to another screen for a Cross-Country Bonus trip. On this trip you choose, one at a time, from a set of five destinations until you encounter a "Stop and Collect" sign. With the selection of each destination, you receive an unknown bonus of credits for that destination.

Now the maximum possible value of the entire Cross-Country Bonus trip is the item that is dependent on the average coin-in. If the entire play in obtaining the interstate signs to obtain the bonus trip has involved wagers of one credit per spin, then the maximum possible value of the bonus trip will be that average, one, times the number 26. Why 26? Only the manufacturer knows that answer. On the other hand, if the entire play in obtaining the interstate signs to obtain the bonus trip has involved wagers of fifty credits per spin, then the maximum possible value of the bonus trip will be that average, fifty, times the number 26 or 1300 credits.

The bonus for a Cross-Country Bonus trip is awarded piecemeal, that is, you receive an amount for each destination you visit, finally ending with a "Stop and Collect" sign. The total for all five of the destinations is the average coin-in times 26. However, each destination awards one of the numbers, 3, 4, 5, 6, or 8 (which sum to 26) times that average coin-in. The point here is that the values of the destinations are definitely not random.

Another observation about the destinations is that the "Stop and Collect" sign in any Cross-Country Bonus trip is always at the destination valued at five times average coin-in. Therefore, the minimum possible value of any Cross-Country Bonus trip is five times the average coin-in. This observation will not in any way help you play Vacation U.S.A. financially better.

Another feature of the Cross-Country Bonus trip, which theoretically should occur and is confirmed in practice, is that the number of destinations visited during bonus trips averages to three.

As an example, if the machine determines that the average coin-in has been three, then the maximum value of the

175

Cross-Country Bonus trip will be 78 (3 x 26) and the values of the individual destinations are 9 (3 x 3), 12 (4 x 3), 15 (5 x 3), 18 (6 x 3), and 24 (8 x 3). The "Stop and Collect" sign is located at the destination valued at 5 x 3, 15. This stuff is getting close to trivia since it is relatively unimportant in the play of the game.

After completing a Cross-Country Bonus trip, you should re-evaluate the status of the machine to determine if it will be, on average, profitable to continue playing.

The most profitable way to play Vacation U.S.A. is to locate a "good" machine and play one credit per spin. There is a temptation to wager ten credits per spin, one credit per each payline per spin, to receive payment for the scatter pays. Playing ten paylines will also make the game seem more exciting with many more pays; but unfortunately in the long run, this is a more costly, less profitable way to play the Vacation U.S.A. machine.

Having determined how to play, we must now explain what constitutes a "good" machine as was alluded to in the preceding paragraph. This determination is actually a somewhat awkward process.

Since the Cross-Country bonus trip is the bonus event that we are striving to obtain by collecting interstate road signs and since the total value of the bonus trip is, as the machine states, based on the average coin-in, a player must consider the coin-in to determine the potential profit from playing the machine.

But on approaching a Vacation U.S.A., how do you know the average coin-in value of the previous play? Plainly, unless you have played the machine or have observed the previous play, you would not know for certain. However, if you look on the lower right of the screen and observe the play button, a yellow circle containing a number, you will learn what the very last play has been. You will generally assume that this number of credits has been played all the way through the current game. This figure is what will be your guide in assessing the value of playing a machine. If, perchance, there is no such figure in a yellow circle, the information regarding the very last play may still be recoverable by inserting a piece of currency into the bill validator.

Let us first assume that you positively know that the previous play has all been at one credit per spin. Then with this information, I can offer the guidance that unless the number of road signs on one of the routes is at least seven, you should avoid playing the machine. This situation of knowing the coin-in occasionally occurs while playing the Vacation U.S.A. to get road signs of the other route. So if you know or suspect that the previous play has all been at the one credit level, then you should only play to obtain the bonus for a route if there are three or fewer of its signs to obtain.

Note: playing Vacation U.S.A. with seven signs under the above conditions is definitely marginal.

Now it is impossible here to examine the value of a Vacation USA for all the number of credits (one to fifty) at which another individual may decide to play. However, commonly amateur players play ten credits per spin, one credit per payline per spin. In fact, certain aspects of the machine's pay schedule, e.g. the scatter pays, encourage this style of play.

If the previous player has wagered ten credits per spin and has obtained five interstate road signs on one of the routes, then the machine should be played until the bonus for that route is obtained. Playing to obtain the five interstate route signs for the one route has the disadvantage that you will obtain numerous interstate route signs for the other route. These will be costly to get and yet you will probably not get enough to warrant finishing that route. The point here is that the above is a somewhat weak play. Far stronger is to play a machine where the indications are that the previous player has wagered ten credits per spin and both routes are developed at least to the fourth sign.

At the extreme high end, let us assume that on examining Vacation U.S.A. slot machines, you find a machine that appears to have been played at the maximum of fifty credits per spin. At this rate of play, the previous player will generally have put so much into the machine in getting only two interstate route signs for one route that you, playing only one credit on one payline, can, on average, profitably finish playing the machine.

As you can tell, these machines are awkward to fully evaluate because you must assume that the previous play was all at the level indicated by the final play. Fortunately, if this is seriously in error, the losses will be well within your pocketbook since almost all the Vacation U.S.A. machines are nickel denominations.

In all cases, you should reappraise the value of continued play after completing a Cross-Country Bonus trip to consider if additional play to obtain a Cross-Country Bonus trip on the other route is warranted.

After you conclude that additional play on the Vacation U.S.A. will not, on average, be profitable, you should make your next destination the change booth.

# Vacation U.S.A. (Tight-Lipped Version)

*Synopsis: Guidelines: In all situations, play one credit on only one payline. When the last bet is one credit and seven or more of either route is completed, play until the bonus for that route is obtained. When the last bet is ten credits and five or more of either route is completed, play until bonus for that route is obtained. When the last bet is fifty credits and three or more of either route is completed, play until the bonus for that route is obtained.*

Vacation U.S.A. now comes in a second variety. I felt the prominent characteristic of this new variety warranted giving this version the title Tight-Lipped Version.

It will be assumed at this point that the reader has read the contents of the chapter entitled Vacation U.S.A. That material, with details about how to profitably play Vacation U.S.A., also applies to Vacation U.S.A. (Tight-Lipped Version) and will not be repeated here.

The only feature of Vacation U.S.A. which seems to have been changed during the remaking is the display of the U.S. map. In the new version, the map is only visible for a short period of time after the player has obtained an interstate road sign.

The result of this variation is that since you must see the map on a machine in order to determine if the machine will, on average, be profitable to play, you must either have observed the previous player or play the machine until you obtain an interstate road sign.

Assuming that you avoid the practice of watching over players' shoulders, you will be forced to play each unknown machine until you obtain an interstate road sign. This could get to be a somewhat expensive item on various occasions. I do not recommend this approach.

A slightly more profitable approach is instead to look at the last bet and determine if the previous player wagered enough (at least ten credits per spin) during his play that the machine might possibly have been left with one or more routes in a somewhat advanced state (at least five signs completed on either route). If the machine indicates that the previous player has wagered at least ten credits per spin, then the Vacation U.S.A. (Tight-Lipped Version) can reasonably be checked by playing one credit per spin on one line until an interstate road sign appears on a paylines.

With the appearance of the first interstate road sign, you can then evaluate the advisability of continued play.

# Wheel of Fortune

*Synopsis: With at least 1201 bonus points, wager one credit per spin on each of the five paylines. Terminate play after selecting letters of the word WHEEL.*

There are several machines that bear the name Wheel of Fortune. Only one of them is a banking machine. The Wheel of Fortune that we are considering here is the machine which involves the collecting of letters to complete a puzzle. If the Wheel of Fortune that you are examining is not of this style, then it is advised that you not play the machine because you are not at an advantageous slot machine.

But, assuming you are at the proper type of machine, there are a few things to note. The first is that there is an incredible amount of information and instructional material on the machine. Indeed, this is one of the most complicated machines commonly sitting around the casinos. This, however, has not interfered with its being extremely popular.

You might think that the item being banked is the letters in the puzzle. True, these letters are a banked item; however, the letters in the puzzle are of minor importance in determining if the Wheel of Fortune machine is advantageous to play. In fact, we will give the puzzle letters virtually no attention in considering whether it is advantageous to play a particular machine.

What is important is the number of bonus points that are banked and posted on the right side of the screen. Some of these bonus points are occasionally just given to you when the machine begins a new puzzle, but usually they are obtained when you receive another letter of the puzzle. These bonus points are important because, on completion of the puzzle, there is a bonus round in which the accumulated bonus points determine how many letters of the word WHEEL may be selected. A random amount of credits is awarded for each letter of the word WHEEL that is selected.

The following chart details the conversion of bonus points to WHEEL letters. This information is also on the Wheel of Fortune slot machine. To profitably play a Wheel of Fortune, you should locate a machine on which the bonus points are in excess of 1200. The chart on the Wheel of Fortune slot machine shows that when the number of bonus points is over 1200, you will receive at least two letters of the word WHEEL. You need to be in a position of receiving two of these letters in order for the machine to be, on average, advantageous to play.

Now, of course, things are never really quite that simple. This required number of bonus points can be lessened slightly. According to my data, if a Wheel of Fortune has bonus points in the high 1100s and the number of blank spaces in the puzzle remaining to be filled with letters will DEFINITELY generate enough additional bonus points to make the final total of bonus points 1201 or more, then the machine will also be, on average, advantageous to play. This is only true, however, if the number of blank spaces in the puzzle does not exceed five.

Reexamining the last paragraph, you definitely need to have a machine where the bonus points will generate at least two letters of the word WHEEL. So the bonus points must go over 1200. Then since this is marginal play, you cannot be trying to fill too many blank spaces; my data says not to exceed five. Then the machine will, on average, be profitable to play. Be assured that this is marginal play and not strong financially.

The most common method used to play an advantageous Wheel of Fortune is on each spin to wager one credit per payline, of which there are five. In other words, play five credits per spin. Playing the maximum of 25 credits per spin only aids the casino's profits.

However, the above method is not the least expensive way to complete the puzzle. There is actually a small savings to be gained by playing a Wheel of Fortune at the rate of one credit per spin. This would mean you were playing only one payline per spin. Like Super 7's, this approach will require a substantially longer time to play. My advice is that you should forego this small financial savings and wager five credits per spin. In all cases, terminate play after selecting letters of the word WHEEL.

### Wheel of Fortune
### Conversion of Bonus Points to W-H-E-E-L Letters

| Final Number of Bonus Points | Number of W-H-E-E-L Letters |
|---|---|
| 1-1200 | 1 |
| 1201-1650 | 2 |
| 1651-2250 | 3 |
| 2251-2750 | 4 |
| 2751 or more | 5 |

**Wheel of Fortune: Average Profit During Advantageous Periods**

| Initial Number of W-H-E-E-L Letters | Average Profit in Credits |
|:---:|:---:|
| 1 | 43.2[1] |
| 2 | 81.6 |
| 3 | 112.3 |
| 4 | 241.4 |
| 5 | 411.7 |

[1]This result is based on very selective play.

# Wild Cherry Bonus Pie

*Synopsis: With five cherries or fewer needed to finish filling the large pie, play the machine. The number of credits to play per spin is dependent on the layout, but you can always interminably play one credit per spin. Terminate play after the large pie is filled.*

Wild Cherry Bonus Pie is a remake of Wild Cherry Pie. At first glance, the remake may appear to be the same game but it certainly isn't. In some major respects, Wild Cherry Bonus Pie departs radically from Wild Cherry Pie.

Wild Cherry Bonus Pie, like Wild Cherry Pie, is one of those games that is so difficult to explain that by the time one completes the instructions, the reader is totally confused. With that in mind, here goes.

The Wild Cherry Bonus Pie machine has three reels. As on most modern slot machines, the areas above and below the payline are visible to the slot player. Therefore, each of the three reels has three areas that you can clearly see: the space on the payline, the space above the payline, and the space below the payline.

Since there are three spaces on each reel that can be seen and there are three reels, there are nine areas visible. These nine areas correspond to the nine sections of a large pie that is displayed above the reels. During the play of the Wild Cherry Bonus Pie machine, cherries are slowly added to the sections until all the sections are filled with cherries. Six cherries are required to fill each of the nine sections of the large pie.

When a wild cherry pie symbol appears on the reels in one of the nine visible locations, the symbol functions in two distinct ways. First, it acts as a wild symbol and as though it were on the payline functioning in standard slot pays. Secondly, the symbol transfers into the corresponding section of the large pie display a number of cherries equal to the number of credits wagered. However, if the section of the large pie corresponding to the location of the wild cherry pie symbol on the reels is already filled with six cherries, then the cherries are instead transferred to a smaller pie located to the left side of the screen.

Additionally, if the section of the smaller pie corresponding to the location of the wild cherry pie symbol on the reels is also already filled with six cherries, then the cherry award is doubled and added to the bonus meter which is located above the small pie. The number on the bonus meter is displayed on a basket.

The complete filling of the large pie with 54 cherries ends the game. At that time, a bonus pie pay, valued between 25 and 500 credits, is displayed with the 'eating' of the large pie. Then the amount on the bonus meter is added to a bonus pie pay and the total is awarded on the machine's credit meter. Another way of saying all this is: on completion of filling the large pie, a bonus pie pay of 25 to 500 credits plus the value of the bonus meter is awarded.

The large filled pie, which has just been eaten, is then replaced by the small pie, which is enlarged to fill the space taken by the former large pie and a new empty small pie appears. The bonus meter is reset to zero. The game is then ready to be played again.

The manufacturer's purpose in having the small pie replace the large pie is undoubtedly to encourage players to continue playing and also to avoid discouraging new potential players who approach the game. Studies have shown that slot players are often dissuaded from playing on slot machines which are clearly in a starting position. The replacement of the large pie by the small pie tends to mask the reality of a starting position by displaying a pie which is only very rarely totally empty.

Clearly, cherries are the item that is banked in this game. However, cherries are handled in so many different ways that the game is difficult to analyze. Trying to analyze Wild Cherry Bonus Pie to predict the average value of a Wild Cherry Bonus Pie machine based on the initial number of empty spots in the pie proved to be clumsy.

From the data I have obtained, it appears that a Wild Cherry Bonus Pie can, on average, be profitably played when there are seven or fewer spots remaining to be filled in the large pie. The size of the bonus meter is generally relatively unimportant compared to the bonus pie pay which is between 25 and 500 credits. If the bonus pie pay is large, you will usually be a winner; if not, you will be behind financially for having played the game.

You should be cautious when deciding to play Wild Cherry Bonus Pie because your success will be very dependent on the unknown bonus pie pay.

The number seven mentioned above should generally not be used as a guide with this game. I have found play at this number to be extremely marginal. Most of the plays were losses with a very few large wins balancing them to a slightly positive average. The high variance with this situation is annoying.

Consequently, the rule should better read: Wild Cherry Bonus Pie can, on average, be profitably played when there are five or fewer spots remaining to be filled in the large pie. Thus, if you play through the bonus round and have a new pie with six cherries needed, terminate play.

The best method to play a Wild Cherry Bonus Pie slot machine can be slightly confusing. The maximum number of credits that can be played on the Wild Cherry Bonus Pie machine is two. If the section of the large pie needing the most cherries requires six, five, four, three, or two cherries, then play two credits per spin. If, however, the section of the pie needing the most cherries needs only one cherry, then play only one credit per spin.

It is probably minutely more profitable, on average, to play one credit per spin all the way through each Wild Cherry Bonus Pie game. I have not checked this; but because I have found other banking slot machines function in this manner, I believe the advice to be true. This wagering approach (one credit per spin) can be incredibly lengthy timewise and boring, but generally there is a stability in playing one credit in comparison to playing two. Playing more than one credit per spin will save consideranle time but will generally generate greater financial swings.

Play should be terminated on a Wild Cherry Bonus Pie slot machine when the large pie is filled.

# Wild Cherry Pie

*Synopsis: With 11 cherries or fewer needed to complete the pie, play the machine. The optimal number of credits to play per spin is dependent on the layout, but you can always play one credit per spin. Terminate play after the pie is completed.*

Wild Cherry Pie is one of those games that is so difficult to explain that by the time the instructions are completed, the reader is totally confused. With that in mind, here goes.

The Wild Cherry Pie machine has three reels. As on most modern slot machines, the areas above and below the payline are visible. Therefore, each of the three reels has three areas that you can clearly see: the space on the payline, the space above the payline, and the space below the payline.

Since there are three spaces on each reel that can be seen and there are three reels, there are nine areas visible. These nine areas correspond to the nine sections of a pie that is displayed above the reels. Each of these nine sections of the pie is initially empty. During the play of the Wild Cherry Pie machine, the sections are slowly filled with cherries. Six cherries are required to fill each of the nine sections of the pie.

When a wild cherry pie symbol appears on the reels in one of the nine visible locations, the symbol functions in two distinct ways. First, it acts as a wild symbol and as though it were on the payline functioning in standard slot pays. Secondly, the symbol transfers into the corresponding section of the cherry pie a number of cherries equal to the number of credits wagered. However, if the section of the cherry pie corresponding to the location of the cherry pie symbol on the reels is already filled with six cherries, then the cherries are instead transferred to a basket located on the left side of the screen.

Completely filling the pie with 54 cherries ends the game. At that time, you will be awarded a random bonus amount and additionally receive one credit for each cherry in the basket. Play should then be terminated on the slot machine.

The above information may take a reading or two to come to understand; but, in other words, the wild cherry symbols that appear in the nine positions of the reels, besides functioning as wild symbols on the payline, put cherries into corresponding sections of the pie. If that section of the pie is already filled, the cherries are instead placed into a basket.

Only one item is banked in this game, the cherries; but they are banked in two distinct ways. First, cherries are banked into the pie itself, drawing the game closer to its conclusion. Secondly, excess cherries are banked into the basket.

Trying to analyze Wild Cherry Pie has been an extremely interesting process with repeated trials and tribulations and more repeated trials. Trying to predict the average value of a Wild Cherry Pie machine based on both the initial number of empty spots in the pie and the initial number of cherries in the basket proved to produce results that were no better or more accurate than using a single variable.

It seems an obvious thing that a machine with a cherry pie with six empty spots and twenty cherries in the basket should be less valuable than a machine with a cherry pie with the same six empty spots and 23 in the basket. But in the analysis, the general variability in the slot activity masks this difference.

From your perspective, the use of a single variable is certainly a good thing, since you do not want to be involved with very complicated information in a casino setting.

The best predictor of the profitability of a Wild Cherry Pie machine seems to be the number of spots in the pie remaining to be filled. From my data, it appears that a Wild Cherry Pie can be profitably played when there are 11 or fewer spots remaining to be filled in the cherry pie. The following table supplies more detail about this matter.

The best method to play a Wild Cherry Pie slot machine can be confusing to explain. First, you should check if the machine you will be playing has a maximum wager of two or three credits. Wild Cherry Pie machines do have this minor variation. For our initial consideration, let us assume your machine has a maximum bet of three credits per spin.

After determining that the machine's maximum wager is three credits, you should examine all the non-completed sections of the pie and note the number of cherries necessary to fill each section. Especially note the pie section (or sections) requiring the most cherries.

If that section of the pie needs all six cherries, then the machine should be played at three credits per spin. The play at three credits per spin should continue until this section only needs three cherries. Then you should pause and make a redetermination of the number of credits to play per spin.

If, instead, the section of the pie requiring the most cherries needs five cherries, then play three credits per spin until that section is reduced to needing only two cherries. Accomplishing that feat, pause and reevaluate the situation to determine how many credits to then wager.

If the pie section requiring the most cherries needs four cherries, and if there is any section of the pie needing three cherries, play three credits per spin until all sections needing three cherries are filled. But if there is no section needing three cherries, but there are sections needing two cherries, then play two credits per spin until there is no section needing either four or two cherries.

If the section of the cherry pie needing the most cherries requires three, two, or only one, then play a number of credits equal to the number necessary to fill that section.

Now was that complicated enough? It continues.

If the maximum number of credits that can be played on the Wild Cherry Pie machine is two, then if the section of the pie needing the most cherries requires six, five, four, three, or two cherries, then play two credits per spin. If, however, the section of the pie needing the most cherries needs only one cherry, then play only one credit per spin.

It is actually minutely more profitable on average to play one credit per spin all the way through each Wild Cherry Pie game. This wagering approach is from personal experience an incredibly lengthy and boring waste of life that only an author collecting data should be forced to endure.

**Wild Cherry Pie: Average Profit During Advantageous Periods**

| Number of Empty Spots in Pie | Average Profit in Credits |
|---|---|
| 1 | 92.6 |
| 2 | 84.1 |
| 3 | 75.7 |
| 4 | 67.2 |
| 5 | 58.8 |
| 6 | 50.3 |
| 7 | 41.9 |
| 8 | 33.4 |
| 9 | 25.0 |
| 10 | 16.5 |
| 11 | 8.1 |

# Wine Cellar

*Synopsis: With five bottles or fewer needed to finish filling the large rack, play the machine. The number of credits to play per spin is dependent on the layout, but you can always interminably play one credit per spin. Terminate play after the large rack is filled.*

Wine Cellar is really just a variation of Diamond Thief and Wild Cherry Bonus Pie. Paris wanted to have a set of slot machines that was different from those of other casinos. For a few dollars of expense in altering the basic design, but not the expense of developing a totally new machine complete with approval of the Gaming Control Board, Paris obtained Wine Cellar.

Wine Cellar, like both of the other two games, is so difficult to explain that by the time one completes the instructions, the reader is usually totally confused. You are about to experience that phenomenon.

The Wine Cellar machine has three reels. As on most modern slot machines, the areas above and below the payline are visible to the slot player. Therefore, each of the three reels has three areas that you can clearly see: the space on the payline, the space above the payline, and the space below the payline.

Since there are three spaces on each reel that can be seen and there are three reels, there are nine areas visible. These nine areas correspond to the nine sections of a large rack that is displayed above the reels. During the play of the Wine Cellar machine, bottles are slowly added to the sections until all the sections are filled with bottles. Six bottles are required to fill each of the nine sections of the large rack.

When a wine cellar symbol appears on the reels in one of the nine visible locations, the symbol functions in two distinct ways. First, it acts as a wild symbol and as though it were on the payline functioning in standard slot pays. Secondly, the symbol transfers into the corresponding section of the large rack display a number of bottles equal to the number of credits wagered. However, if the section of the large rack corresponding to the location of the wine cellar symbol on the reels is already filled with six bottles, then the bottles are instead transferred to a smaller rack located to the left side of the screen.

Additionally, if the section of the smaller rack corresponding to the location of the wine cellar symbol on the reels is also already filled with six bottles, then the bottle award is doubled and added to the bonus meter which is located under the large rack.

The complete filling of the large rack with 54 bottles ends the game. At that time, a bonus wine rack pay, valued between 25 and 500 credits, is displayed with the removal of the bottles from the large rack. Then the amount on the bonus meter is added to the bonus wine rack pay and the total is awarded on the machine's credit meter. Another way of saying all this is: on completion of filling the large rack, a total comprised of a bonus of 25 to 500 credits plus the value on the bonus meter is awarded on the credit meter.

The large wine rack, which has just been emptied, is then replaced by the small wine rack, which is enlarged to fill the space taken by the former large wine rack and a new empty small wine rack appears. The bonus meter is reset to zero. The game is then ready to be played again.

The manufacturer's purpose in having the small wine rack replace the large wine rack is undoubtedly to encourage players to continue playing and also to avoid discouraging new potential players who approach the game. Studies have shown that slot players are often dissuaded from playing on slot machines which are clearly in a starting position. The replacement of the large wine rack by the small wine rack tends to mask the reality of a starting position by displaying a wine rack which is only very rarely totally empty.

Clearly, bottles are the item that is banked in this game. However, bottles are handled in so many different ways that the game is difficult to analyze. Trying to analyze Wine Cellar to predict the average value of a Wine Cellar machine based on the initial number of empty spots in the rack proved to be clumsy.

From the data I have obtained, it appears that a Wine Cellar can, on average, be profitably played when there are seven or fewer spots remaining to be filled in the large wine rack. The size of the bonus meter is generally relatively unimportant compared to the bonus wine rack pay which is between 25 and 500 credits. If the bonus wine rack pay is large, you will usually be a winner; if not, you will be behind financially for having played the game.

You should be cautious when deciding to play Wine Cellar because your success will be very dependent on the unknown bonus wine rack pay.

The number seven mentioned above should generally not be used as a guide with this game. I have found play at this number to be extremely marginal. Most of the plays were losses with a very few large wins balancing them to a slightly positive average. The high variance with this situation is annoying.

Consequently, the rule should better read: Wine Cellar can, on average, be profitably played when there are five or fewer spots remaining to be filled in the large rack. Thus, if you play through the bonus round and have a new rack with six bottles needed, terminate play.

The best method to play a Wine Cellar slot machine can be slightly confusing. The maximum number of credits that can be played on the Wine Cellar machine is two. If the section of the large rack needing the most bottles requires six, five, four, three, or two bottles, then play two credits per spin. If, however, the section of the rack needing the most bottles needs only one bottle, then play only one credit per spin.

It is probably minutely more profitable, on average, to play one credit per spin all the way through each Wine Cellar game. I have not checked this; but because I have found other banking slot machines function in this manner, I believe the advice to be true. This wagering approach (one credit per spin) can be incredibly lengthy timewise and boring, but generally there is a stability in playing one credit in comparison to playing two. Playing more than one credit per spin will save considerable time but will generally generate greater financial swings.

Play should be terminated on a Wine Cellar slot machine when the large rack is filled.

# X Factor

*Synopsis: With 6X, 7X, 8X, 9X, or 10X, play the maximum credits per spin. Terminate play when the multiplying factor is used.*

X Factor is, to say the least, an unusual game. On the X Factor slot machine, the X factor is a value that multiplies certain winning combinations on the payline of the three-reel machine when maximum coins are wagered, and then resets to the minimum value of 2X. During the play of the game, the X factor grows from 2X to 3X to 4X to a maximum value of 10X. This growth is accomplished by obtaining power points. Obtaining ten power points will raise the X factor one unit unless the maximum of 10X has been reached, in which case the power points are banked to be used to raise the value of 2X after the current maximum value of 10X has been used.

X Factor is advantageous to play whenever the X factor has reached 6X, 7X, 8X, 9X, or 10X. Usually players do not leave the machine when the X factor is that high. The proper method of play under these conditions is three coins per spin terminating play when the multiplying factor is used.

# Odds & Ends

## Slot Machine Anomalies

Slot machines have anomalies, oddities that set them apart from other slot machines, items that are so trivial that they seem unimportant; yet these trivialities can have repercussions in the play of the machines themselves. I have often wondered if some of these oddities are purposely designed into the mechanism or if they are simply accidental consequences of the programing that became apparent after the machines were widely distributed.

Williams Gaming, Inc. has produced a slot machine called MULTI-PAY on which the game of blackjack appears. In this particular game, the oddity is that if you play coins without having any credits in the machine, you cannot double down or split. During any particular blackjack hand, coins cannot be added to the machine. Only credits already in the machine can be used for such purposes. This, of course, certainly will affect your play at this particular game.

A couple of times, I have seen individuals stung because of this oddity. Say a player had perhaps 15 credits and wagered ten on the next hand. Then as chance would have it, the player had two cards he wished to double. Well, he just plain couldn't. The machine would not accept additional coinage. Also the MULTI-PAY machine would not permit him to double for less.

If you happen to get caught in an oddity like this and lose extra coinage because of it, don't hesitate to complain and ask for the extra that you would properly have received. The Reserve, where I first noticed this, did compensate me for an unnecessary $2.50 loss (a win that I did not properly obtain) the first time I experienced this anomaly. Casinos tend to be fair about these unusual things, especially when the oddity is first brought to their attention. They, in turn, often pass this type of complaint back to the manufacturer.

After you experience this type of snafu and are reimbursed, you do have to be cautious about continuing to use the machine. The casino will not reimburse a player who knowingly elects to continue using a machine with this type of syndrome.

Generally on slot machines, blackjack games that pay three to two on a natural 21 all require you to wager an even number of credits to be paid properly without being shorted. You must continually be careful.

Another type of anomaly that I have found while playing a wide assortment of slot machines occurs on the Safe Cracker. This particular machine is very slow to show you the pertinent information concerning its status as the machine runs through a sequential display on its visual. However, you can obtain the information almost immediately by inserting currency into the bill acceptor as though you were preparing to play.

Similarly on Fort Knox (Max Bet Version), you cannot obtain the information about the game's status by simply selecting the game on the Odyssey. Nor can this information be accessed by selecting the game and then inserting a bill. Instead, with this game you need to insert a bill while the Odyssey machine is in the menu mode. Then when the Fort Knox (Max Bet Version) is selected, the game will often (but not always) appear with the desired information. This technique always works if the last bet was three credits but not necessarily if the last wager was one or two.

Another very unusual anomaly is on most of the Boom slot machines. It seems that an individual can continuously play one credit per line by simply holding a finger on the "PLAY 1 PER LINE" button. The oddity is that on slot machines as a general rule, you must repeatedly press the spin button in order to repeatedly play. One can play this machine by taping this button down through repeated spins until the firecracker award is hit. I personally use a small pin to wedge the button into a down position. This anomaly seems to go against the unwritten tradition that a player must make some overt action or gesture to play a slot machine. Apparently, sitting motionless can now be considered a form of slot play.

An unusual feature built into a number of slot machines can be seen at the Spacequest Casino in the Las Vegas Hilton in conjunction with their Star Trek: The Experience. These machines have a device with a gap of about two inches. If you place your hand in this gap and break a beam, the slot machine plays in the standard manner as when a handle is pulled or a button is pushed. Futuristic, yes! But unfortunately, no advantageous slot machines are equipped with this device.

As another item, let me mention an anomaly that can actually be exploited to the advantage of the knowledgeable player. On Odyssey machines, if you touch the screen in a spot other than the indicated standard positions, nothing will happen. In fact, the standard locations will not respond if there is already another finger on the screen distorting the tube's magnetic field.

Such information can be useful when you see a non-player seated in front of an Odyssey machine which you know has a game worth playing. You can sit at an adjacent Odyssey and repeatedly pretend to try calling games by touching the screen. Furtively having your other hand holding the side of the Odyssey with the thumb touching the screen will prevent the working of the touch sensitivity device and the generation of the standard machine response. Drawing the individual's attention to the "broken" machine, you can politely ask to play his machine instead. He may respond positively to the predicament, thus eliminating any delay and allowing immediate access to his machine.

Is playing slot machines always a disgusting, deceitful, vulgar, tacky, dirty practice? If you can't answer that after this many pages, you need to reread most of this book.

Another anomaly has to do with the slot machines at Money Maze; so these comments are currently exclusive to Bellagio. The machines in this set are all extremely similar in appearance. There are some minor differences in the various pay schedules but these are of little long run significance.

The unusual quality associated with these machines is their locking mechanism. It is plainly poor. In a period of sixteen days at the Money Maze machines at Bellagio, my wife and I located sixteen open slot machines (more irregularly than one each day). This is an incredible number of slot machines to find open because they were not shut properly by the floor persons during routine hopper fills, etc. It takes a considerable amount of ineptness on the part of the floor persons to perform their duties so poorly that a customer can freely help himself to the very lifeblood of a casino, the money.

The locking mechanism has some sort of plastic catch that was not always holding when the floor persons shut the lid after entry. This failure of the lock required no more than a simple checking by the personnel to verify that the machine was secured. The fact of the matter is that the slot employees were not closing the machines properly. To close a machine properly means to lock a machine and then try to open it without, of course, using the key. This is similar to locking your dwelling and then, after removing the key, turning the doorknob and trying to reenter. This simple security practice of checking, which is a very appropriate procedure to use when leaving your abode, was not being done by any of the slot personnel to our knowledge. They would only press down on the lid, believe it had snapped in place, and never attempt to lift it back up.

Let me assure you that leaving slot machines in an unlocked and unsecured status is an extremely serious matter. Individuals have been fired at various casinos for such gross neglect.

At first, the supervisory personnel at Bellagio were very grateful to be notified of the problem and responded with comps to their restaurants and buffets. By about the tenth finding of an improperly secured machine, the supervisory staff was getting damn good and tired of the ineptness of their underlings being pointed out. By the sixteenth find, Charles Price, assistant slot shift manager, didnít even have the courtesy to say, ìthank you.î But you have to remember that he has a busy schedule and canít really work in two extra words.

Eventually, with this much of a mess repeatedly occurring at Bellagio, I wrote to Bob Oseland, Vice President of Slot Operations, and his supervisor, Bill Bingham, Vice President of Table Games, primarily because the incidents kept repeating, no effective remedial measures seemed to be taken, and plainly the upper management may not have been informed of these ongoing incidents.

Of course, neither Bob Oseland nor Bill Bingham had the time to answer their mail. Actually, now that I think about it, I really donít feel that Charles Price, Bob Oseland, and Bill Bingham are that busy. No, I think theyíre just rude. Since some of these individuals are management personnel and set the tone and standards for Bellagio, I feel we can safely conclude that rudeness is becoming the norm at Bellagio.

Now this machine anomaly may still be present since it would have taken some significant output of funds to properly correct all of the original fifty slot machines (now currently twelve). If you play at Money Maze, you very possibly will locate an open slot machine. In the experience of my wife and me, we only reported the machines and asked for comps to the buffets and restaurants. We never scooped up the money. Our final reward showing Bellagioís true appreciation was our 86íing. With our experience as a guide, you will have to personally decide how to handle the matter when you find such a machine.

# Intermittent Bonus Slots

Intermittent Bonus Slots? Well, hardly anyone calls them that. It is simply a term to describe a type of slot promotion. The setup for one of these promotions usually involves a small set of slot machines in some section of the casino. The machines are generally standard reel machines that are also used elsewhere in the casino. Customers are then expected to play these machines; at times, a light on top of each of these particular machines will indicate that the machines are in a special pay mode.

When the slot machines are in the special pay mode, pays on the slot machine are generally either doubled (2X), tripled (3X), quadrupled (4X), or even quintupled (5X). All the machines in the special area or zone use the same multiplication factor during any special pay period. However, different special pay periods will randomly use different multiplication factors. Occasionally, the slot setup is such that only one machine of the group will receive a bonus award of credits on the machine.

Another feature of a promotion involving Intermittent Bonus Slots is that the machines all go into the special pay period simultaneously. Commonly, a special light on the top of the machine will indicate that the special pay period is in effect for the machine.

Whenever a machine is in the special pay period, the machine should be played as rapidly as possible and at bets of the maximum credits per spin.

Another common characteristic of this type of promotion is that the machine must have been played immediately prior to the start of the special pay period and usually at the maximum wager.

In order to play one of these promotions profitably (not all can be profitably played), you need some type of special information. This can be information of many types: the time interval between the special pay periods (which can be structured in many forms), the amount of play necessary prior to the special pay period, the size of the next multiplication factor, etc. There must be some information in order to work these promos profitably. If you attempt to just play all the time, or randomly, you will, on average, end as a loser.

# Slot Progressives

Just as there are progressives on linked video poker machines, there are also progressives on linked slot machines. Linked slot machines such as Megabucks, with perhaps the ultimate in high jackpots, are examples of such progressives.

On a far more modest scale, many casinos have linked slot machines which all have the potential to hit a select payout and win an extremely large jackpot. These systems bank a small amount of money from each play on the numerous slot machines in the system. Some of these progressives max out, i.e. reach an ultimate high level, and cease growing at that point, even though play on the machines continues. In a jurisdiction such as Nevada, if such a progressive ceases to grow at some point, there must be signs or information to that effect on the machines.

Many of these progressives may be advantageous to play at some unknown value. However, unlike video poker where it is possible to estimate the average number of hands until some particular winning hand occurs (because cards are required to be dealt randomly), it is impossible on a slot machine to make such estimates about the average number of spins until some particular valuable alinement of the reels occurs.

True, we do make such estimates based on unknown internal settings on many of the machines mentioned in this book. However, the events involved occur relatively often by comparison, and so are subject to repeated verification. However, on most progressives the special event simply occurs too rarely to be worthy of investigation as a potential profit-generating tool. With that insurmountable difficulty, it is my current suggestion that you should always avoid playing progressives on slot machines.

# Questionable Slot Promotions

Slot promotions can often be valuable events in which to participate. Many casinos occasionally make slot offers of various sorts to the public. Probably the most common is to give double slot points during some specified period.

In the Las Vegas area, the Imperial Palace has for some time offered double slot points during the hours from midnight to 8:00 A.M. Clearly, the purpose of this is to induce slot play at odd hours. The promotion certainly must be somewhat effective because the Imperial Palace has had this offer for some considerable time.

Now the Imperial Palace also had an offer whereby if you collected twenty points on your slot card in a 24-hour period, you would receive a free buffet. If you played during the aforementioned time period, you could earn the twenty points for the free buffet with only half the slot play.

The above was not a slot promotion to avoid. In fact, most slot promotions offered by major casinos are run in a proper manner. Major casinos generally have a reputation to uphold and strive to be more than fair in dealing with their customers.

However, there are occasions when you should consider avoiding a slot promotion. This is generally when the slot offer is made by a small bar, tavern, or restaurant. And even more so if the establishment is a small, privately run business.

As an example of what can happen to you, consider what did happen to my wife and me at a local establishment in the Las Vegas area. It seems the proprietors at Madison Ave. Bar and Grille made an offer to the public by hanging signs in the establishment and also by a rather large distribution of fliers in the area immediately surrounding the bar. The offer, named Rack Pack, was that anyone playing ten racks of dollar tokens (one hundred tokens per rack) through a slot or video poker machine would receive an eleventh rack free, which also had to be played through the machine. All play had to be completed within a thirty-day period. This offer was really ridiculously generous and, as came to be seen, was very poorly structured.

The first type of problem that arose involved changes in the rules. The first of these involved a requirement that five coins per wager or spin be made rather than simply single-coin play. Later, this rule was altered to max bet at all times, which on some games was a wager of ten dollars per play or spin. The final alteration was a rule change that an individual had to play certain one dollar slot games rather than a game of his choice. Then the entire offer was abruptly canceled.

I and several other individuals who had played somewhat under ten racks were not permitted to complete our play and receive the free eleventh rack to also play. We were simply told that the offer was canceled. In my case, even the record of my play could not be located.

Checking with the Nevada Gaming Commission, my wife and I were informed that the Commission is primarily concerned with the actual gaming, in this case the operation of the machines, and has very limited authority over promotions. The Commission is also sometimes limited by the standard restriction placed on most promotions, i.e., "management reserves all rights." This or a similar statement gives broad leeway to the establishment to modify the promotion, especially regarding problems and inconsistencies that arise or require clarification.

The Nevada Gaming Commission does have somewhat broad powers under a proviso of protecting the reputation of gaming in general. After about a week or so, the Gaming Commission informed Madison Ave. that they would be required to permit individuals to complete their play with regard to the promotion. Superficially, this would appear to rectify matters.

However, the upshot was that Madison Ave. Bar and Grille had told individuals for a period of many days that the promotion was canceled, but now that they were required to permit those same individuals to complete their participation in the promotion, the establishment was not required to reinform those individuals they had just sent away or to extend the play time by the amount of time that the offer had been suspended.

Of course, many of the individuals who had played partially through the ten-rack requirement simply left the establishment and never knew that they could have finished the promotion. This type of remedy clearly favors the establishment.

There were additional problems at Madison Ave. Some customers' records of play could not be located and in a few cases were in dispute as to the accuracy of the number of racks played. The bar had one employee I personally caught attempting to short me during a transaction. Probably the most telling physical item in this establishment that should have acted as a warning of the shenanigans to come was a sign that read, "PLEASE SHOW SOME CLASS AND LEAVE THE GLASS" giving some indication of the general ambiance.

One tragedy is that there are many bars and restaurants throughout the Las Vegas area that have slot promotions and handle the offers in a fair and equitable manner. They are, by loose association, the ones who are sullied by the actions of the proprietors like those at Madison Ave.

An underlying problem at most small establishments is that they can't take heavy losses. Any losses suffered are not the losses of some abstract multi-million dollar corporation. Losses of even a few thousand dollars could in some establishments have a serious impact resulting in employee layoffs or closing.

My advice in cases involving an extremely generous offer at a small business is that you should be very careful and thoughtful about investing any serious money or time into the promotion. You may find yourself in a continually changing or totally defunct offer. In the current climate, be extremely cautious when becoming involved in slot promotions at small establishments that have gaming as a sideline.

# The Slot Point Fiasco

I sat next to my wife at the Stardust, watching her play two multigame Odyssey machines both with Buccaneer Gold and both at two daggers. She was playing these two side-by-side machines at this level not because we expected to make a significant profit but to gather more data for my book. What we don't do for the readership!

During her play on one of the machines, I noticed that our slot card seemed to accumulate too many slot points. After we left the machines, we began to analyze just what had happened.

We decided to return to the one machine that had an overly generous slot card reader and give it some play to see just how we would fare. By playing single-deck blackjack (called Top Hat 21 on the Odyssey), we will be assured of losing at a rate of at most 5%, since naturals pay even money and doubling is restricted to 10 and 11.

Beginning to play blackjack at one dollar per hand on this machine, we soon discovered that the machine was awarding five slot points for every dollar played. Since slot points in the Stardust Slot Club are each worth ten cents, this could be a losing situation. In fact, we were so confident that we began playing at two dollars per hand, thus benefitting by ten slot points per hand. Of course, we could have played at 100 credits ($25) per hand on this quarter Odyssey, but that would have made for very big financial swings (for a slot machine) as we variously won and lost. At four thousand points, we took a breather while I went to the slot club booth.

On arriving and presenting my slot card and ID, somehow I came to appreciate that I was being treated as a special valued customer. I asked for complimentary dinners, and I sensed a certain disappointment in the Stardust personnel when I told them we already had room accommodations elsewhere. I also requested and received $400 for the 4000 accumulated slot points.

To emphasize how extreme the situation is getting here, let us examine certain other pieces of information not mentioned above. In order to get a single slot point on one of these quarter Odyssey machines, a player must play thirty dollars through the machine. In order to accumulate 4,000 slot points, he would have to put $120,000 through the slot machine. Even though the machine will take $25 wagers on this blackjack game, a player would have to play 4,800 $25 hands to obtain 4000 slot points. This would have been somewhat awkward because this Odyssey machine had a broken bill acceptor and the initial wagering required hand-feeding of coins.

But the numbers are almost extreme beyond belief. If my wife and I had played in shifts all through the night playing $25 hands of blackjack, we could definitely have run the number of slot points to a total over 1,000,000. Imagine asking the slot club personnel for $100,000 when they opened the booth in the morning!

But slot clubs aren't run by total ninnies. The amount of action necessary to generate one million slot points at the Stardust on a quarter slot machine would be $30 million of cash in. They would never go for this in any way. The Stardust can be beaten, but not quite that way. Let me assure everyone, there would have been no $100,000 payment to us in the morning because of a computer foul-up.

Slot clubs can and do at times confiscate an individual's slot points and refuse to honor their debt to the customer. I personally had this happen to me at the Tropicana as an outgrowth of a tacky scheme that some of their security force were pulling. That incident was discussed in the local newspaper, *Valley Explorer,* to the Trop's displeasure, but the upshot was that the Tropicana has retained all of my slot food comps ($206). But crookedness at the Trop (such as the nine-count complaint filed by the Nevada Gaming Control Board leading to a $250,000 fine *[Las Vegas Review-Journal, August 21, 1999]* which makes my $206 in lost food comps seem insignificant) is an old story by now and not the point of this discussion.

So just how should a player handle this situation at the Stardust? We decided to add 10,000 points to the slot card. That would look like we played only $300,000 through the machine and with $25 hands of blackjack would appear to require only 12,000 hands. Even that was stretching credulity.

Returning to the Odyssey, we then ran the slot points, now at six, up to over 10,000. The next morning, while receiving the paperwork for two complimentary breakfasts, I removed the entire amount from the slot card. After breakfast, we added another 6514 points to this slot card without incurring a net loss while playing this blackjack game. We then took a break and went to Westward Ho and the Riviera.

Returning to the Stardust about an hour later, we found that the slot point dispensing mechanism on this Odyssey had been adjusted. The mechanism functioned in a standard manner and the "bonus period" was over. Ironically, the bill acceptor was still out of commission.

Roughly 20,000 slot points had been accumulated in about 12 hours on one single account. The loss from the actual play was $68.25. Without a quibble, the Stardust honored all the slot points earned by us and other individuals from this aberrant machine. At this point, I might comment that if you or your spouse has an ID in a maiden name, then you could also obtain an additional slot account in that name and collect additional funds.

In retrospect, I have come to believe that the computer personnel never informed the slot club that they had made a gross error. Instead, the computer technicians simply let the the Stardust Slot Club think of us as valued customers.

You should note other facts in this situation. Part of the success here may have been the result of playing many hands of only two dollars which each generated ten slot points. To have played $25 hands each generating 125 slot points might have caused the computer to trigger certain alerts for supervisory personnel. One must be careful when being greedy.

Also, note that this entire incident does not involve any malfunction of any machine. This episode is all the result of ineptness on the part of some Stardust computer programmer(s) in improperly installing and overseeing the components of their system. This situation is similar to incidents in which slot machines have accidentally been improperly adjusted by casino technicians and then dispensed too many jackpots. Such a casino would certainly not be able to claim that it did not owe payment for a jackpot because its own employees had made a boo-boo. However, slot club benefits are not in the same category as direct winnings.

The easiest casino defense against this type of incident is to have a slot card system that does not directly inform the player about how many slot points he has or how many he has just earned. Forcing the player to continuously inquire at the slot booth for such information might give the casino an opportunity to adjust the player's slot data without his knowledge. Alternatively, a casino slot club could have a system where slot points are not convertible to cash. This also would have negated our actions in this situation. However, both of these defenses are alternatives that a good slot club would generally prefer not to implement because such a change would adversely affect relations with their many regular customers.

This gross error has certain qualities that have made me wonder if, perchance, instead of a simple mistake, there was some underlying misconduct and an unusual attempt by insiders to drain the casino. This is purely speculation on my part, but casinos can be strange places.

From this incident, there is one thing that I came to realize beyond a shadow of a doubt: slot points are not just some petty pieces of nonsense. They can add up to real value in the right situation.

# Free Slot Play

Free slot play is a gimmick that casinos use to attract potential customers into their establishments. Usually, but not always, the prizes are trivial or virtually nonexistent. Bally's has one where the prize is $1,000,000, but don't hold your breath. At the other end of the spectrum is the free play machine at Slots-A-Fun, which quite often dispenses fifty cents during the two free pulls any person over 21 can receive. Other places like the Riviera dispense numerous free logo items but nothing in cash except for very large wins.

But below is actually a method to get totally free slot play on a regular quarter or nickel slot machine. Let me assure the reader, before continuing, that this technique is probably the cheapest legal scam I have learned about. It even plays on the casino's generosity (yes, they do have that quality sometimes). But apparently, it does work successfully and so it is included for your consideration.

At least three of the casinos in the Las Vegas area (Bally's, Caesars Palace, and Sunset Station), have a policy of giving the recipient of any hand pay on a slot machine enough extra funds to get to the next dollar. For example, if the player has $113.75 in credits on a quarter machine (presumably from winnings) and presses the Cash Out button, the slot machine will lock up and an attendant will arrive and hand-pay the player $114.00. So the player will get an extra quarter.

To get free slot play at one of these casinos, one can follow the following format. First choose a machine, such as a quarter Odyssey which has the game of blackjack. Insert one dollar and play a single 25¢ hand. If you win and are at $1.25 on the credit meter, then you are ready for stage two. If perchance you should lose this initial hand of blackjack, continue playing 25¢ hands until the credit meter is either at $1.25 or unfortunately $0.25.

Then you are ready for stage two.

Insert somewhere between $100 and $150 into the bill acceptor. Let us use $110 for our discussion. You will now have either 441 or 445 credits on your slot machine. Then press the Cash Out button. The Odyssey machine will not attempt to pay with coins but instead will indicate a hand-pay is needed. A floor person will be along shortly to assist you. Generally, you will receive either $111 or $112. The quarter is rounded up to the nearest dollar. So you either make 75¢ cash or have had a small amount of free slot play. There is generally no checking to verify any significant slot play. At the worst, you will receive either the $110.25 or $111.25 which is due. Also remember not to tip the floor people in this situation. You simply can't afford it.

I warned you this was petty and cheap, but absolutely legal. This activity may seem extremely worthless, but be assured it will at least be more valuable than that $1,000,000 free slot pull at Bally's.

# Token Scams

Strictly speaking, token scams are not a part of this book's material; but since the metal casino tokens are a consequence of slot machines, we will discuss the tokens to some extent.

Many years ago, real silver dollars were used in slot machines and at the gaming tables. However, with the termination of U.S. silver coinage, these all passed from the casino scene. The casino needed a substitute for the passing of the silver dollars and initiated legislation enabling them to issue metal chips to be used only for gaming purposes.

Consequently, casinos began to have metal chips issued for their customers' use. Also with the passage of time, inflation entered the picture and made the playing of dollar slot machines more inviting.

An outgrowth of all of this is that there are individuals who collect the metal chips of the various casinos. With the spreading of casinos across the country, this collecting has grown considerably.

Every casino will, in time, need additional chips because there is a drift of the chips away from the establishment. Consequently, a casino will eventually decide to obtain more metal chips. Sometimes, the casino will simply elect to use the old pattern with a new date; but more likely in recent years, the entire to-ken will be redesigned. Thus, the casinos generate additional material for souvenirs and collectors. This, of course, benefits the casino.

In the course of changing token patterns, sometimes things go a little haywire. The alteration of the tokens can create unforeseen problems. The most recent problem of this sort occurred at the Flamingo Hilton. It seems that the thickness of their old tokens was significantly different than the thickness of their new tokens. Well, so what?

The difference in thickness of the tokens was such that you could sort the tokens that were dispensed on cashing out on a dollar machine. If you were to make a stack of 19 of the older thicker tokens and a stack of twenty of the newer thinner tokens, both stacks would be close to the same height.

Now, the problem was that the racks for dollar tokens at the Flamingo could be filled in such a manner that they appeared full while, in fact, each of the five rows or only some of the rows were short by a single one dollar token.

Initially, the problem only affected the Flamingo Hilton itself. Various ne'er-do-wells would move chips around the casino to obtain an extra dollar or so when exchanging a rack of dollar tokens for currency. It should be noted that at that time, except at the main cashier cage, the Flamingo Hilton did not have coin counting machines that would count dollar tokens.

After a bit, the change booth personnel came to realize that they were being victimized by certain regulars. The change booth personnel were being forced to remember these particular individuals and to always check racks from them. But change booth personnel shouldn't have to busy themselves repeatedly counting racks of tokens.

After a while, the Flamingo, rather than replace many of its tokens, made all of its racks identical and to exacting standards. The measurements were such that twenty new tokens would fit snugly while 19 of the older thicker tokens would wobble a noticeable amount.

This helped the Flamingo deal with the problem, but many of the surrounding casinos became the new recipients of the thicker tokens. Nineteen of the thicker Flamingo tokens began to show up in racks at these casinos.

Eventually, the Flamingo put change counters that could count dollar tokens into all its change booths. Other casinos either had already done so or followed suit.

Racks of dollar tokens are now almost invariably dumped into a counter and not handled in the former manner of visual inspection of the rack. So the problem ended. Well, mostly it ended. You can still sort out 19 older thicker Flamingo dollar slot tokens, place the 19 as a row in another rack of tokens (in the Flamingo or a nearby casino), carry the rack to a dollar carousel (which usually doesn't have a counting machine) and get an extra dollar for the effort.

Welcome to Las Vegas.

# The Over-Payer

When I finished playing the machine, I pressed Cash Out and the 37 quarter credits ($9.25) were converted into coins, which toppled into my bucket. I took my bucket to the person at the change booth and was given the $10.75 that the counter indicated. What happened? Well, I'd found an over-payer.

An over-payer is part of the casino's war on poverty. Unfortunately for the casino, it doesn't generally know it's fighting. Basically, an over-payer simply releases too many coins when it dispenses sizable numbers of coins. As a general rule, an over-payer only gets worse from the casino's perspective. The payout system does not right itself and most slot machines do not have a backup system to double-check the dispensing of coins.

An over-payer can exist for a surprising amount of time in the casino. This is, in part, because many of the customers do not know exactly how many coins they are supposed to have when they visit the change booth or cashier to change their coins into paper currency. Usually, any discrepancy the customer may notice tends to be associated in the customer's mind with the cashier's counting device. In actual fact, the machines that the cashiers use are far more accurate than most slot machine payout systems; also the cashiers' machines are checked periodically for accuracy.

If an over-payer is small in its over-payments, it will, in the routine course of things, go undetected by the casino.

As I understand the current law, it is illegal (in fact, a felony in Nevada) to simply bleed these machines of funds. Whether anyone has ever been prosecuted for this type of activity, I have no idea. Nonetheless, most players consider over-payers a delight to find and definitely worth the effort if handled properly.

There are really four common ways a person can handle an over-payer.

First, if the over-pays are small, one could simply wait for the slot machine's payout system to become worse, monitoring the machine by inserting a ten dollar bill every few days. The slot machine may take some time, depending on the amount of play it receives, to become much worse. If it doesn't break down fast enough to accommodate one's schedule, simply forget it. An over-payer that returns too little is simply not worth the effort.

Now if the over-payer is fairly strong (5% to 10%), one has three more options. In the first case, one can simply insert bill after bill and cash out the coins. This bleeding of the machine will almost certainly irritate those in charge; even if a person isn't prosecuted, he will be thrown out on a permanent basis. But if an individual does do this, it is best to have a partner to assist with taking the cupfuls of change to the cashier. In fact, the couple should take turns at this part of the activity. After a few hundred dollars, the machine will need what is called a hopper fill, which is a reloading of the machine with more coins. Casinos monitor the refilling of machines, so this will create a problem if done too often.

When the attendant comes to fill the slot machine, a bleeder will casually ask just how much is in the bag that is being emptied into the machine. This information is important because the player needs to calculate just how much can be inserted into the machine before it will need another refill. The draining can then be stopped prior to such a need. Then another unknowing customer can perchance be the one to call for the next hopper fill while the bleeder will be off elsewhere until tomorrow.

Of course, the bleeder can simply bleed the machine until he is thrown out by the casino personnel. But that is seldom done by any rational person.

The alternative to straight bleeding of the machine is to be an honest person. After discovering the over-payer, simply report the malfunctioning device to an appropriate casino employee. Make certain to take special note of the person informed and the time. If the casino personnel do not respond and close down the machine immediately, then I believe the illegality of removing funds from the machine becomes blurred. This is because the casino, through its personnel, has indicated that the matter is of little or no concern, or perhaps is the way the casino wishes the machine to be.

The tragedy from the casino's outlook is that reports of this nature to their personnel are often simply ignored. I myself have reported the same over-payer on three separate shifts before the machine was finally properly repaired by a slot mechanic.

Finally, the most lucrative method of draining an over-payer is to actually play the machine. This requires a rather strong over-payer. The individual simply plays the machine and cashes out rather often. If this activity is worked as a team, the action can continue around the clock. The average losses suffered as the reels are spun are small compared to the benefits received on cashing out. What makes this so effective is the play itself. The casino wants the action on the machine. As the hopper is refilled again and again, the casino senses that this is a part of the normal course of events associated with standard heavy play.

There is one other type of over-payer that has so far passed unmentioned here. With this type of over-payer, the problem is not in the payout system but in the bill acceptor. On extremely rare occasions, a slot mechanic will repair the bill acceptor system incorrectly by putting a critical component designed for one denomination of machine into the system of a larger denomination of machine. In such cases, the bill acceptor will recognize the paper currency properly but will convert the information into credits based on the denomination of a different machine.

The only time I have heard of this occurring was at a Piggy Bankin' machine at the Flamingo Hilton in Las Vegas. It seems that a repair person put a convertor designed for a quarter machine into a dollar denomination machine. This created a situation whereby a player, on inserting a paper bill, e.g. twenty dollars, would receive four times the proper number of credits, i.e. eighty credits instead of twenty.

The day the repair error on this machine was discovered, several knowledgeable individuals had drained the machine and left after extracting a small bundle of free funds. Many other regular customers also played this machine, I'm sure, but with a play involving only tokens from a bucket, the problem was not noticed by them.

If you think that hopper fills of $400 each are a substantial loss for the casino, let me assure you that it is possible to extract even more with a little additional patience. One does this by playing the machine for a rather long period of time (perhaps an hour or two) while inserting bills every now and then to raise the credit meter higher. Then when the credit meter is near a thousand dollars, simply cash out. The player will receive the amount that is dispensed into the tray; but rather than finish paying him by repeatedly refilling the hopper, the casino personnel will elect to complete his pay with paper currency. The slot play will be thought of as simply a gradual buildup of winnings. With this procedure, a player can actually receive more than the number of coins in the bag of a standard hopper fill while the situation is recorded as a single fill.

And, of course, the Flamingo Hilton had at least one friendly customer do that little trick also. There were by early evening already four hopper fills made on this particular slot machine. When you realize that the previous fill on that machine prior to its "repair" had been three days earlier, you start to sense how extreme this situation was. Numerous fills on dollar slot machines in such short periods of time are uncommon.

After the fifth hopper fill, a slot mechanic was called to check the machine. At the Flamingo Hilton and many other major casinos, standard procedure requires that a machine be checked after five hopper fills within twenty-four hours. The mechanic glanced through the machine, making a few routine checks. Happily, he did not tamper with the "luck meter." The machine passed his cursory test and the couple at the machine resumed play.

After the sixth fill, the floor person commented, "This must be the luckiest machine in town!" He wasn't exactly wrong, but he wasn't exactly right.

After the seventh hopper fill, a surveillance team of at least six people (change people, slot personnel, floor people, slot mechanics, etc.) was hurriedly put together to watch the action on the machine from a distance. The overhead video surveillance crew was asked to quickly review previous film footage. The feeding of five dollar bills into the bill acceptor still was passing as the feeding of twenty dollar bills because twenty was continuously appearing as the number of credits purchased. But the entire scene was getting out of hand.

Then suddenly another couple arrived at the wayward machine. The two couples exchanged greetings; one team cashed out and moved off the machine while the other took over the play. The replacement team continued at the machine, but it was too late. It had gone on far too long. After a little over a half-hour, the casino personnel simply took the machine away from the second couple and crammed a dollar bill into the bill acceptor, finally confirming their suspicions when four credits appeared on the meter.

So after seven hopper fills resulting in the dispensing of at least $2800 of casino funds in less than twenty-four hours, the machine was shut down. This type of gross error in slot repair is the type of mistake that gets slot mechanics fired. He'll be dearly missed by many people. But more importantly, now you're ready. You can start looking for an over-payer of your own.

# The Open Machine

Open, says me! And lo, the locked doors on the slot machine opened to those magic words. Well, don't you wish?

Open machines come in two varieties: the machines that you find already open and the machines that happen to open while they're being played. The latter are far more valuable.

If you happen perchance to find a machine that is already open, there isn't really much you can do except call over security; they in turn will get the floor personnel to properly lock the machine. Your reward will probably be a free meal (for two if you ask), since some people wouldn't hesitate to unload not only the hopper but also the far more valuable bill acceptor. Let me assure you that this is a serious crime and getting caught will result in a trip to the metropolitan police department.

Instead let us assume that you are actually playing a slot machine and it comes open. This has never happened to me but did happen to the person on the machine next to mine. In this case, the player may think that he has hit a special jackpot by lining up some mystery pay combination on the reels. Some slot machines do have extremely weird pay schedules and mystery payouts. In such a case, couldn't the player reasonably take his winnings from both the hopper and the bill acceptor with a clear conscience? After relieving the machine of the "winnings," he'd be sure to close the door. Some machines are wired into the computer system to alert personnel if a slot machine door is open for too long. So, he'd try not to disturb the friendly folks who service the machines by taking the winnings quickly and quietly without a lot of hoopla. He'd also consider the pleasant idea of taking a break from all that good luck and dropping by another casino for a while! *[Ed. note: He'd also better have a good attorney in case he was caught on video!]*

# Meltdown

The total collapse of a slot machine is a meltdown. A meltdown doesn't happen often. In fact, in all the countless machines that my wife and I have played over the years, only three times have we experienced a meltdown. All three actually happened to me.

The first meltdown occurred at the Flamingo Hilton. My wife was playing a dollar Piggy Bankin' slot machine and I decided to examine the surrounding Piggy Bankin' machines which were also of the one dollar denomination. I pressed the spin button on an adjacent machine to trigger the illumination of the screen. But something happened and the machine did not respond properly. The machine generated an error message. I was so inexperienced that I did not understand what had transpired. A change girl was passing by and I asked her to call a floor person.

In a few minutes, a floor person arrived and I explained that the machine was not responding properly. She made some minor cursory adjustments but also was unable to get the machine to respond properly. She explained that the Piggy Bankin' machine would have to be turned off until a slot mechanic could examine it. She noted the only number on the screen, 521, which happened to be in the rectangle marked credits. She taped up the machine, called in the malfunction, obtained the $521 in U.S. currency, and counted it out to me.

My wife had by this time finished playing her machine and she watched this fiasco. I never really tried to cheat the Flamingo. They just simply cheated themselves. I have such mixed feelings about myself in this matter. I know now that the 521 was an error message; and the floor person, in a state of inexperience, read the message as credits due to me. I doped this all out as we headed out the door with $521 from a machine I hadn't put a cent into.

I realize now what I should do to right this matter. If the Hiltons ever lose all those hotels they own and need some help making ends meet . . . well, you've got it, guys.

The second meltdown I ever experienced occurred when I was playing at the Stardust on a Piggy Bankin' machine of the one dollar denomination. Amazingly, I had just hit the jackpot by alining three pigs on the payline. It was the first time I had ever made such an alinement. The machine started to pay me the first part of the jackpot in tokens (the second part is hand paid) and was dropping tokens into the tray. Suddenly, the machine stopped and a cryptic numerical message appeared on the exterior area where the play information is posted.

I naively thought the machine only needed a hopper fill, so I gathered up the 59 tokens in the tray and began playing another machine nearby. When the floor people finally arrived, I came to realize that a win of a thousand dollars (based on one credit per spin) was in serious jeopardy. The slot machine did not need a hopper fill. There had been a meltdown. The error message on the machine indicated that the slot machine had lost its memory. The machine had stopped paying the thousand dollar jackpot because it couldn't remember why it was paying out money. The slot machine couldn't remember the three symbols alined on the reels.

I learned that evening that modern slot machines have a memory of the last ten games. These are stored and can be accessed by the casino personnel if need be. But in my case, the coded message meant, "I don't remember anything."

Gaming Control was called; Williams (the Piggy Bankin' company) was called; and the machine was locked up until it could be examined by expert technicians. Many weeks later, I was finally paid the rest of my winnings, $2441. $2441! That's twenty five hundred dollars less the fifty-nine the machine had already dispensed.

When the Piggy Bankin' slot machine lost its mind, it generated an error message that, among other things, placed a two in the area indicating the number of credits wagered. That was a design flaw and I was the accident waiting to happen. With no memory and a two in the credits played area, the decision by Gaming was that I was a $2500 winner.

A fifteen hundred dollar bonus! You might think I love meltdowns. In a way, I do; yet I realize that they have the potential to work the opposite way and possibly some day I'll suffer a loss because of a meltdown. Sometimes I hate to think of the future.

The third meltdown I experienced was at the Imperial Palace on a Buccaneer Gold machine. It was far less dramatic. I was playing a machine which someone had left in disgust, although I wasn't certain exactly why. There were three daggers (an advantageous play) and I inserted a twenty dollar bill. Somewhat over eighty spins later, I was inserting another twenty dollar bill. In just a few spins, I received the fourth dagger on the payline. Then suddenly the machine blanked out with the screen going totally dark. When the machine came back up, I had no additional dagger.

Surprisingly, the change girl had seen the blackout, and after working through several supervisors, I was granted my request by the return of my entire forty dollar investment. In this case, I was fortunate that the change girl had noticed the failure. Although it was not mentioned to me, I sensed from the supervisory personnel that I was not the first person to have had trouble with that particular machine. The machine was shut down and the slot manufacturer called.

Casinos despise such machine failures because not only can the situation alienate customers, but the machine downtime is a cost to the establishment. In the Stardust situation, the machine was down for four days while Gaming Control investigated.

Although it is rare, if you ever do have a meltdown on a slot machine you're playing, tell the slot department personnel. My experience is that they will try to do right by you.

# The Search

In every casino, there is a coin which is lost. Your job is to find it. It's on the floor, under a seat, between the machines; it's somewhere. Locating it may take days, so don't put too much effort into the search. I have heard, even read, that there are individuals who make a living looking for lost funds in the casinos. If that's so, let me assure you that they don't have a very high standard of living.

Searching for funds in casinos has gotten the nickname silvermining. Besides being weak financially, this can be very boring. However, if you are visiting numerous casinos anyway, I definitely recommend casually integrating this activity into your routine.

While silvermining, you can incorporate such things as looking for Marlboro miles. This current promotion supplies a good example of another item you can readily find discarded in the casino setting. In the course of many months, you will eventually accumulate more Marlboro miles than people with acute lung cancer. These will, in turn, change into an array of Marlboro gear through their catalog.

Returning to silvermining, it is possible to find funds that have plainly been abandoned. Near the cashier's cage or the change booth, you can occasionally find discarded pennies. I know it's small, but I've always gathered them.

More valuable spots to find droppings are around the slot machines. It is interesting to me that it is perfectly proper to find and keep coins that are on the floor; and yet I was once actually told by a security officer to leave the Tropicana for the day because I had found some coins on the floor. However, I believe the Tropicana security department was riddled with so much crookedness and corruption as mentioned elsewhere, that my expulsion was, I believe, based on othetr matters.

Another spot to locate coins in a casino is in the coin returns at the bar. Although I have heard that there are individuals who actually go by the bar and endeavor to check all the coin returns, I do not recommend that you follow that procedure. I understand that the bartenders have had individuals removed from the establishment for this activity. This searching is not an illegal act; it's just usually done by the type of customer the casino does not want, i.e. one without money.

My wife and I do not go around poking in all the coin returns at the bars; but if we do happen to go to the bar for a while, we always check where we are seated. That type of activity will be tolerated, just as it is quite acceptable to check the coin returns on pay phones when making a phone call.

Another overlooked spot in a casino at which to find funds is at the crap table. Occasionally, slot players drift over to shoot craps and find it convenient to use the lower shelf designed for drinks as a place to set a bucket full of coins. Not surprisingly, when they leave the crap table, the bucket of coins is easily forgotten.

The most profitable place in a casino to find funds is at and in the slot machines. First of all, you will in time find coins and tokens left in the trays of the slot machines themselves. Unlike the coin returns on the bar-top slot machines, removing this coinage is illegal as it's not yours. However, if you insert a coin into the slot machine, then that machine is your machine and you can take all the money in the tray as your own. A slightly cheaper way to become the owner of the funds in the tray of the slot machine is to insert a bill into the bill acceptor. This act of inserting value into the machine also makes the machine yours. However, in this case, you can simply cash out the credits and everything is properly yours.

The single most valuable find, short of locating a purse or wallet, are credits left on a slot machine. This again is a situation in which it is illegal to simply cash out the credits and take the coinage as your own. In fact, as I understand the law, this act would be a felony. However, if again you insert a coin or alternatively a bill into the bill acceptor, the machine becomes your machine and the entire amount is yours.

I have heard of individuals placing their hand over either the spot where coins are inserted or alternatively the spot where bills are inserted, thus simulating the insertion of funds before playing or cashing out the machineís credits. I assume that is as close to the minimum as one could do to fake properly obtaining the machine.

Of course, for you to properly do this, the machine must actually have been deserted. Don't try this action when you know full well that the machine is being played by the woman who was sitting next to her husband and has just gone to the restroom for a moment. I am talking about machines that are plainly deserted.

The last thing to deal with in this chapter has to do with finding valuables such as purses or wallets. These, of course, are not yours and will in no way ever properly become your property, unless you follow the proper procedure. Initially, you might think that such an item should be taken to the security podium in order for that department to locate the legitimate owner. This sounds simple enough, and yet it is not the thing to do.

The trouble with this approach is that the security department will take the item and endeavor to locate the owner. That part is still okay. But if the security department fails to find the owner because, for example, the item contains no ID, then the item reverts to the casino. Many casinos have rules like this which they religiously follow. If the item is a coin purse with paper currency and no ID, the unclaimed item will revert to the casino as owner. The casino has no obligation to return an unclaimed item to you.

If that type of rule-making by the casinos irritates you, let me suggest the following two approaches. First, you can yourself open the purse or wallet, seek an ID, and finding one, then page the owner. With this approach, any tip given for returning the item will flow to you rather than an intervening party. If you do not wish to page the individual for some reason (time constraints, etc.) or if this approach is tried and fails, then take the item to the police department and transfer it to them with the stipulation that if the item is unclaimed, you wish to receive it. They have procedures to accommodate that request and will handle the matter appropriately. You may sometime find yourself several hundred dollars ahead by handling the matter in this manner.

Another method of handling a found purse/wallet is to toss it into an official mailbox. In this regard, I should stress that I am talking about an official Postal Service mailbox. Many casinos have "mailboxes" that are simply collection sites from which the cards, letters, etc. are taken and then transferred to a postal official. Tossing the purse/wallet in such a receptacle is akin to handing it to the casino security department. So you must be certain to place the item into a U.S. Postal Service mailbox. The postal authorities will examine the contents for indicators of ownership and route the item on its way.

Of course, you could take the purse or wallet home with you and ponder the great question, "Why did this person throw away a seemingly valuable item?"

# Hopper Fill Heists

Hopper fill heists must happen every day in a large city like Las Vegas. A few are the result of thieves, but most are the result of plain ignorance on the part of novice players.

A hopper is the part of a slot machine that contains the coins or tokens which are dispensed during ordinary play. The hoppers must routinely be filled because the slot machines empty of money. This filling is even more common on the current scene than in the past, because many customers use bill acceptors rather than hand-feeding coins. And lastly, a heist is the improper taking of funds.

Most hopper fill heists occur because a novice player simply cashes out on a slot machine; when the machine stops dispensing coins or tokens, the player thinks he has been paid in full. The player then departs, leaving a machine that needs additional coinage in order to complete the payout. When slot personnel find deserted machines in need of a hopper fill, they have instructions to fill the machine, and when the pay process is completed, to play the dispensed coins back into the slot machine until all the coins and generated credits are used, thus returning the entire amount to the casino.

Sometimes a machine that needs a hopper fill is approached by another novice player and in the confusion, the hopper fill occurs and the dispensed coinage winds up in his possession. This act of receiving the dispensed coinage is improper; but in the great scheme of things, the occurrence passes unnoticed. Technically, there has been a theft; but since some totally inexperienced players have no idea what is happening, it is difficult to treat such individuals as thieves.

On a few occasions, I have seen an individual who completely understood that his machine needed a hopper fill but elected to leave the machine because he considered his time too valuable to be spent waiting for a hopper fill that was for only one or two coins.

Sitting down at a deserted slot machine that needs a hopper fill and obtaining or attempting to obtain the funds that will be forthcoming is a criminal act. Yes, I've seen plenty of individuals get away with this activity, but I suggest that you avoid such things.

I even know a few individuals who have been caught attempting a hopper fill heist. In each case, the film footage clearly showed that the individual had not been playing the machine. None of them was prosecuted; but each was expelled from the casino on a permanent basis, because if there is one thing a casino cannot tolerate, it's theft.

More valuable than improperly obtaining a simple hopper fill is obtaining jackpots that another player has won. This has, to some extent, fallen on hard times because most modern machines attempt to clearly indicate to the player that he has won a significant amount of funds. Even if the player were to leave the machine because perhaps he understood English poorly and could not read the signs, another individual who tried to obtain the jackpot would find himself in serious trouble because, at most major casinos, all large jackpots are subject to video verification.

# Till Tappers

Till tappers are bold and aggressive, to say the least. A till tapper is an individual who helps himself to a token or two from the till of someone else's slot machine.

I once caught a till tapper at the Tropicana in Las Vegas when he was reaching into the till on the slot machine that my wife was playing. I collared him and he dropped the swag; but one of the tokens fell on the floor, so I'm sure it was clear just what had almost transpired. While he didn't get away with tokens, the change girl came by, noticed the fracas and notified security. When security arrived, they separated the two of us.

I was asked a few questions and told the officers the above information. I presumed that they were going to have the individual transported away by the local police department. Some few minutes later, the security personnel came back and suggested that my wife and I should leave, since the other party "may have some friends around." Although I balked at this idea, they insisted we depart and so we did. I learned a day or two later that nothing happened to the other party and he had remained in the Tropicana Casino. That was really the very first experience we had with the Tropicana security force.

If you don't understand what's wrong in the above situation, let me fill in some information. It is not the Tropicana's decision as to whether criminal charges are filed; it is my wife's right to decide if charges are pressed. What security may have been covering up in this situation, we never did learn. But requiring us to leave instead of the thief indicates misconduct on their part.

But I always try to learn from any situation, no matter how distasteful, and so I did here. The proper response on our part should have been to call the police department and explain the situation that had occurred. They have the right to enter the casino and confiscate the video tape of any serious incident. (In major casinos, slot machines are under video surveillance. In smaller casinos this is not necessarily so. In absolutely every casino, the gaming tables are required by law to be under video surveillance.) If the police find the actions of security out of line, that will be noted and might entail further action.

So if you have some crazy incident arise in any casino and the situation is handled in a questionable manner or in a way you feel is improper, contact the local law enforcement. The police are not about to let serious matters just slide. The casino authority is not the last resort.

Returning to our discussion of till tappers, there are very few who will plainly reach under your nose to try to swipe some coinage. Yet my wife had this happen at the Flamingo. A woman was playing an adjacent machine and boldly reached into my wife's tray and removed a couple of quarters as my wife was cashing out. The cashing out is important because my wife knew exactly how many quarters were involved. My wife spoke to the lady, who feigned poor English. My wife then flagged a floor person who dealt with the lady and told her that if she didn't return the coins, a security officer would be called. Somehow the lady understood his English better than my wife's and returned the two quarters before she departed. Do not be surprised that till tappers have a lot of gall. It's part of the territory.

A variant approach is one in which a team of two will sit on opposite sides of an unsuspecting target with one distracting the customer while the tapper on the other side grabs a little. Even this is not very common because the take is far too slow.

The ideal time to tap is when the player goes to get a cup or bucket. To initiate this, the tapper removes all the cups and buckets in the surrounding area. Then on cashing out, the customer will need to get a container. Those few moments can easily cost the player several dollars.

This style of till tapping is easily avoided by getting a change bucket prior to playing at a machine. In other words, you can anticipate needing this item before playing.

Far more common than till tapping is the simple snatching of a bucket containing some coinage. I've personally seen the results of this several times as I watched security personnel wrestle and struggle with one of these characters. So you are advised not to be cavalier with your change containers. However, this last type of incident is not, strictly speaking, till tapping.

## Strings and Things

Stringing is a very old technique designed to cheat vending machines. Its application to slot machines is only incidental to the use of this technique elsewhere. Stringing, as its name suggests, involves attaching a string to a coin and lowering it down through the coin slot. In some cases, a hole was actually drilled through the coin to attach the string or thread to the coin. On entering the slot machine, the coin would trigger the mechanism as though it had passed through the entry system and then was definitely safely within the confines of the machine. However, the string permitted its user to, if not remove the coin from the machine, at least use the coin to repeatedly reactivate the entryway system.

Slightly more sophisticated was the procedure to attach the string to the coin with a strong adhesive. If the stringer were interrupted during his attempt to gain free play, he could possibly jerk the string, breaking the connection with the coin. He would then, at most, be caught holding in his hand a string not connected to any coin (not exactly a criminal act). If the coin contents of the machine were to be sorted through (involving hundreds of coins), only a dirty coin with some dried glue might be found.

Several defenses were incorporated into machines to combat stringing. One was to always have the slot mechanism firmly grip the last few coins that had been inserted. An alternative was to incorporate a scissorlike device into the entry way system to slice through any thread attached to the coin. If the stringer were alternatively to string using wire, then the scissorlike device would jam and effectively terminate additional slot play. In more modern times, stringers have plied their trade using magnetic tape such as is used in tape recordings. This tape is extremely thin, and flexible enough to thwart the cutting action of the scissorlike device in many slot machines.

Perhaps the two biggest deterrents to stringing were the application of video cameras to the entire gaming area of the casinos and not just to table games, and the introduction of maximum coin wagering where the maximum is greater than one. In most modern slot machines, the stringer would do best by maneuvering the coin and string up and down within the slot machine entry way two or three times, and five times on most video poker machines, which is a lot of work for a single max bet spin or hand. These two deterrents have caused the activity of stringing to fall on very hard times.

An activity similar to stringing is spooning. In spooning, a device like a flattened spoon is inserted down the slot machine entryway. The slot machine could then be played by repeatedly maneuvering the spoon up and down. Manufacturers easily combated this technique by making the entryway have a turn near its start. Spooning also involves using devices to violate slot machines by movement through the pay chute. This route into the machine has been found to be far more lucrative.

Stringing and spooning. If you mention them to most people nowadays, they'll just say, "Huh?"

# Stuffing

Stuffing is exactly what it sounds like. It is a method of blocking the pay chute on a slot machine. Often a very soft rubber ball is placed up into the pay chute to block the dispensing of coins. I have never found a rubber ball or part thereof used to block the pay chute. I have found folded cardboard that was inserted into the pay chute to block payment.

What has happened in all the cases that I have seen is that a player presses the Cash Out button on the slot machine and receives absolutely no payment. This generally causes the player to call over a change person who will in turn call over a floor person. The floor person usually runs a small screwdriver into the dispensing tube and removes the blockage. The process takes about five seconds.

If you're on the machine when the blockage is found, the coinage which topples out is considered to be yours. The casino personnel do not consider any of the funds to belong to the casino.

The buildup of the coinage in the pay chute occurs in a special fashion. The machine is generally a model that dispenses all winnings, or perhaps has been set to dispense all the winnings, by a button selection on the machine. Then when stray individuals play a coin or two into the machine and spin the reels, they will receive no payment because the coins won are only part way down the pay chute. The customer then either thinks he hasn't won or that the machine is broken. The customer usually moves to another machine and leaves his trapped winnings for the stuffer's arrival.

Instead of blocking the pay tube with folded cardboard or other foreign matter, a stuffer could block the pay chute with coins of the proper denomination for the machine. These can, in some cases, be forced into the pay chute to prevent other coins from being paid properly.

Blocking the pay chute with foreign matter could lead to a prosecution. Blocking the pay chute with coins, however, is a situation that it is difficult to show didn't occur accidentally. This is even true if the coin blockage is of a different denomination, because such coins are supposed to fall through the machine and return to the customer. If the stuffer can block the pay chute with a few pennies, the stuffer has very little invested financially. By stuffing in the morning and retrieving later that day, if the stuffer does only three machines in each of ten casinos, that's a good bit of potential.

As far as most people who read this book are concerned, this is a warning that if you don't get paid properly on a slot machine, call a floor person. Watching for improperly working machines is part of their job. And remember: if the floor person does remove a blockage, it's your machine and consequently your money.

# Slugging

Sluggers aren't generally very bright. In fact, as a group they tend to be definitely on the dumb side. Sluggers are people who pass slugs. No, not one or two! Hundreds of them. But just where does one get hundreds of slugs? Well, most sluggers have to make them.

The entire process usually starts with the individual gathering a vast number of lead weights. These are generally the lead pieces from the wheel balancing done at tire sales outlets. After gathering a few pounds of lead (which can legitimately be used to make sinkers for fishing), the individual then has to obtain a few metal one dollar casino tokens (most sluggers do not go to the high roller [$5 and up] slot section of the casino) and purchase some filler material. By filler material, I am referring to the material used to fill damaged fender areas on autos. This material is used to make a cast of the casino tokens.

These casts can then be filled with molten lead by heating the lead on a stove or hot plate. After cooling, the molds can be emptied and the rough edges filed down if necessary. The new lead "tokens" will be smooth on one side. Actually, the original casino tokens are primarily used for their size. The manufactured tokens are not designed to fool anyone visually. Their dull lead appearance makes them easy to spot and they cannot be passed through the gaming tables or to the cashiers in sizable quantities.

Sluggers then take their work (which is no small effort) to the casino and introduce the tokens into the slot machines and, in the course of play, cash out legitimate tokens from the numerous small pays. These legitimate tokens are then transferred to the cashier for currency.

The play of the slugger does have two particular qualities and, fortunately, these are something that many people do naturally. First, he must enter the casino with his tokens. However, many people bring in tokens from surrounding casinos and so that in itself is not noticeable. Secondly, the slugger must continuously cash out his credits. This is because he must be on guard against the possibility of a coin jam. If a coin jam occurs, he will simply depart.

However, two main problems confront the dedicated slugger in the modern scene. First, he may actually hit a large hand-paid jackpot. Then he is forced to choose between immediately departing and alternatively getting paid. If he elects to get paid, he runs the risk that the machine will be opened, and sitting on top of the legitimate tokens in the hopper will be his creations. These are so easy to spot that they cannot be missed. Also, some slot machines have a special tube that retains the last few coins introduced into the machine. If detected, the slugger will be making a trip to the local slammer.

As I understand, sluggers who get caught usually get probation on the first offense. However, if the slugger tries his trade again, he will usually get a prison sentence.

The second problem that the slugger faces, alluded to above, is being monitored on video camera. Generally, the video camera will not distinguish the slug from a legitimate token. The camera is actually used in quite another way.

At virtually all casinos, the slot machines are individually emptied of their surplus coinage once a day, usually during the early morning hours. This is then taken to a counting room where, among other things, the "foreign" tokens (from other casinos) are separated.

When in the course of this activity, a sizable number of slugs is found in any one machine, the machine number is noted and sent to the surveillance camera crew. They, in turn, check the film footage on that machine to see just who the customers were. A set of photos is then sent to security and the floor personnel.

If someone who resembles any of the photos is seen entering the casino and playing any slot machine, the casino personnel take note. However, they do not interfere with his play. The personnel give him free reign for some considerable time with no disturbance to unload his stash of slugs. They then politely come over, open the machine on the pretext of checking something, and if they see a layer of slugs, escort the individual to other environs.

So, sluggers don't usually last long.

A more successful method of playing slugs is to walk around a casino playing one here and there in assorted machines. It is common among slot players to circulate, trying various machines, so this activity goes unnoticed and has the advantage that the slugs do not accumulate in any particular machine. Therefore, the slugs may pass unnoticed in the counting room. Even if they are noticed, the outcome would be to check film footage of literally dozens of machines and that would be a huge undertaking.

In the course of slot play on various denomination machines, a player will occasionally come across a slug or two or sometimes even a foreign coin. I always transfer such material to the change booth personnel or the cashier and they, in turn, give me a proper coin or token of the appropriate denomination. I believe that if you spend enough time in casinos, you can eventually sell the cashiers your entire foreign coin collection.

# Soft Slugging

Soft sluggers are generally rather bright. In fact, as a group they tend to be employed individuals who are unfortunately suffering extremely from a common but severe character defect, excessive greed.

Unlike common sluggers, they aren't moving hundreds of crudely made slugs into slot machines. No, instead they just insert four or five small pieces of paper into their favorite slot machines, and, after a number of plays, cash out and leave. They can, in a very few minutes, make far more than any common slugger.

Soft sluggers use copying machines. In the privacy of their office, they can create choice pieces of imitation currency that will fool many bill acceptors. With the highest tech machines, soft sluggers can duplicate even the small writing around the picture of Ben Franklin on the older issues of one hundred dollar bills. With double-sided printing, they can inflict a nasty sting into a casino's profit.

But this is counterfeiting and you can be sure the federal officials will be called into the matter. There is a bright side to all this, of course. The federal penitentiaries are far nicer than the state-run facilities.

# Casino Responses

You may wonder if casinos have any policy with regard to individuals who routinely play advantageous slot machines. As a general rule of thumb, the answer is, "No."

To some extent, casinos are in the process of learning how to deal with the impact of this type of machine. Virtually from the installation of the first banking machines, casinos sensed individuals hanging around waiting for certain select machines, especially particular types of dollar and higher denomination machines. These were being played by customers who were clearly novices, as the knowledgeable persons could tell by observing the method of play in use.

Sitting around waiting for a particular machine certainly wasn't in itself a bad thing, but soon these waiting individuals began to use verbal means of encouraging novice players to depart from desirable machines. This type of encouragement, much of which occurred unbeknownst to the casino personnel, often required certain conditions to be implemented successfully.

So, verbally encouraging players to leave soon altered into pestering individuals into leaving their machines. This usually required a team effort. One team member would sit on either side of the victim player and talk to each other across and in front of the novice. Smoking was another favorite to annoy the person on the desired machine.

Of course, no casino could tolerate customer harassment; teams of individuals who did such shenanigans were soon expelled from the casino. But still the problem remained — the problem of having slot machines that could easily and quickly become extremely valuable.

The common casino responses to this situation have been twofold. The first is that casinos have drifted in the direction of having banking games of nickel and quarter denominations in preference to those of dollar and higher.

The second casino response is that at many casinos an individual cannot hang around obviously waiting for customers to vacate their slot machines. This is primarily because past experience has shown that this situation leads to other problems, as previously mentioned.

Now, to some extent, the casino doesn't care who plays its slot machines. The casino gets on average a certain percentage from every spin of the reels. The situation is somewhat analogous to a poker room. In a poker room, the casino takes a small amount from each pot for dealing and monitoring the game. The casino doesn't care who wins any particular pot. In a similar way, a casino gets a small percentage from each spin of the reels and doesn't really care which of its customers hits a jackpot or wins or loses on its slot machines.

In other words, unlike blackjack where card counters are attacking the casino's funds, advantageous slot play only results in one customer besting another customer through proper slot play. This is the current status of playing advantageous slot machines at most casinos.

Now, of course, there are a few casinos that have tried other tactics. The Tropicana has been through several stages in its handling of the presence of such slot machines until currently the casino has no banking machines. The scenario is rather interesting.

Initially, the Tropicana had the usual situation of teams pestering customers. This harassment of customers ended rather quickly with the teams being expelled.

But after this, something unusual happened at the Tropicana. Apparently, some of the security personnel were impressed that these slot machines (dollar denomination) were significantly valuable to play. But how could these machines in any way benefit them? Well, of course, there was a solution that was imposed.

The situation at the Trop was that the security personnel got into the practice of 86'ing individuals who did not tip and tolerating individuals who did. Not really that complicated a scheme. Definitely, the machine "privileges" were worth some tipping to have. Surprisingly, this type of activity was not illegal nor contrary to any of the conduct codes of the Tropicana Security Department since security people (unlike at many other casinos) were permitted to accept gratuities from customers. As a result of my newspaper article calling attention to this tacky situation, the Tropicana cleaned up their casino by throwing out the people giving tips and retaining their employees who accepted the gratuities. (This was the Trop's version of cleaning up.)

The Tropicana casino then monitored the valuable machines in a very aggressive manner. The machines were relocated to a position where the officer at the security podium could see players at the set of machines. Security personnel then removed individuals who played at these banking machines and seemed to become a little too much like a permanent feature. Even with this approach, the casino had, on at least a couple of occasions, teams come in and selectively play the machines without disturbing the customers as had previous teams. The casino removed these teams when it realized the individuals involved were not ordinary novice customers. As I understand, the casino removed anyone who frequented the machines for more than a couple weeks and played them to the exclusion of others.

This was the Trop's way of dealing with the valuable slot machines. Even this seemingly strong approach was subject to problems of corruption in reacting to who was observed. Were officers at the podium letting their friends play "unnoticed," etc.? Is an individual who comes to Las Vegas from California every weekend and clearly plays the machines in a profitable manner just an ordinary customer? Security must have hated dealing with the situation, even with this format.

Nonetheless, the point here is that the Tropicana tried to cope with having valuable high denomination slot machines by monitoring the people playing the machines. This was done for a while in preference to downgrading their machines to a lower denomination.

Finally, the Tropicana removed all the banking machines. Not just the dollar and the quarter machines. Just plainly all. Then for certain, the problem was gone. It's a radical step but an effective one and in recent months we have not known of a single banking machine in that casino.

The Tropicana is really in a class by itself.

Beyond the Tropicana, no casino had a policy of tossing out individuals who knew how to play slot machines. Then Bellagio opened its doors. For roughly a month or so after the opening of Bellagio, everyone was welcome to play at the casino. Then the casino began tightening the machines to the extent they could. (There are limits on tightening machines.) Although this made the machines at Bellagio less profitable to play, the primary effect was that the machines only became less profitable but were, however, still profitable.

Then Bellagio simply began evicting people who knew how to play slot machines profitably. The security department, following the instructions of the slot department, began telling anyone and everyone who knew how to play slot machines profitably to leave Bellagio. My wife and I were, of course, tossed out in the general melee.

Now I seriously doubt that Bellagio has a written policy with regard to this type of expulsion. Nonetheless, even though the management voices denials, it is a policy that the casino personnel have put into motion and are implementing at this time.

According to Al Hedges of the security department, if you "play better and have an advantage [over the other slots players]," you are not welcome at Bellagio. What was more interesting to consider and went unmentioned was the significant advantage that the casino has over those very same players.

Through Barbara Shull-Brown of Bellagio's Security Investigations, we learned that the slot department is "uncomfortable" with winning strategies being used at their slot machines.

Of course, both of these individuals, in removing knowledgeable slot players from Bellagio, are only responding to directives from the slot department. Note that these expulsions may all have been an indication and a response to Bellagio having some possibly unannounced financial difficulties. Indeed this later appeared to be a correct assessment to some extent.

Bellagio in and of itself made a profit. It did not, however, live up to its projections, which were undoubtedly too high in the first place. Casinos are successful either by generating new business or by taking business from competitors. That was where the rub was. Bellagio did take business away from competitors; unfortunately, it was largely taken away from the sister properties, Mirage and Treasure Island. The high end business was to some extent overbuilt.

With high debt from borrowed funds, Bellagio was under some pressure to produce revenue. Again it did this, but never as had been hoped.

Of course, selectively evicting individuals who profitably play banking slot machines from Bellagio did not solve any financial problem. Those who played machines profitably were soon replaced by others who played similarly. The profit motive is too well entrenched in our society for such a solution to be effective.

If profitable machines are causing a problem in a casino, then the solution is to remove or alter the machines. Other solutions fail in the long run as they did at Bellagio. Later, many machines were either reduced in number or downgraded in denomination.

But when Bellagio's slot department got into the business of tossing out individuals who inform customers how to best play the various slot machines, they really indicated that the casino only wanted plain suckers at Bellagio. Coupled with the fact that Dan Paymar (noted video poker expert and publisher of *Video Poker Times*) described Bellagio's video poker as "the worst video poker in the entire valley" [*VPT*, Volume 6, Number 6], it became clear that the machines at Bellagio, both video poker and slots, were only supposed to be for complete suckers.

Currently, MGM Grand reportedly plans to purchase Bellagio and related properties, which will undoubtedly alter Bellagio's handling of knowledgeable advantageous slot machine players.

With all of this discussion, I should probably explain how to be properly 86'ed from a casino. First, never show any security personnel a form of identification. True, you are required by law to have positive identification when in a casino. However, you are not required to show it to anyone in the casino unless you win a large jackpot and must complete federal paperwork such as a W-2G tax form. Instead of presenting an ID, always elect to leave. If you have done nothing illegal, the casino personnel cannot restrain you from leaving.

The advantage of not showing ID is that the situation is about a hundred times more difficult for the casino to handle if a customer refuses to show ID. The casino is then always in the position of saying, "This person looks like someone we threw out before." That is a very weak position.

Of course, as you're leaving, the security personnel will read you the Trespass Act and ask if you understand it. Always tell them that you don't and ask if they would repeat the Trespass Act and clarify some of its implications as all of you head to the door.

As far as staying away, that's a little up in the air as to how long you should remain away. If you're just told to leave in an informal sense without the reading of the Trespass Act, you should probably stay away for the rest of the day or at a minimum the rest of that shift.

Reading someone the Trespass Act would certainly mean that the individual should stay away for the rest of the day. I would recommend two or three days. Then it's your decision. But remember that on reentry you are subject to possible arrest. If you do decide to reenter, I would suggest you be cautious about playing any machine because you might instill value into the machine and be dismissed before obtaining the bonus.

If the casino personnel have good memories and are really disgusted with you, they will wait until you are playing. Then you will be have to go through the same scenario again, relearning that your presence is not desired.

On a really technical basis, here is how I understand the meaning of the reading of the Trespass Act to someone. First, any reading of the Trespass Act to an individual is good forever.

In theory, the individual is permanently barred for all eternity. Now on a practical level, I understand that the courts do not generally enforce such a reading if done more than a year prior to the reentry. In other words, every year one can reenter the establishment and discover if he's still an undesirable. As a second part of all this, I understand that the Las Vegas Police Department doesn't generally bother with reentries in disregard of the Trespass Act reading if more than six months have transpired. The police will simply direct security to reread the Trespass Act to the errant visitor.

I insert 'generally' in the above statements because if an individual has a significant criminal history (purse snatching, pick pocketing, etc.), the police and courts might feel inclined to react harshly to any revisit.

An interesting aside to all of this is that if one is 86'ed from a casino and later receives an invitation to return from some other part of the casino, then one can properly reenter. In my case at Bellagio, after being dismissed, I received an invitation about two months later from the slot club, inviting me to return to play and enjoy the facilities. Such an invitation, even if computer generated, negates an 86'ing and one can properly reenter the casino.

The most unusual 86'ing of an individual that I personally know about occurred to Mike Schaefer. Mike is a Nevada lawyer and that may have influenced the method of his 86'ing. According to Mike, he was notified by mail not to visit Bellagio, Mirage, Treasure Island, etc. He actually showed me the letter. In order to visit any of the properties involved, Mr. Schaefer was directed to first contact the lawyer who, representing his client, had signed the letter and absolutely no one else.

Being 86'ed by mail was totally new and amazing to me. When I quizzed Mike Schaefer about what he believed had precipitated this action, he stated that it was in response to his twice insisting at Bellagio that his check writing limit needed to be raised. He had absolutely no history of any bad checks. Bellagio just didn't want to deal with the matter.

Mike Schaefer has repeatedly run for public office and is a former assemblyman. So if you ever get trespassed from a casino for some nonsensical reason, don't be upset. You're in very respectable company.

One thing did come out of Mike's dismissal. Mike went to court and the judge ruled that an individual can only be dismissed from the activities that are properly a part of the casino itself. In other words, if Mike Schaefer were to be invited to a wedding in the chapel of a casino from which he had been barred, he would have every right to attend and to be a part of any festivities related to that affair. Such functions are not the domain of the casino. This means that the power of the casinos in trespassing individuals from their property is not as Draconian as they would have it appear. As of this writing, this ruling is being appealed by Mirage Resorts.

Does this have anything to do with being told to leave a casino because you're too good at playing their slot machines?. Not really very much. But the story is interesting, somewhat enlightening, and shows that things are changing.

## Conclusion

With this material under your belt, you'll find that the casino changes into an entirely new place. Instead of somewhere to try to hit an elusive jackpot, the casino becomes a place to play hide-and-seek. You can spend vast amounts of time looking for and playing advantageous slot machines that have been vacated. And while you're walking around looking for a good machine, you may find credits left on machines, coins left in the tills, money lost on the floor, discarded funbooks and other casino promotional material.

Advantageous slot play can be integrated into many other casino-related activities. For example, if you play blackjack, take a break at the slot department when the deck goes strongly negative. Advantageous slot machines work well into a vast array of casino-draining activities.

If you stay in Las Vegas and visit the casinos long enough, you will eventually learn to count cards at blackjack, set dice at craps, clock roulette wheels, case big six, play advantageous slot machines, beat video poker, exploit coupons and promotions, aggressively use slot cards, stuff drawing ticket boxes, and resell the free promotional items from the casinos. But those things are in other books. This book is just a strong beginning.

As I finish this book, I have come to realize that I am getting into an endless task of examining and reexamining advantageous slot machines. Manufacturers will continue to produce machines to appeal to the public and I, in turn, will be running around playing those slot machines and informing the public about how to most profitably play those particular machines.

The ludicrous part of all this is that the manufacturers have all this information at their finger tips and with greater accuracy. For many reasons, they will not divulge their information or trade secrets. So here I am trying to solve the artificial mysteries which other men have created. Is life really so shallow?

Yet the manufacturers have created all those games and machines to entertain and please the public. And I, in turn, am producing these results to please another segment of the public, the ones who just want the money.

The information contained herein will, with sufficient play, produce positive cash results. In fact, my books are currently the only books on earth about slot machines that will definitely produce positive cash results. When you win a sufficiently high stack of paper currency, look back and ask yourself, "What is all this insanity?"

# Appendix

## Technical Methods

This chapter is placed at the end of this book for exactly one reason; most people do not care about the manner in which any of the previous results were obtained. Most individuals will only be concerned as to whether the results are correct and if the cookbook procedures given herein actually work. Basically, this chapter deals with how some of the data was analyzed and the origin of many of the numbers mentioned in the text.

I began playing advantageous slot machines by an incredible fluke. I had read in Stanford Wong's *Current Blackjack News* about the Piggy Bankin' and Shopping Spree slot machines (December 1996). I was walking through the Tropicana Casino in Las Vegas and a lady enthusiastically said to her husband, "Oh, look! They've got a bunch of Piggy Bankin' slot machines."

She sat down at one of the slot machines and within three or four spins "broke the bank." She was roughly twenty dollars ahead and I was impressed.

I went home and reread *Current Blackjack News.* Within roughly two weeks, my wife and I were playing Piggy Bankin' slot machines to the near exclusion of playing coupons and other gaming promotions. The profit from playing dollar banking slot machines was so extreme that nothing compared to it. Playing coupons, which gives an individual an incredible edge over the casino, suddenly paled. My wife and I began doing nothing else but looking for and playing these slot machines. (Okay, okay, we did do one other thing.)

When we began playing Piggy Bankin' machines, we kept records of our performance on each machine. We would record the initial bank on the machine, the coin in, and the coin out. By subtracting the coin in from the coin out, we had a measure of the profit or loss on each machine. Then it was a simple matter to use linear regression with the initial bank as one variable and the profit or loss amount as the other.

With this analysis, my wife and I soon found we played better than many other people. While there were sizable numbers of other individuals who were examining the same machines, these others would be reluctant to play dollar Piggy Bankin' machines that had less than 25 credits in the bank. We, however, would play banks with numbers as low as 18, 19, and 20, knowing that although we would lose on many of these games, on average they would be financially beneficial to play. In other words, we played to win on average and in the long run, and became relatively unconcerned about winning on every machine.

With the passage of time, I eventually sorted our data by casino. Wong's newsletter (January 1997) mentioned that the Piggy Bankin' slot machines had four settings. I confirmed this with my data, noting that the Tropicana had the lowest hold on its one dollar Piggy Bankin' slot machines, while the Flamingo and Stardust seemed to have the next two settings respectively on their dollar denomination machines, and finally the fourth and tightest setting seemed to be used universally on all quarter denomination Piggy Bankin' machines.

Certain pieces of understanding came with the intense examination of these particular machines through linear regression. First, the initial banks could clearly be used to determine the average profitability of the various machines. Second, the cutoffs, the size of the initial banks which were, on average, of zero profitability (depending on the machine setting), differed very little from roughly 17 to 20.

If a casino changes its hold by a small percentage by using different machine settings offered by the manufacturer, this will cause the cutoff, the value of the initial bank which is on average of zero profitability, to change by only a small amount. Fine-tuning to sort out these variations in casino hold is often of very little practical value. Also as a general rule, no casino will make its hold so ridiculously high or low as to radically affect these cutoff numbers.

The third item that became clear was that extremely large wins distort the data in a radical way. It took several months to realize this fact, and the realization came about with our experiencing an actual win of a very sizable magnitude.

I struggled with how to handle these rare anomalies created by large wins. Let me clarify the situation here. We are dealing with a win in the order of a thousand credits, whereas most other pieces of data were easily in the -50 to +100 credits range. A single inclusion of an extremely large win will distort the regression line into a result that leads one to say, "Play every single machine no matter what the initial bank is."

Such a conclusion from numerically distorted data is, of course, ludicrous. But being a purist, I wanted to have everything fit. Indeed everything can be made to fit if you play virtually endlessly through a good part of eternity. There would then be a set of data containing large numbers of these very large wins.

But no one can collect that much data and there is simply no way to generate the data on a computer to simulate results as is done in blackjack. Eventually, for the purposes of this book, I realized that these large wins would plainly have to be removed from the data and ignored. I chose this course of action because the large wins are not a part of common short-term play. If you are playing a dollar machine, inserting a single dollar, and win 1000 dollars (1000 credits), you are not dealing with an ordinary situation as portrayed in this book. In a similar way, if you are playing a nickel slot machine, inserting a nickel or even five nickels, and win 50 dollars (1000 credits), you are again not dealing with an ordinary situation as portrayed in this book.

The methodology in this book is based on common occurrences. Extremely large wins were, of necessity, removed from the sets of data about the many individual games. However, losses were never removed from the data. This does definitely make the data biased. This removal makes the results given herein somewhat conservative from the player's perspective, although very slightly so. In other words, if you play long enough, you should actually have better results than the numbers in this work indicate.

After using linear regression to examine Piggy Bankin' slot machines, I used the same approach in obtaining results for Buccaneer Gold, Lady of Fortune, and Fort Knox. Both the regular and max bet versions were examined in this manner. Games such as Red Hot 7's, Royal Hot 7's, Super 7's, Safe Buster, and one of my favorites, Boom, were all treated by simple applications of linear regression procedures.

These games could equally well have been examined by using a weighted average to determine the cost of obtaining a single dagger, letter/symbol, digit, or whatever and comparing that with the average value of the bonus. The results would have been virtually identical.

But the last game mentioned above, Boom, was a real turning point for me. I fully realized just how petty the profit from some of these advantageous slot machines could be. Playing a Boom at 36 for an average profit of 20.0 credits would be terrific if these were dollar machines. But since this game is rarely seen in a quarter denomination and usually is in a nickel denomination, we are talking about a very petty amount of average winnings: in most cases, one single dollar.

Two things changed on the gaming scene that began to affect the handling of the data. First, the games began to grow in complexity to where such relatively simple statistical techniques were not possible to apply in examining the games. And the games themselves began to diminish in value.

Banking machines of the dollar denominations were replaced by those of a quarter denomination. There also suddenly began to be a proliferation of nickel denomination machines of various sorts. The upshot was that the playing of many banking slot machines began to be of much more limited value.

With the reduction of the denomination of the banking slot machines and thus the general decrease in the value of the machines, there was still a need to give the public a set of rules about how to properly play the various slot machines, but no longer a need to dispense sharply detailed results. The slot machines began to not be worth such intently detailed examination. For example, in the preceding work, it can be noted from the tables that playing a Boom at 28 will result in an average profit of one tenth of a credit. On the common nickel machine, that's one tenth of five cents.

A question became very apparent: are some of these games really worth detailed examination?

As the games grew in complexity (there are even more complex games in the first supplement to this book, already available) and generally decreased in value, the direction of the analyses changed. Instead of searching for an ultimate answer as to when and how to play some of the machines most profitably, I elected to create rules describing conditions and methods of play which 1) were easily remembered and 2) would lead to winning results, on average, if suitable machines were located and played properly.

With games such as Double Diamond Mine, the rule about the shaft contents, i.e., one 9 or two 8s or three 7s, was simply created as an easy-to-remember rule. The rule was found to yield positive results, on average, with a sufficient amount of slot play and this was checked using standard hypothesis testing techniques. However, with this game, no serious attempt has been made to determine some ultimate set of rules which will form a border between machines which can be played for positive values on average and those which will be of negative value on average.

Remember, we are not studying the wonders of nature and some eternal values related to subatomic particles. We are dealing with a bunch of stupid slot machines which can quickly be in a junk heap when (no "if" about this) the public loses interest in the machine. Detailed examination of most (maybe all) banking slot machines is simply not warranted.

Then there is the vast array of machines such as Empire, Isle of Pearls, Spacequest, etc., that are all virtually alike. After a limited amount of play, I devised the rule described in the text. That this rule works was checked with additional play. Again with standard hypothesis testing, it was confirmed that the average profit from properly playing Empire machines of the population which satisfy the criterion given herein, is greater than zero.

However, the play of Empire machines, et al., under the detailed conditions is so much like playing a regular slot machine that you don't experience a winning sensation. Many of the machines will lose modestly with this rule, but every now and then you win to an extent that overcomes all of the previous losses and puts you plainly ahead.

The closest comparison that I can give is that it is like playing a sort of short-run video poker. In video poker, a player is usually losing and then a royal flush comes and compensates financially for the previous negative play, plus there are some considerable extra funds. The difference with the game of Empire is that the rule given herein will not require you to wait nearly so long to have the negative situation from previous play turn into a positive financial experience.

Also of interest is that most of the people who compete for banking machines are too unsophisticated or impatient to bother with these machines. Basically, the competition to find and play these machines isn't there in any sizable amount. And maybe now you see that some banking machines are subtle, and then inside the subtleties are even more subtleties.

All the rules in this book have been checked and will yield winning results with a sufficient amount of play. If any readers attempt to play enough machines and record the data, they should get comparable, although certainly not exact, results. Those experiences on the machines will be clearly different, but not alarmingly so, with enough play.

As mentioned above, on several games, after a limited amount of play, I simply manufactured a rule and then with my wife went and checked its performance. Fortunately, I never fabricated a rule that didn't work. The previous play had functioned as a rule-making guide.

Much of my data carries serious weaknesses. On some of these games, I have at the very most a few hundred plays. That is more than sufficient to make a good analysis. However, most of the games have been examined using data from far fewer plays. That doesn't make the results wrong, or the guidance given incorrect. It is just unnerving to offer results on game after game that carry varying degrees of confidence.

For example, I have roughly one hundred pieces of data from the play of the game Empire. That is a good bit of data. You will be a winner if you play following the directives given in the text.

However, I have played Isle of Pearls six times. The game is not in many casinos and, as fate would have it, not in the casinos that I tend to frequent. That is an incredibly small amount of data to analyze with confidence. I have had to extrapolate and claim that Isle of Pearls which has the same pay schedule as Empire, looks like Empire, seems to play like Empire, etc., is, except for cosmetic differences, the same game as Empire. And therein you begin to see the weakness of the situation and the opening for significant error.

Yet I have an extreme amount of confidence in the results.

## SUMMARY TABLE

| GAME | REQUIREMENTS FOR PLAY | METHOD OF PLAY | PLAY TERMINATION CRITERIA |
|------|----------------------|----------------|---------------------------|
| An American in Paris | any figure 1 step from 50+ OR 2 steps from 100+ OR 3 steps from 150 | 3 credits/spin | requirements for play not met |
| Balloon Bars Balloon Race | | *NEVER PLAY* | |
| Big Bang Piggy Bankin' | 40 or more credits in piggy bank | 1 credit/spin | 3 "Break the Bank" symbols alined |
| Bingo | fixed position bingo at least half done OR adding marks = to spotcredits will form a bingo | 1 credit/spin | a bingo is obtained |
| Blackjack | generally not a banking game on slots | | |
| Blackout Poker | 40 or more credits in group bonus meter & 2 or fewer low (or 3 or fewer high) cards remaining | maximum credits/hand | appropriate bonus(es) eliminated |
| Bonus 5 Line | | *NEVER PLAY* | |
| Bonus Bank | 1 or more blinking "HELD" symbols | determined by hold pattern | no blinking "HELD" symbols |
| Bonus Spin | | *NEVER PLAY* | |
| Boom | 30 or more firecrackers displayed | 1 credit/spin | no row of firecrackers |
| Buccaneer Gold | 2 or more daggers | 1 credit/spin and max/spin during double pay period | no daggers displayed |
| Buccaneer Gold (Max Bet Version) | 3 or more daggers | maximum credits/spin | no daggers displayed |

246

| GAME | REQUIREMENTS FOR PLAY | METHOD OF PLAY | PLAY TERMINATION CRITERIA |
|---|---|---|---|
| **Build Your Bonus** | 10 valued puzzle needs a single piece OR the 25, 100 or 200 puzzles need two or fewer pieces | 1 credit/spin | bonus is obtained |
| **Chuck Wagons** | remaining distance for Your Wagon = 3/4 remaining distance for Their Wagon | maximum credits/spin | mileages read zero or clear that Your Wagon cannot beat Their Wagon |
| **Diamond Thief** | 5 or fewer diamonds needed for valise | layout dependent OR 1 credit/spin | valise requires more than 5 diamonds |
| **Double Bonus** | DB symbol present | hand feed coin(s) for spin | no DB symbols present |
| **Double Diamond Mine** | 9 diamonds in one shaft OR 8 diamonds in each of two shafts OR at least 7 diamonds in each shaft | 1 credit/spin | diamond shafts do not meet requirements for play |
| **Empire** | time remaining in seconds = 2 times the floors remaining to climb | maximum credits/spin | climb completed or remaining time is insufficient to complete climb |
| **Empire (Enlarged Bonus)** | time remaining in seconds = 2 times the floors remaining to climb | maximum credits/spin | climb completed or remaining time is insufficient to complete climb |
| **Empire Deluxe** | time remaining in seconds = 2 times the floors remaining to climb | maximum credits/spin | climb completed or remaining time is insufficient to complete climb |
| **Empire King** | time remaining in seconds = 2 times the floors remaining to climb | maximum credits/spin | climb completed or remaining time is insufficient to complete climb |

247

| GAME | REQUIREMENTS FOR PLAY | METHOD OF PLAY | PLAY TERMINATION CRITERIA |
|---|---|---|---|
| **Fireworks** | 100 points/question mark | *Avoid Play* (1 credit/spin) | obtaining bonus |
| **fishin' for Cash** | 9 fish in one stack OR<br>8 fish in each of two stacks OR<br>at least 7 fish in each stack | 1 credit/spin | fish stacks do not meet requirements for play |
| **Flush Attack** | Flush Attack mode | maximum bet/hand | termination of Flush Attack mode |
| **Fort Knox** | 4 or more obtained digits in combination | 1 credit/spin | new combination created |
| **Fort Knox<br>(Max Bet Version)** | 4 or more obtained digits in combination | maximum credits/spin | new combination created |
| **French Dough** | 9 loaves in one window OR<br>8 loaves in each of two windows OR<br>at least 7 loaves in each window | 1 credit/spin | loaves in windows do not meet requirements for play |
| **Greased Lightning** | distance remaining for Your Car =<br>3/4 distance remaining for Their Car | maximum credits/spin | mileages read zero or clear that Your Car cannot beat Their Car |
| **Isle of Pearls** | time remaining in seconds =<br>2 times the feet remaining to descend | maximum credits/spin | dive completed or remaining time is insufficient to complete dive |
| **Jewel in the Crown** | 2 jewels in any row labeled 25, 100, or 1000 | maximum credits/spin | after obtaining 3 jewels of the same color |
| **Jungle King** | time remaining in seconds =<br>2 times the feet remaining to ascend | maximum credits/spin | climb completed or remaining time is insufficient to complete climb |
| **Jungle King<br>(Enlarged Bonus)** | time remaining in seconds =<br>2 times the feet remaining to ascend | maximum credits/spin | climb completed or remaining time is insufficient to complete climb |

| GAME | REQUIREMENTS FOR PLAY | METHOD OF PLAY | PLAY TERMINATION CRITERIA |
|---|---|---|---|
| **Jungle King** (Random Bonus) | time remaining in seconds = 2 times the feet remaining to ascend | maximum credits/spin | climb completed or remaining time is insufficient to complete climb |
| **Kool Kat** | head is crowned OR any pile = 99 OR two piles each =75 OR all piles = 51 | 1 credit/spin | no crown & piles do not meet requirements for play |
| **Krazy Keno** | special ball next in tube | *Avoid Play* (max bet 3-spot) | next ball in tube is not special |
| **Lady of Fortune** | 5 or more highlighted letter/symbols | 1 credit/spin | 12 letter/symbols to obtain |
| **Lady of Fortune** (Max Bet Version) | 5 or more highlighted letter/symbols | maximum credits/spin | 12 letter/symbols to obtain |
| **Lost City Adventure** | 5 diamonds displayed | 3 credits/spin | bonus round completed |
| **Merlin** | time remaining in seconds = 2 times the feet remaining to traverse | maximum credits/spin | trip completed or remaining time is insufficient to complete trip |
| **Merlin** (Enlarged Bonus) | time remaining in seconds = 2 times the feet remaining to traverse | maximum credits/spin | trip completed or remaining time is insufficient to complete trip |
| **Merlin** (Random Bonus) | time remaining in seconds = 2 times the feet remaining to traverse | maximum credits/spin | trip completed or remaining time is insufficient to complete trip |
| **Money Factory** | bundle of 200 or more on conveyor belt | *Avoid Play* (1 credit/spin) | no sizable bundles on conveyor belt |
| **Money Maze** | many strategies available | # credits/spin = # of spaces gargoyle is from pay spot | when tired from exhaustion or told to leave the casino |
| **Monopoly** | | *NEVER PLAY* | |
| **Mystery Treasure** | 2 sections of map completed | 1 credit/spin | completion of map |

| GAME | REQUIREMENTS FOR PLAY | METHOD OF PLAY | PLAY TERMINATION CRITERIA |
|---|---|---|---|
| Neptune's Treasure | 1 figure 1 unit from chest OR 2 figures each 2 units from their chests OR 3 figures each 3 units or less from chests | 1 credit/spin | machine does not meet play requirements |
| Pay-Roll | 2 coins in any tube labeled 25, 100, or 1000 | maximum credits/spin | after obtaining 3 coins in any tube |
| Piggy Bankin' | $1, $2, & $5 machines: 18 or more credits in piggy bank | 1 credit/spin | "Break the Bank" symbol on payline |
|  | 5¢ & 25¢ machines: 21 or more credits in piggy bank | 1 credit/spin | "Break the Bank" symbol on payline |
| Pirates Treasure | 2 sections of map completed | 1 credit/spin | completion of map |
| Playoff: Deuces Wild |  | NEVER PLAY |  |
| Playoff: Jacks or Better | 145 or more credits in pot | 5 credits/hand | winning of playoff |
| Pushers | shelf density is substantial with coins layered and overhanging the front edge | slowly play 1 coin at a time | after winning 8 coins or more from shelves OR losing 8 coins |
| Racing 7's (5,10,20 Version) | some 7 two marks or fewer from end | 1 credit/spin | race is completed |
| Racing 7's (10,25,200 Version) | 4 marks or fewer remain for blue 7 | 1 credit/spin | race is completed |
| Red Ball | 20 under either 3x3 OR 15 under both 3x3's | 3 credits/spin | play requirements not met |

| GAME | REQUIREMENTS FOR PLAY | METHOD OF PLAY | PLAY TERMINATION CRITERIA |
|---|---|---|---|
| Red Hot 7's | 3 or more 7's completed | 1 credit/line on 5 lines | 5 free spins have been obtained |
| Red Hot 7's (Symbol Score Version) | 3 or more 7's completed, i.e. 600 or more points accumulated | 1 credit/line on 5 lines | 5 free spins have been obtained |
| Riddle of the Sphinx | 3 matching symbols topping any column | 4, 5, or 6 credits/spin (column dependent) | no column top has 3 matching symbols |
| Ring 'Em Up | | *NEVER PLAY* | |
| Road Rally | time remaining in seconds = 2 times the miles remaining to travel | maximum credits/spin | trip completed or remaining time is insufficient to complete trip |
| Road Rally (Bonus Version) | remaining distance for racer = 3/4 remaining distance for pace car | maximum credits/spin | mileage reads zero or clear that racer cannot beat pace car |
| Royal Hot 7's | 3 or more 7's completed | 1 credit/line on 5 lines | 5 free spins have been obtained |
| Rue de Riches | 2 coins of each of 3 or more denom. OR 2 coins of each of 2 denom. and 1 of the 2 denom. is 50 | *Avoid Play* (3 credits/spin) | requirements for play not met |
| Safe Buster | 2 X's | 3 credits/spin | bonus spinning ends |
| Safe Busters | 2 X's | 6 credits/spin | bonus obtained |
| Safe Cracker | $1 machine: 20 or more coins in safe | 1 credit/spin | opening of safe |
| | 25¢ machine: 25 or more coins in safe | 1 credit/spin | opening of safe |
| Shopping Spree | 29 or more shopping credits | 2 credits/spin | bonus spinning ends |

| GAME | REQUIREMENTS FOR PLAY | METHOD OF PLAY | PLAY TERMINATION CRITERIA |
|------|----------------------|----------------|---------------------------|
| Slot Bingo | 50 or more numbers on either flashboard | 1 credit/spin | bingo on appropriate card |
| Spacequest | time remaining in seconds = 2 times the number of lightyears left to ascend | maximum credits/spin | ascent completed or remaining time is insufficient for completion of ascent |
| Super 7's | 3 or more square 7's | 5 credits/spin | 5 free spins have been obtained |
| Super 8 Line | | NEVER PLAY | |
| Super 8 Race | | NEVER PLAY | |
| Super Double Diamond Mine | diamond shafts: 9 diamonds in one shaft OR 8 diamonds in each of two shafts OR at least 7 diamonds in each shaft | 1 credit/spin | diamond shafts do not meet requirements for play |
| | diamond dust shafts: within 2 credits of top of shaft | 2 credits/spin | diamond dust shafts do not meet requirements for play |
| Temperature's Rising | number of degrees remaining = bonus | 1 credit/spin | after winning bonus |
| Tour de Slot | any cyclist 1 space from 50+ OR 2 spaces from 100+ OR 3 from 150 | 3 credits/spin | requirements for play not met |
| Treasure Quest | 3 or more completed treasure chests | 1 credit/line on 5 lines | 5 free spins have been obtained |
| Triple Cash Winfall | 9 coins in one stack OR 8 coins in each of two stacks OR at least 7 coins in each stack | 1 credit/spin | coin stacks do not meet play requirements |
| Triple Diamond Baseball Diamond | 25 or more runs and indicated runs displayed | 1 credit/spin | HOME RUN on payline |

252

| GAME | REQUIREMENTS FOR PLAY | METHOD OF PLAY | PLAY TERMINATION CRITERIA |
|---|---|---|---|
| **Triple Diamond Mine** | 9 diamonds in one shaft OR 8 diamonds in each of two shafts OR at least 7 diamonds in each of the shafts | 1 credit/spin | diamond shafts do not meet requirements for play |
| **Vacation U.S.A.** | guidelines: last bet 1 & 7 interstate symbols on one route OR last bet 10 & 5 interstate symbols on one route or 4 symbols on both routes OR last bet 50 & 3 interstate symbols on one route | 1 credit/spin in all cases | guidelines indicate continued play will be unprofitable |
| **Vacation U.S.A. (Tight-Lipped Version)** | guidelines: last bet 1 & 7 interstate symbols on one route OR last bet 10 & 5 interstate symbols on one route or 4 symbols on both routes OR last bet 50 & 3 interstate symbols on one route | 1 credit/spin in all cases | guidelines indicate continued play will be unprofitable |
| **Wheel of Fortune** | 1201 or more bonus points | 5 credits/spin | after selecting W-H-E-E-L letters |
| **Wild Cherry Bonus Pie** | 5 or fewer cherries needed for large pie | layout dependent OR 1 credit/spin | large pie needs more than 5 cherries |
| **Wild Cherry Pie** | 11 or fewer cherries needed to complete pie | layout dependent OR 1 credit/spin | pie is completed |
| **Wine Cellar** | 5 or fewer bottles needed for large rack | layout dependent, or 1 credit/spin | large rack needs more than 5 bottles |
| **X Factor** | 6X, 7X, 8X, 9X, or 10X | maximum credits/spin | X factor less than 6 |

# Complete Blackjack Basic Strategy
## One Deck, Dealer Stands on Soft 17

| Player's Total or Hand | 2 | 3 | 4 | 5 | 6 | 7 | 8 | 9 | X | A |
|---|---|---|---|---|---|---|---|---|---|---|
| 5-7 | H | H | H | H | H | H | H | H | H | H |
| 2, 6 | H | H | H | H | H | H | H | H | H | H |
| 3, 5 | H | H | H | D | D | H | H | H | H | H |
| 9 | D | D | D | D | D | H | H | H | H | H |
| 10 | D | D | D | D | D | D | D | D | H | H |
| 11 | D | D | D | D | D | D | D | D | D | D |
| X, 2 | H | H | H | S | H | H | H | H | H | H |
| 9, 3 | H | H | S | S | S | H | H | H | H | H |
| Other 12's | H | S | S | S | S | H | H | H | H | H |
| X, 3 X, 2, A | H | S | S | S | S | H | H | H | H | H |
| Other 13's | S | S | S | S | S | H | H | H | H | H |
| 14 | S | S | S | S | S | H | H | H | H | H |
| X, 5 | S | S | S | S | S | H | H | H | G | H |
| 9, 6 | S | S | S | S | S | H | H | H | G | G |
| Other 15's | S | S | S | S | S | H | H | H | H | H |
| X, 6 | S | S | S | S | S | H | H | H | G | G |
| 9, 7 | S | S | S | S | S | H | H | H | G | H |
| 16's containing 6 with 6, 7, 8, 9 & X, 2, 2, 2 & unsplitable 8, 8 | S | S | S | S | S | H | H | H | H | H |
| Other 16's | S | S | S | S | S | H | H | H | S | H |
| 17-21 | S | S | S | S | S | S | S | S | S | S |

| | 2 | 3 | 4 | 5 | 6 | 7 | 8 | 9 | X | A |
|---|---|---|---|---|---|---|---|---|---|---|
| A, 2 | H | H | D | D | D | H | H | H | H | H |
| A, 3 | H | H | D | D | D | H | H | H | H | H |
| A, 4 | H | H | D | D | D | H | H | H | H | H |
| A, 5 | H | H | D | D | D | H | H | H | H | H |
| A, 6 | D | D | D | D | D | H | H | H | H | H |
| A, 7 | S | d | d | d | d | S | S | H | H | S |
| A, 8 | S | S | S | S | d | S | S | S | S | S |
| A, 9 | S | S | S | S | S | S | S | S | S | S |
| A, X | S | S | S | S | S | S | S | S | S | S |

## Pair Splits

|  | 2 | 3 | 4 | 5 | 6 | 7 | 8 | 9 | X | A |
|------|---|---|---|---|---|---|---|---|---|---|
| 2, 2 | W | B | B | B | B | B | H | H | H | H |
| 3, 3 | W | W | B | B | B | B | W | H | H | H |
| 4, 4 | H | H | W | w | w | H | H | H | H | H |
| 5, 5 | D | D | D | D | D | D | D | D | H | H |
| 6, 6 | B | B | B | B | B | W | H | H | H | H |
| 7, 7 | B | B | B | B | B | B | W | H | Y | H |
| 8, 8 | B | B | B | B | B | B | B | B | B | B |
| 9, 9 | B | B | B | B | B | S | B | B | S | S |
| X, X | S | S | S | S | S | S | S | S | S | S |
| A, A | B | B | B | B | B | B | B | B | B | B |

# KEY:

B (Break) = Split
D = Double Down  (Otherwise Hit)
d = Double Down (Otherwise Stand)
G (Give Up) = Surrender (Otherwise Hit)
H = Hit
S = Stand
W (With) =  Split with Doubling (Otherwise Hit)
w (with) =  Split with Doubling (Otherwise Double)
Y (Yield) = Surrender (Otherwise Stand)

## Modifications if Dealer Hits Soft 17:

Hit  A,7  v.  A
Stand  X,2  v.  6
Split  9,9  v.  A

*See next page for early surrender chart, plus a simplified basic strategy for easy memorization.*

# Basic Strategy for Early Surrender

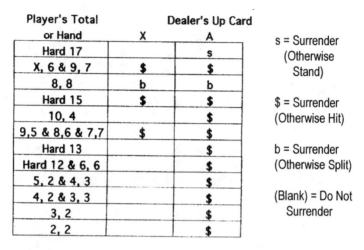

| Player's Total or Hand | Dealer's Up Card X | Dealer's Up Card A |
|---|---|---|
| Hard 17 | | s |
| X, 6 & 9, 7 | $ | $ |
| 8, 8 | b | b |
| Hard 15 | $ | $ |
| 10, 4 | | $ |
| 9,5 & 8,6 & 7,7 | $ | $ |
| Hard 13 | | $ |
| Hard 12 & 6, 6 | | $ |
| 5, 2 & 4, 3 | | $ |
| 4, 2 & 3, 3 | | $ |
| 3, 2 | | $ |
| 2, 2 | | $ |

s = Surrender (Otherwise Stand)

$ = Surrender (Otherwise Hit)

b = Surrender (Otherwise Split)

(Blank) = Do Not Surrender

**Early Surrender Modifications if Dealer Hits Soft 17:**
Surrender 6,2 & 5,3 & 4,4 v. A

---

**A Simplified Blackjack Basic Strategy, Less than Perfect, But Easy-To-Learn, Modified from Arnold Snyder's Blackbelt in Blackjack, Copyright 1998, Used With Permission:**

1. Always stand with hard 17 and higher.
2. Stand on all stiffs (12-16) v. 2-6.
3. Hit all stiffs (12-16) v. 7 and higher.
4. Always double down with 11.
5. Double with 10 v. 2-9.
6. Double with 9 v. 2-6.
7. Double with soft totals of A-2 through A-7 v. 4, 5, and 6.
8. If not doubling with a soft hand, always hit A-7 or less, and always stand on A-8 and higher.
9. Always split Aces and 8s.
10. Never split 4s, 5s, or 6s. (Just play two 4s as a hard total of 8, two 5s as a hard total of 10, etc.)
11. Split all other pairs v. 3, 4, 5, and 6.
12. Never take insurance.
13. Surrender hard 15 and 16 v. ten, if allowed.

# Complaints Welcome!

I have tried to make this not only an informative book but also an entertaining one. The information contained herein has been examined and reexamined not only to make it correct but in a useful form.

What I hope to obtain from the assorted readers is input concerning items that you find of interest or wish to question. Also, I would hope that if you have a few ideas about how to improve this text, you would jot those ideas on even something as innocuous as a postcard and send them to me through the publisher.

It is difficult to improve a publication without hearing detrimental comments. This, in particular, is something I hope to extract from the readers. I especially crave well-thought-out criticism.

As a final request, since new banking machines are always on the drawing boards, I am asking that if you find banking slot or video poker machines that are not mentioned herein, again please contact me through the publisher. Slot machines are sometimes test marketed in other locales before being introduced to the national or Las Vegas arena. I will, in turn, send you any information I may currently have about how to best play such machines.

If, additionally, you have any information about anomalies on various machines, please inform me. I will try to confirm your observation(s) and perhaps expand on the material.

And lastly, if you feel that any of the directives about how best to play a particular advantageous slot machine can be improved or should be modified, again please inform me through the publisher.

Thank you for obtaining and reading this book. I hope it leads you to pleasurable experiences.

*— Charles W. Lund*

Write to Charles W. Lund
c/o RGE Publishing
414 Santa Clara Avenue
Oakland CA 94610

# About the Author

Charles W. Lund earned a Bachelors Degree in Mathematics at the University of Colorado. He continued his studies and earned an M.S. in Actuarial Science (Insurance Mathematics) from the University of Nebraska, followed by an M.S. in Statistics from the University of Florida, and finally, a Ph.D. in Statistics form Virginia Polytechnic Institute and State University. With his extensive background in mathematics, he has been able to bring considerable ability to the analysis of data collected from slot machines. Charles is currently the gaming columnist for the *Valley Explorer* in Las Vegas, and has also written numerous articles for *Blackjack Forum* magazine.